DIALECTIC VS. TECHNOCRACY

DIALECTIC VS. TECHNOCRACY

HIGHER REASONING FROM ANCIENT GREEK RATIONALISM TO MODERN GERMAN IDEALISM

Tommi Juhani Hanhijärvi

Algora Publishing
New York

Library of Congress Cataloging-in-Publication Data —
Names: Hanhijärvi, Tommi Juhani, author.
Title: Dialectic vs. technocracy: higher reasoning from ancient Greek rationalism to
modern German idealism / Tommi Juhani Hanhijarvi.
Description: New York: Algora Publishing, [2023] | Includes bibliographical references
and index. | Summary: "Low reason is about coping in the world in the world's terms; but
our freedom, morality, and enlightenment require the higher, more speculative faculty. Dr.
Hanhijarvi (Humboldt Univ.) invites us to explore the great thinkers and re-activate the
profound abilities of the human mind that so importantly out-shine today's mechanistic
thinking" Provided by publisher.
Identifiers: LCCN 2022056119 (print) | LCCN 2022056120 (ebook) | ISBN
    9781628945003 (trade paperback) | ISBN 9781628945010 (hardcover) | ISBN
    9781628945027 (pdf)
Subjects: LCSH: Dialectic   History. | Reasoning   History.
Classification: LCC B105.D48 H36 2023 (print) | LCC B105.D48 (ebook) |
    DDC 153.4/3   dc23/eng/20230213
LC record available at https://lccn.loc.gov/2022056119
LC ebook record available at https://lccn.loc.gov/2022056120

Printed in the United States

Die Vernunft ist das ganz frei sich selbst bestimmende Denken.

(Reason is thought conditioning itself with perfect freedom.)

— Hegel

Table of Contents

Human life is being gradually mechanized as we sleep. There are now few open confrontations, because there is no systematic polarization between real and artificial intelligence (AI) any more than there is between a political Left and Right. All parties now are for technological progress, though no one knows what this may mean but for thoughtless convenience. Hollywood clichés are more swiftly circulated and in greater volumes — and people are for this? We should be in a state of crisis, offended to be viewed as predictable machines, asking ourselves how we might prove at least to ourselves that there is more to us than this.

Here in *Europe* we get most of our news in this area from California, for that is where all the giant computer corporations are housed and where the rhetoric is least inhibited. But in California they do not often seem to know what is being lost. Traditionally Europe has of course prided itself on being more cultured, and a few generations ago we still had skeptical voices as from the Frankfurt School, but these are no longer so often heard. For now European and even German philosophers tend rather to go with the tide. It is generally accepted that also in the area of critical thought the standards and paradigms are increasingly American, and the German Idealists and the ancient Greeks are read in these domesticated ways. Now everyone is middle class and mediocre.

However, in the streets of *Berlin* this still raises questions. Google is building a skyscraper in the east of the city which will employ thousands of computer professionals to mechanize further areas of culture, but typically for Berlin this still triggers a protest movement. (In my native Finland this would not occur, and more likely Helsinkians would rush to rename their city Googledorf.) The street protesters still often live in squats, and many are maladjusted to society and the economy. There are still little wagon towns inside the city, little utopias by their own lights. The standard packaged fashions are not quite everywhere, and all the music in the streets is still not pop. Thus the city has not quite given up — and here is why this book is devoted to it.

Personally I moved here alone as a 21-year-old history student (from Heidelberg), not knowing anyone here and never having visited the city. I came purely for the sake of adventure, in search of a larger reality. That was not long after the fall of the Berlin Wall, and there were plenty of windy wastelands inside the city. Living was very free and cheap, but Berlin was also a harder and ruder city then. Shocks were everywhere: street dogs ran freely, punks threw stones at the police, lunatics and bohemians wandered around aimlessly — bullet holes on the walls, monuments of idealistic or romantic culture and of totalitarianism, all the extremes of the world in ruins. I lived in around 20 different addresses and changed my philosophical beliefs as frequently. My head was spinning and it still is. I am interested in all of these things. The city is my labyrinth. To Berlin! In gratitude.

TJH, in Berlin, November 2022

Introduction

> Industrial society possesses the instrumentalities for transforming the metaphysical into the physical, the inner into the outer, the adventures of the mind into adventures of technology. The terrible phrases (and realities of) "engineers of the soul," "head shrinkers," "scientific management", "science of consumption", epitomize (in a miserable form) the progressing rationalization of the irrational, of the "spiritual" — the denial of the idealistic culture.
>
> [P]hilosophic thought is necessarily transcendent and abstract. Philosophy shares this abstractness with all genuine thought, for nobody really thinks who does not abstract from that which is given, who does not relate the facts to the factors which have made them, who does not—in his mind—undo the facts. Abstractness is the very life of thought, the token of its authenticity.
>
> —Herbert Marcuse, *One-Dimensional Man*, 1964

This book is about *reasoning*. Is it scientific and technological? I cast doubt on that now-conventional view by presenting readers with a more traditional style of reasoning which is dialectical and philosophical. True, mechanical computation is impressive in its efficiency and precision, but these count only for so much in the total view. We are now so impressed with quick computers and brightly lit space shuttles that they blind us to many other things, indeed to superior things. The technocratic culture has its merits, but it is merely useful and servile. It is like a body without a head.

The *contemporary context* for this discussion arises because the sphere of automata is constantly expanding. Robots steer airplanes, invest in stock markets, and generate algorithms for advertizing to affect predictable consumer behavior. The popular keyword is Artificial Intelligence (AI). But it is less often noted now that computation requires no *real* intelligence, no interpretation, intuition, mind's eye, natural light, self, personality, or consciousness of any kind. There is no ghost in the machine.[1] With automata much can occur — or at least seem to occur — in life and the universe without anyone really being there. Not only are there no Gods and no heroes anymore but there is not even a free will or a self. You think you decide? Well, it is your blood vessels that do it, or the wiring inside your skull. This prospect is totalitarian or dystopian according to some authors because increasingly the mechanical model threatens to control all of life and reality. But the word 'totalitarian' can also be misleading, given that there can now be no great dictator with a plan: even he would be a puppet of impersonal forces. No one is in control.

However, it is crucial for this book's discussion that this general type of threat is in fact *not new*. In ancient Greece, Democritus and Leucippus already formulate the atomistic and materialistic lines of thought that can in major respects only be copied in milder versions in this, our very modern age, and they have their cousins in ancient China and India. Ancient Greece is also already well rehearsed in all types of atheistic ridicule of a *deus ex machina.* Cynics parade their views openly in public. Of course, the ancients do not fly to the moon or possess an electrical tooth brush, so the specific tools we now enjoy are comparatively new. But the general lines of thought are old. This is the reason why the main replies to the reductive manners of thought that are considered in this book are familiar already from ancient texts. They show us how it is still a long way from here to the mechanization of life and thought *in toto.*

What then is the opposite force? What is *philosophical or foundational* reasoning? And what is its relation to the technocratic model that has just been sketched?

In this book the cues concerning this are taken from the dialectical philosophers of ancient Greece and modern German Idealism, though similar lines of thought are familiar also from India, China, and numerous further cultures. In India there is what is called Hinduism as well as

---

[1] This phrase is taken from the Oxford philosopher Gilbert Ryle who argues in the Cold War period that human mental lives are explainable in behavioral terms. See Rey for the place of Ryle and behaviorism in the more recent computationalist landscape. Behaviorism is only one way to try to mechanize human mental life.

Buddhism. From China we have Daoism but also Confucianism. The main Greek philosophers include Pythagoras, Socrates, and Plato. In German Idealism the two dominant names are Immanuel Kant and Georg Wilhelm Friedrich Hegel. Beyond these, there are dozens of further -isms and personalities.

Fundamental to all these dialectical perspectives is a distinction between merely *relative* things and *absolutes,* or in other words between *conditional* or dependent things on the one hand and *unconditional* and independent ones on the other.

The former class is lower because it is always qualified: If A is true *only if* B is, then that means that A needs backing up by B. Therefore A by itself is not quite true yet, and so it is true and not true, or true and false at once.

This already is an authentically dialectical thing to say, in both the East and the West, and in ancient as well as modern times.

But the perspective does not concern only truth: unconditionally real things form a higher order because they are real on their own. They do not need outer aid. The lower things are not real in themselves, so they are like servants or illusions. (The Hindu word for them is *maya.*)

We can generate hierarchies also for many further topics: freedom, the self, kindness, beauty, etc.

However, in a way the *chief* dialectical topic is reasoning itself, for it is the *generative principle* behind all the different uses. If you can reason dialectically, you can use your skill in many places at will. Thus dialectical reasoning comes first, and then there is a range of topics where it can be used.

Here is why this book focuses on reasoning.

Why should this relativity extend to *science and technology?*

One key thought is that mechanical computation can be so efficient *only because* it is so obedient. If the robot, the slave, and the soldier act in straight-forward manner, they must follow predetermined instructions. The instructions must be black-and-white or the machines will not compute. This is what is required for the culture of efficiency. There cannot be an option to pause and think.

But this is not binding, authoritative, or obligatory, because it is all only conditional on the predetermined instructions. It gives us results in vast quantities but only because all the difficult questions about priorities and principles get left out. Such questions are simply dropped and everything is made straight-forward and servile. To what? And what for? What are the priorities and where are their compelling foundations? And what do these questions even properly mean? All this is already unscientific and philosophical.

Dialectical thought seeks the unconditional archetypes which do *not* depend on any ulterior givens. But then we do not get efficiency or loud machines and flashy cities.

Is this *socially elitist?*

In some hearers' ears it always is, at least at first. But in principle this could go either way, and there are historical references on both sides of the question.

Let us take the anti-elitist side first. *Kant* argues that each of us has the capacity for higher as well as lower reasoning, which he calls *Vernunft* and *Verstand* respectively.[1] Our freedom, morality, and enlightenment require the higher and more speculative faculty, he says. We come to our own with it and we are freed. Mere *Verstand* makes us too much like marionettes. With *Verstand* we can do physics and navigate on a sail boat, for instance. *Verstand* or low reason is all about coping in the world in the world's terms. It is not about transcending it.

This has largely been my own experience as a teacher. Youths can do sciences and languages and history but they can also step up to the level of *Vernunft* if only they are presented with the needed tools.[2]

What is the elitist side to this issue? The Hindu caste system is certainly elitist, and so are Plato's utopias, Atlantis, Kallipolis, Magnesia. In texts like these, hierarchies of things become hierarchies of people. Then there are upper classes and lower classes, not only higher and lower types of reasoning or thought. Yet Plato's different utopias are only more or less elitist. Kallipolis is that, yes, but Magnesia not so much. Moreover Plato may offer his utopias mainly as models for the *psyche* (Greek for soul), not for the *polis* (Greek for city), saying that the real hierarchy must always reside inside the individual person. You have (or you are) your higher and lower parts, and you need your higher self to figure out their relation. You can flourish only if you find your priorities. The utopian city is only the individual psyche writ large, Plato says, a useful model for

---

[1] Kant's two German words literally mean 'reason' and 'understanding'. But these are not fitting translations philosophically, because 'understanding' is no longer in use (unlike in Kant's eighteenth century, cf. Locke and Hume) and what now tends to be called reasoning would rank as mere *Verstand* in Kant: mechanical computation, physical science, economic rationality, etc. *Vernunft* has largely vanished from both the wider culture and from scholarly works on Kant (see Chapter 3).

[2] I should add that such tools are *not* in circulation now. This book is written with a sense of *crisis* in mind because the necessary materials and conventions are missing (see Preface).

individual thought. If so then it is not literally a political program at all. (In Greek the higher self is called a *daimon*.[1])

On a different level, Hollywood entertainment is of course by far more *popular* than any dialectical studies. Everyone at present does not like to read books. Moreover some logical riddles are too much pretty nearly for everyone. But how much does that mean? There are persons who say that the only way to be culturally democratic is to go by the lowest common denominator, but in my view this is to sell oneself short.

Is dialectic *culturally biased?*

Many a technocrat has posed as a liberal, saying that science or technology exhausts all the neutral facts and that beyond them only subjective value choices remain. It is popular now to say that this is democratic, so only the technocratic means are seen as objective. Ends are private, means are public. We have a world of tools, that is all, and then we have our private fictions.

It could be that this is correct, but it is not. Why not? Well, the dialectical patterns are not subjective, I will show, and technological knowledge is not unquestionable. The popular generalizations are often not true.

Are dialectics not *impossible* in a material world? To be sure, if we are determined by scientifically known laws then we can leap out of their reach only in our imaginations.

However, the dialectical perspective is that we may *voluntarily* hold up the materialistic edifice. It is not true on its own. We choose to act in what the French existentialist Jean-Paul Sartre calls *bad faith* (French: *mauvais foi*): the waiter pretends to be merely a waiter, playing that role. We only make believe that we do not notice or think of all kinds of things in order to stay inside the normal and convenient range, *as if* we had to.[2]

If this is true, then we may do rather many things we do not honestly need to do. *Surely* people will seek even more wealth, and *of course* they will adapt to the social climate, or our thoughts are *guaranteed* to accord with our times. Yes? Well, not quite, not always.

---

[1] This is the origin of our word 'demon'. In Greece a daimon is a higher self, and the happy or flourishing individual lives in accordance with the daimon. The Greek word for happiness is *eudaimonia*, where the prefix *eu-* standards for coherence, accordance, or harmony. 'Happiness' in this sense is not so much about smiling and eating sugar cakes as doing the things one is properly built to do. One 'finds oneself' in the daimon.

[2] See Appendix A, quotation 1.

It is necessary now to explain that low, mechanical vocabularies or types of order do not suffice *even for considering* completely independent things. They are not competitors or candidates at all on the grand questions dealt with in dialectics. For to be at all concerned with the extreme issues about, say, free will, God, or absolutes or archetypes of any kind, belongs exclusively to higher reasoning. Low reason cannot reach them. This is to say that it does not even negate them! If the low reasoner does pretend to reach conclusions about these topics and to pronounce about them with authority, then this is always only an indirect indication of his limitations. For he then only presupposes what he claims to show. For example, in physics one does not *discover* that each thing has a cause in some other thing, and rather this is assumed at the start of physical inquiry. That is how physics operates. It is monocular.[1]

To be fair, there is of course a sense in which it is not only low reason that is monocular. For the freedom and nobility of the high thinker comes at a price: he cannot confront reality as it simply happens to be. Every kind of contingency eludes him. Pure reason is utterly deaf and blind to what actually happens now.

The *overall picture* then is like this. Neither half of reason, the high or the low, can dominate the totality. For neither can do the work of the other. There is a division of labor, and the lessons run both ways. For example, the high mind sketches utopian science as it ultimately ought to be with a perfect hierarchy of laws, but the low mind does the actual dirty work in the field, considering how animals or germs operate in fact,

---

[1] In other words physics proceeds to research *external nature* based on certain premises, but its research does not concern these premises. The premises are blind spots to the physicist because they are not out there in nature. They are integral to the physicalistic *perspective*. They do not have mass or energy, for example. (Similarly, the astronomer views the stars but astronomy is not one of the stars.) In contrast with this, the philosopher of science does study the premises of the sciences, but not scientifically. The foundational or absolute questions arise for the philosopher but not for the scientist. Science works only *based on* its presuppositions, and it would be much less efficient if it turned philosophical. Thus there is an either/or. But this is very much in keeping with the dichotomy of this book. One can be impressed with the efficiency and determinacy of science, but dialectical philosophies and theologies will have other merits. Kant explains this best, see Chapter 3. (*That everything that happens has a cause, cannot be concluded from the general conception of that which happens; on the contrary the principle of causality instructs us as to the mode of obtaining from that which happens a determinate empirical conception. Critique of Pure Reason A301/B357.*)

The great source on *causality* specifically, however, is Hume, who sees that constantly conjoined properties (as in statistical regularities) are not causally related. (For example, on a hot summer more ice cream is consumed and more people drown, but eating ice cream does not cause you to drown — even though these phenomena co-vary statistically.) Hume knows that empirical science presupposes a conception of causation which is actually false. What then is real causality? This is again a philosophical question, not a scientific one.

based on observation, or in general what can be done, not merely what should be. Similarly, the high demand is for perfect morality and sublime beauty, but the low impulse is to adapt to the weather and mood of the day. Hence, without high reason, low reason is a cheap and opportunistic thing, adrift and directionless, because it has no proper standards or priorities.[1] But then on the other hand high reason by itself is too proud for the world, being foolishly ignorant about what happens on the streets, like a Don Quixote who mistakes windmills for giants. Thus each half has its place. We need animal utilitarianism *and* high culture.

In our day, it is this *higher* half that has become exotic.

Now the first thing to understand is how dialecticians typically *get started* with their reasoning.

Dialectical Questions

Even small children master the rule or principle which is involved in generating dialectical questions: it is to just keep asking until asking no longer makes coherent sense. The three-year-old's version of this is to keep repeating *Why?* If the child is presented with (a), the child says *Why a?* and receives the answer (b), and again she says *Why b?* and we say c(), etc. In this way we come to form a series like this:

- a BECAUSE b BECAUSE c BECAUSE...

But where does this series end? Is there some final z?

This already is a first little sketch of dialectical questioning.

However, it is only a first sketch, for in fact there are *numerous meanings* to questions *Why?* and correspondingly to explanations *because,* and accordingly dialectics have diverse topics. The chief ones in this book are:

- a CAUSES b CAUSES c...
- a AIMS AT b AIMS AT c...
- a IS MADE OF b IS MADE OF c...
- a PROVES b PROVES c...

Obviously the same chain can be *turned backwards,* so the first one of the preceding four could be ... c IS CAUSED BY b IS CAUSED BY a. (If R = CAUSES and Я = IS CAUSED BY, aRbRc means much the same as cЯbЯa.) The meaning would be the same, though we would then begin from the last point in time and not the first. This is typical, so dialectical

---

[1] See Appendix A, quotation 2.

series do not have to be presented in any particular direction. We can flip them around depending on our interests.

Switching the *wording* is also always possible, as in a MOVES b instead of a CAUSES b. This may slightly alter the meaning or at least the style, but not drastically for we will still be dealing with what since Aristotle has been called an *efficient* cause or a moving cause. His terms for the other causes are: the aiming relation is called a *final* cause, the make-up is a *material* cause, and proofs or definitions are *formal* causes. These are philosophers' standard technical terms for stereotyping series.

Another way to form such series would be by shifting between different question words. Instead of *Why?* we could ask *What?*, *Where?*, *When?*, or *Who?* However, already Aristotle knows that questions *What?* actually fall into his four kinds just like questions *Why?* What a chair is, for example, is a piece of wood by its material cause, but by its final cause it is a portable seat for one. A heart has the final cause of pumping blood but it may be made of organic tissue or synthetic plastic: hence the final and the material cause are not the same. Thus there are numerous meanings to questions *What?* just as there are to questions *Why?*, and this tells us that shifting between these question words makes for only superficial differences. Deeper down we have the typology of causes, so it is more dependable. (*Where?* etc. are a little different and I will come to them in Ch. 3.)

If these are your typical dialectical questions, what are their typical answers?

Dialectical Answers

Let us begin with Plato's theology in this final work, the *Laws*:

- *PLATO'S GOD:* Plato's God (*theos*) is *self-moved*, so a MOVES a MOVES b MOVES c, et cetera, and a = *theos*. Thus the chain does not begin from a sudden, blank point a but from a pattern, a MOVES a. (If MOVES = R then aRa.)

The chain of movers does not begin from a mystical leap out of the blue, for rather it has a self-conditional, circular structure. a MOVES a goes from a back to a. We would have a different circle if x is self-evident, so that x proves x, or if y is self-ruled, so that y rules y, or if z is intrinsically valuable: valuable for its own sake as in z for z. But this is the general way to solve the extreme riddles generated in dialectical questions.[1]

---

[1] This book, like some of my other books, is something of a rebellion in this regard.

Two millennia later *Kant* takes us back to the same design:

- *KANTIAN AUTONOMY:* A free will is not merely a sudden leap from nowhere in Kant's books but rather an act of self-legis-lation (in Greek *auto* = self, *nomos* = law). Thus there is again no arbitrary jump or miracle but rather a specific and rational structure. The free person states his ideal law and acts on it, that is the law which he would impose on all the world if he were a king, dictator, or God, though he is not. But this makes for a familiar chain: a MOVES a MOVES b MOVES c ... (Kant's more specific version reads: a COMMANDS a COMMANDS b COMMANDS c ...)

In fact a similar pattern is found in ethical codes throughout the world:

- Jesus and Confucius articulate a GOLDEN RULE which says to treat others like you would like to be treated.
- Ancient Indians present a law of KARMA which says that your next life will accord with your choices in this life: if you act like a monkey you will be reborn as a monkey.
- Pythagoras says justice amounts to a ratio of EQUALS FOR EQUALS or for x, x^2.

Numerous sayings echo the same:

- Tables are turned.
- Reap what you sow.
- Practice what you preach.
- Eye for eye.
- Measure for measure.

Can you see what I am doing? In each ethos the agent becomes the patient, so a does what it does *to* a, as in aRa. Hence we keep getting the same circle format.

In more fashionable terms you might do this even in *programming*:

- If you were to *program yourself* then what rules should your future selves obey? If you simply command them and expect them to obey blindly, they may rebel! But if again you are too mild then you do not *have* a program — a vague dream is no plan.

- *What language* would you use? Which kind of code is suited for your soul? What might be a perfect language? Or is there any particular language one must use, and if so why?

There is here a shift of levels from programming oneself to programming programming itself, and this takes us nicely to the world of dialectical *Ideas*.

Ideas are undeniably the highpoint in all the major Western dialectics — Plato's, Kant's, and Hegel's. Plato's term for an archetype or absolute is usually this (Greek: *idea, eidos*). Kant adopts this term into his own philosophy consciously from Plato, and Hegel adopts it as consciously from Kant (their German equivalent term is *Idee*).

The rough idea of a Platonic Idea can be intuited as follows:

- *PLATO'S IDEAS:* These have the characteristic of being both general standards or scales and the best things as measured by those standards or scales. Thus the Idea of Beauty is the measure of beautiful things everywhere and the most beautiful thing (*Symposium*), and the Idea of Justice is most just, and not only the yardstick of justice (*Republic*). Each Idea has a kind of double structure: it is both the measure and the best measured thing. It has the one function and the other.[1]

The Platonic Ideas are a little different from theos or autonomy in being of a higher order: they are not like aRa but like RR or RRR. (There is an identity purely of identity, a law of laws, and a harmony of harmonies: the *Kalon.* Commonly in both Greece and India there is a God of Gods, and Plato even has an Idea of Ideas: the *Agathon,* the Idea of the Good.) However, the main thought is largely as before, for Ideas are perfect by their own lights, and this is why they do not pass the buck. (If you come to x, x does not push you further to some y, but back to x.) They do not generate further questions because they are self-referential — like closed circles again. Plato typically views his Ideas as timeless, changeless, and insensible archetypes. They are cognized by the mind's eye.

---

[1] For more on this see my *Plato's Logic.*

Plato is not always of this view, however, cf., e.g., *Republic* 596A. Here the Idea of a Bed is a perfect model for beds, but if all Ideas are abstract and superempirical — as Plato usually says — then this Idea cannot itself be a bed. Similarly he says there is an Idea of the Large, but if Ideas are nonspacial then that Idea cannot itself be large. These are the sorts of complications I must here omit to reduce complexity.

Hegel's Ideas are similar:

- *HEGEL'S IDEAS.* These are both concepts and the uses of those concepts, so that for instance the Idea of Right in Hegel's *Philosophy of Right* (§ 1) is both the concept of right and a thing that is right. It is a standard and an instance which satisfies that standard, at once. But likewise for all other Ideas in Hegel: an Idea of Truth would be the yardstick for truth and one of the truths. About what? Itself. Thus each Idea is again a perfect circle of its own, much as in Plato.[1]

However, it is characteristic of Hegel to add a *processual* twist to this, so that we get each Idea in a temporal series of steps:

- *a thesis:* one of the functions (for instance a subject),
- *an antithesis:* the other of the two functions (for instance an object),
- *a synthesis:* both functions at once (a subject *and* an object).

In this way we are *freed*, Hegel teaches: freed from the anomalies of the animal world, and to a higher world of perfect harmonies. Accordingly, dialectic has been called the *pulse of freedom.*

But now the reader already has the main concepts of this book.

The idea is, it should be clear, that just as dialectical questions *Why* can be asked everywhere — East and West, by ancient and moderns, and in all kinds of styles — so these dialectically circular answers are also possible everywhere. The principle is the same. It is not uniquely Greek or German, or Indian or Chinese, etc.

In this text I will need to focus on the principle, and this will lead to a regrettable neglect of many local colors and experiential or emotive aspects of dialectics. (I have to avoid detours.)

Dialectical Contradictions and Negations

I hope inexperienced readers understand that dialectical reasoning is now not a common or commonly acknowledged thing at univer-

---

[1] Not that *Hegel* sees this analogy: he views Plato's Ideas merely as general concepts or universals and Plato as a kind of theorist of theorists or purest planner who never puts any of it into practice, see especially Hegel's *History of Philosophy.* (Writing about dialectics tends to be like solving a jigsaw puzzle in this way.)

sities, schools, or the publishing industry. In fact it is popular among twentieth-century philosophers and logicians to say that dialecticians commit a *logical error* in saying that a negation of a negation (which is Hegel's phrase) is anything but a return to the same. The larger problem is supposed to concern the place of contradiction in rational thought and also in outer reality. (The most aggressive attacks have probably been by Karl Popper.)

Let us now sort this out.

If standard, non-dialectical logic[1] is used, then negations or contra-dictions work in a black-and-white fashion, like this:

- if p = *I am seated on a horse,* then
- not-p is that it is false that I am seated on a horse, and then
- not-not-p is that it is false that it is false that I am seated on a horse, in which case I am seated on a horse.

If p is false, not-p is true, and if not-p is false, p is true. The possible values are only two: true/false, black/white, 1/0.

Due to this, if we read in Hegel that there is a negation of a negation, then the logical interpretation is to say that this is all he means: p, not-p, p. (For not-not-p is just p.)

However, this is *not* what Hegel means, and it is also not what other dialecticians mean when they reason dialectically. Rather, the pertinent thing is to distinguish *more levels,* and *more values,* not only two (as in black/white, 1/0). Thus compare:

- a ‹ b ‹ c, or
- white, gray, black.

Already these three levels require more than binaries like true/false or black/white, but this need only increases once we approach passages where the levels are more numerous — four, ten, etc. (Logically simplistic background theories are too poor for dialectics: dialectics deal in greater complexes.)

The profitable way to read dialectical texts is in terms of *hierarchies.* Compare this hierarchy for beginners:

- a DEPENDS ON b DEPENDS ON c...

---

[1] Like Aristotle's, which dominated Western thought for two millennia; see Kneale and Kneale.

Here we have a series of becauses, causes, or reasons from a to b to c. Crucially, the variables have *more and more weight* as we move to the right. For if a DEPENDS ON b DEPENDS ON c..., then there is an increase in dependability in time. In other words that a, b, c, ... form a hierarchy as in in a < b < c... and not an even or equal series.

To this background we can make sense of contrariety as *relativity*.

In accordance with the above hierarchical thinking, if for instance a IS CAUSED BY b IS CAUSED BY c IS CAUSED BY d, c is more of a cause than b, but even c is caught in the middle — in cross-fire as it were — for its role is also to be the effect of d. c both pulls and is pulled or pushes and gets pushed in turn, as it were giving as well as taking.

This is the kind of contradiction or negation that one finds in dialectical books. (Hence, instead of clinging to black/white, 1/0, true/false, one needs the hierarchies, and on that basis one makes sense of relatives.)

But is this then not illogical? (Is it not illogical to reason in ways that is not coded or captured in logic?)

Logical *relations* show that the scope of logic can be extended to these complexes. Compare:

- *DIALECTICAL QUESTIONS* are series, as in aRbRcRc... xRyRz, where R is a relation like IS MOVED BY or IS PROVED BY and a-z are its relata.
- *DIALECTICAL ANSWERS* are circles, as in aRa or zRz (a MOVES a, z PROVES z) or else as in RRR, RRRR. We can also shape more complex expressions out of these elements, like ((aRb) R (cRd)), where two R-relations relate to each other as R, and ((aRb) S (bRa)), where R and the reverse of R relate to each other as S. In ((R) R (RR) R (RRR) R (RRRR)) R continually demands higher powers of itself in time as we move towards the right. (Beyond these there are many more, but I will keep them to a minimum in this book.)

Why am I bringing up relations of all things? What are relations? Logical relations are predicates with at least two places, so for instance x IS ORANGE is not a relation because it has only one place (x), whereas x IS TALLER THAN y is a relation because the places are two: x and y. Similarly with x GIVES y TO z: here there are two relations — GIVES and TO — and three places — x, y, z.

Now it is in relations that we can have many levels as dialectic requires, so here is a way to make logical sense of dialectics. (More on relational logic in 3.2.[1])

ADDENDUM. Here I need to insert an explanation that is required from the *opposite* corner. For as soon as we begin to make logical sense of dialectics, some readers will suspect that dialectics are *too* logical — in short too mechanical and robotic to be interesting in real human life.[2]

Or why not?

First let me note this. Typically, of course, machines only obey their programs, so they do not compare, critique, or polish them. They are not programmed to do so, because their business is to be useful slaves, not free or autonomous beings, let alone self-thinking Gods or Ideas.[3] However, in dialectics there is no interest in the useful and one explores the higher questions without limitations.

But then what is the role of symbols like R? This is easy to see from a few examples. Take it that a MOVES a. Then this surely begs the question *how* a manages to do this, so the aRa pattern only leads us down the right tracks. Similarly, if someone keeps asking *Why?* about something then we can ask *Why do you ask?* and expect reasons. He cannot merely parrot *Why? Why? Why?*, no matter what happens. That will not be reasoning. Thus aRbRc... is only the dead bones. It is not the living flesh. And thus with all the R formats.[4]

---

[1] I will not be discussing zRz or RRR etc. in 3.2, however. These are not standard topics in relational logic, and instead logicians tend to avoid the issue or logical relations. If p IMPLIES q, for example, then IMPLIES is a relation. Similarly CONTRADICTS, etc. Hence a thoroughly self-conscious relational logic should not only discuss sentences like R IMPLIES S, where R and S are relations, but also R T S, where IMPLIES = T and T is one of the relations. Instead of this, authors like Tarski only reason about relations, not *in* them. That is mechanical, not philosophical. (The wider issues include Russell's Paradox and according to some authors even Gödel's Incompleteness Theorem. For more on this see my *Plato's Logic*.)

[2] Cf. Horkheimer and Adorno's *Dialectic of Enlightenment*, a dialectical book without a great deal of logical order.

[3] But could they be programmed to do these higher things too?

The reason I do not focus more on AI in this book is that now it seems to have no *representative theory*. (Hence it is hard to specify what would be anti-AI.) Church and Turing, classic generalizations about computation from the 1930's that are still so often referred to as the pioneering formulations, do not represent what is called 'deep learning', and when deep learning is discussed it is too often surrounded with Californian hyperbole. In reality I see daily that the algorithms on the internet get my preferences wrong because they simplify and stereotype excessively, and if I know that the algorithms are designed in Google's secret laboratories then I also know that the people or the machines in those laboratories are not always quite as clever as they are made out to be.

[4] Here one can keep pushing: Do dialecticians obey the R logic or not? If they obey it, how are they different from machines? (continued)

Reading Dialectical Texts

In saying the things I have said in this Introduction, I have constantly already assumed that dialectical texts should be read according to what can be called their *deep structure*. The easiest way to explain this is by reference to the composer Johann Sebastian *Bach* (1685-1750).

By all accounts Bach is an amazing creator of musical harmonies but, genius that he is, he merely wings it every time. He creates countless harmonies out of the blue. He has few predecessors and no musical theories to build on. And crucially for my argument: he never states a musical theory.

The point is: his melodies instance musical harmonies, they do not state them. If the songs have words, they are typically Christian. The words do not say "Chord C, then F, and Am, and play this part softly..." but "Jesus, O joy..." and "My God..."

After Bach, musicologists have been busy trying to explain his know-how, and my musicologist friend tells me that this is so even today. They can hear from Bach's work that there is more to map. More things fit together than has hitherto been explained.[1]

But all the great dialecticians are like Bach! Each is another genius, another intuitive creator who spins out coherent patterns which he never names or defines. On this comparison I am the 'musicologist' who runs after the heroes and tries to keep up, explaining their magic away and imparting their skills to the people.[2]

It makes a great difference what *kinds* of rules one obeys. An Idea or a Golden Rule is a rule, but it does not mechanize or demean you because it mainly guides your imagination in your search for ideals. In contrast say factory workers may need to follow strict guidelines about exactly where to be and when, how dressed, which functions to perform at which machines, etc. Such lower functions are the more mechanizable ones (cf. Marx in Ch. 4).

[1] On genius see 3.9.

[2] *Why* do the dialectical stars not manage to explain their own inventions? The reason is a little different in each case.

With Hegel the trouble is with his term choices, so he is liable to confuse readers when he says — as he often does — that there is a *negation of a negation* when one moves from a thesis and antithesis to a synthesis. This is but one of hundreds of examples one could cite. Hegel is not good at explaining himself, and his more readable texts consist of his students' lecture notes. (Often Hegel's confusions seem to result from his attempts to use Aristotle's logical categories for higher patterns.)

With Plato, the problem is not that there is a misled theoretic vocabulary as in Hegel but that there is none, and deep insights are presented only poetically or very briefly. With Kant, the main shortcoming is that his theoretic vocabulary is suited for *Verstand* but not for *Vernunft*: it is Aristotelian, not relational. Kant cannot reason properly about his higher half. (There are shortcomings also in the lower half but it is not dialectical, see 3.2.)

What is the *opposite* of this book's interpretive strategy?

That would be to require that all dialectics occur verbatim. If a text contains the word 'dialectic' (or 'Idea' or some other keyword) then it is dialectical, and not otherwise. Obviously this is false because for instance Popper writes at such length *against* dialectics, so he brings it up to oppose it.

A more serious omission, however, would be of books that are dialectical but only unofficially. I will give two examples.

First the *Tao te Ching* (§ 19). See if you do not find a pattern here:

> If we could renounce our sageness and discard our wisdom, it would be better for the people a hundredfold. If we could renounce our benevolence and discard our righteousness, the people would again become filial and kindly. If we could renounce our artful contrivances and discard our (scheming for) gain, there would be no thieves nor robbers.

The *dao* emerges thus from living examples such as this, not from any official formula, but anyone can see that a recipe is hidden in the text. (The code may be cracked.)

As another example compare the literary ironies of Søren Kierkegaard (1813–1855):

> What the philosophers say about reality is often as deceptive as when you see a sign in a second-hand store that reads: Pressing Done Here. If you went in with your clothes to have them pressed you would be fooled: the sign is for sale.[1]

The great realists are not real, so the deeper coherence is absent. It is as if the fire department were on fire, the doctors were sick.[2]

---

[1] *Either/Or*, p. 50.

[2] Kierkegaard's irony is based on a *lack* of the kind of completeness or coherence that one finds in dialectics proper. *If* we had complete coherence, then also books on comedy would be funny, so they would practice what they preach. But things get ironic or paradoxical as soon as this is *not* so: we have unpoetic lectures on poetry, astronomers who have never been to outer space, etc. For more examples see Appendix B.

CHAPTER 1. SOCRATES: QUESTIONING ATHENS

> Socrates is one of those eternal figures who have become symbols ... He became the leader of all versions of modern Enlightenment and philosophy; the apostle of ethical freedom, who was bound by no dogma or tradition, who stood on his own, and who obeyed only his inner voice of conscience; the originator of the new religion of the this-worldly, of an inner power to create happiness in life without any need of mercy, and of an interest in its own perfection through its own relentless efforts. Still, these formulations do not communicate his meaning in the post-medieval world. No new ethical or religious thought has appeared, and no spiritual movement has taken shape, without calling on him as its true founder.
>
> —Werner Jaeger (1939)

Socrates is known primarily for his culture of philosophical questioning in Plato's dialogues, and it is often thought that the real Socrates is present only in Plato's earlier and youthful works which Plato writes when he follows the old Socrates around the streets of ancient Athens to witness the next thing he will do.

As we will see, Plato's own views in his middle and later periods are not so much about questioning as answering.[1] He presents us with confident visions of immortality, the perfect *polis* (city) or utopia, the archetypal Ideas,

---

[1] Plato's corpus is usually divided into three main phases, each of which has its version of dialectical reasoning:

and God. Socrates himself by contrast has zero confidence in anything.[1] He is an intellectual trouble-maker who cannot sit still and buzzes around town questioning everything and everyone, including himself. (He is the only one who knows that he does not know, he quips.) In time the democratic Athenians come to have enough of him and have him killed, but this only contributes to his heroic status among young idealists like Plato. His cultural status in later antiquity status is Christ-like or (to compare a different region of the world) Buddha-like. He becomes immortal. Like Jesus and Buddha, he is the speaker and teacher who never writes or forms any official school or church. He is a kind of street purist, a barefoot reformer — the real thing before all the traditional stories and canons are formed.

So much for the historical setting. For Socrates is not only a fascinating personality but the originator of a philosophical method. His tool for reasoning is the dialectic. Now what exactly is this? The key to this lies in Socrates' quest for *definitions* of core ideals (1.1). Thus, he questions others systematically by first asking what some x is, such that x = y. So y is to define x. For example, take it that x = knowledge. Then Socrates' question is, What is knowledge? What does it equal? What is this y which exposes it as it really is? We know for instance that *the Morning*

His *earlier* dialogues are said to instance an "elenchtic" method in which the historically real Socrates refutes views by finding that they contradict themselves. This is commonly seen as a negative, destructive tool and the motive for its use is taken to be skeptical (cf. Woodruff). However, I will not view the early period as this negative, as the reader will soon see.

Plato's *middle* dialogues contain what he officially presents as a "dialectic". This is a more constructive manner of reasoning than the elenchus. 'Socrates' is now Plato's mouthpiece who actively presents Plato's own ideas instead of looking for them primarily from his interlocutors, and the interlocutors need usually only to nod in assent. In the *Phaedo*, the *Symposium*, and the *Republic* Plato presents his boldest and most distinctive views. This is unquestionably his high point also as a literary artist.

In Plato's *later* period dialectic is tamer, a method of collection and division which anticipates Aristotle. This method is at its plainest in the *Statesman*, the *Sophist*, and the *Philebus* (beyond a brief statement in an otherwise much wilder work named the *Phaedrus*). However, it is hardly there at all in the *Theaetetus*, let alone in the *Timaeus*. As I read Plato's last work, the *Laws*, in Ch. 2 it is not about collection and division but largely like the middle-period dialectic. According to Hegel a further later Platonic work, the *Parmenides*, is the cardinal achievement in ancient dialectics, and its patterns seem actually to escape this triple typology altogether.

On the current clichés about Plato see Fine, ed. On Aristotle's dialectic see Irwin, *Aristotle's First Principles*.

[1] To anticipate, the relation between Kant/Hegel below will be similar to that between Socrates/Plato: questions/answers, problems/solutions.

Star = Venus and that $E = mc^2$. But what then is knowledge, or knowledge itself? What do we insert for the blank variable x?[1]

To this background, what is really new with Socrates is his critical culture. It consists of assessing the truth of definitions by bombarding them with counter-examples. Before him others had generalized widely, for instance Thales about water and Heraclitus about fire, but Socrates introduces criticism. For example, if we hear that someone says that to be moral is to cause pleasure, then Socrates equips us with the tools to *test* this proposition. For he knows the logical make-up of the proposition. The definition is false if there is at least one moral thing which does not cause pleasure or if there is at least one pleasing thing which is not moral. In a rudimentary sense this is already dialectical. It is a yardstick for critical thinking.

But next, if we ourselves think critically *about* criticism, then this leads to some further questions. If Socrates seeks definitions, what *kinds* of definitions does he want (1.2)? And how exactly are hypothetical definitions to be tested? Here is what I mean. Socrates does not experiment in a chemistry laboratory, for example, so he does not assess anyone's views by seeing whether they square with the experimental facts in that field. Nor is he a geographer, so he does not sail off like Homer's heroes or wander to unknown lands like Alexander the Great. But then what does he do? Where does he get his evidence? The prominent view among current scholars is very mild regarding this, namely that Socrates goes by mere common sense (much like many current Anglo-American scholars themselves do!). On that view, some x = y is true exactly if x = y squares with what is ordinarily thought or said by people on the street. Why is this mild? Well, to give but one of the reasons now, it fails to explain how rebellious Socrates is. If he relied on everyday intuitions of ordinary people then he would hardly be a trouble-maker in Athens and there would be no need to silence him by getting him killed. But these things actually happen. Hence the omens are that he has some higher standard which is not merely ordinary or commonsensical.[2]

---

[1] Notice already that if the *word* 'knowledge' sufficed for this then obviously there would be no reason to require y — the secret equivalent. We would only say like Dr Johnson: knowledge is knowledge, each x is just x, that is all.

[2] A contrast with the French Enlightenment is illuminating: Voltaire, the star of that movement, is often said to have said something like this: *I disapprove of what you say, but I will defend to the death your right to say it.*

Now this is emphatically not like Socrates, for he goes out and questions others. He is killed because he does *not* leave individuals alone to maintain and express whatever views they wish. Voltaire wants each individual to have a private sphere — somewhat like a suburban home, perhaps, in modern American idioms — But Socrates is for a public sphere. We should not form separate islands

A more rational Socrates needs to be closer to the dialectical tradition which forms after him, I explain (1.3). He is after deeper symmetries. This is to say that Socrates' definitions are not really as much like scientific formulas as it can seem at first, and accordingly Socrates should not be read as any kind of pre-scientist. For scientific formulas are always much too contingent. Why should water equate with two molecules of one type and one molecule of one type, for example? Regular as scientific formulas are compared to children's stories or dreams for example, they are still not all that regular. And why would sociological statistics confirm any hypothesis with a stamp of authority at all? Hear-say is not truth, and trendy beliefs are often false. If empirical or social scientists report what is ordinary then that is to say that they compromise with the accidents of the low world. They are for sale: they serve. Socrates does not, for he is from a higher world. But this means only that we need to keep questioning *him*. Where does he get this superior authority? Does he cheat? (The ancient world is crowded with false prophets. Here comes Empedocles wearing a purple cape, pointing to his home in the sky!) As suggested I argue that Socrates relies on the symmetric intuitions we have all encountered from diverse traditional and holy texts. (These do not carry authority because they are traditional but because they are so neatly symmetrical. Their authority and calm symmetry accounts for their traditional popularity.)

One way to corroborate this way of reading Socrates is by considering it in the light of what is certainly his central paradox, namely his professed ignorance ('I know I do not know'). If his conception of knowledge is analytical then this must be insincere, for analytical truths are too obvious to be unknown, but on a dialectical reading Socrates has more depth. This becomes clearer with reference to the so-called 'paradox of inquiry' (from Plato's earlier works, the *Euthydemus* and the *Meno*, 1.4). The paradox is that one cannot inquire into any x because one needs first to know what x is in order to inquire into x, but if one does not what x is then one need no longer inquire into it. (Say you want to know about the foraging habits of bees: you cannot study them unless you can identify bees and observe the foraging. You cannot begin from a blank *tabula rasa*.[1]) The solution is that the object of inquiry needs to be described on two levels, and I can illustrate this first again with water.

---

but have some kind of new continent together. (As Kant will say in Chapter 3, the free have duties, not simply rights.)

[1] This is again to anticipate *Kant* (Ch. 3). Against empiricist philosophies of science he argues that scientists must actively interrogate nature, somewhat like witnesses must be interrogated in a court of law. Scientists cannot simply observe and report what happens to come their way. They must plan, structure, etc.

To study water you must already have a type-1 conception of water, so you must be able to locate it, distinguishing it from other things. Then you know that water is a transparent and tasteless liquid on planet Earth, which may also turn into steam, snow, and ice depending on the temperature. But then the knowledge you seek is type-2 knowledge, and here we need Socrates' ideal of knowledge. In chemistry we would use H and O, hydrogen and oxygen, but Socrates' type-2 knowledge is divine (in Plato's *Apology* in 1.5). It is an Idea (in Greek *idea* or *eidos*, both terms are introduced in Plato's *Hippias' Major* in 1.6). It is structured much like the Pythagorean 'equals for equals' (in Plato's *Gorgias* in 1.7). Thus the paradox of inquiry is solved by noting the difference between the two types, type-1 and type-2, and chemistry leads us to understand in mundane terms that there is such a difference at all. But Socrates' type-2 is not chemical, and this leads us deeper into the world of dialectics.

Finally for this chapter we will take a peek at *Platonism* proper (1.8). In his *Phaedo*, Plato begins to extend Socrates' comparatively austere and rigid little program into what is with justice describable in certain ways as a dominant philosophy in the Western world. Here we see that the Idea of the Equal equates perfectly with itself, that a psyche which recollects it reaches immortality in separating from the body, that psyches are reincarnated in new bodies depending on the choices they make in this life, that virtue is its own reward, and more. These views have similarities with Pythagorean as well as Hinduist teachings, and they influence Christian theology heavily from ancient times. Thus Socrates ultimately only sketches and initiates a certain pattern which for Plato is elementary, like mother's milk, and then it is Plato who brings dialectical reasoning out into the open.

From Questioning to Defining

As noted the center of Socrates' philosophy is his dialectical method (or *elenchus*). But there is plenty of life spinning around the center. He is the great questioner in Western philosophy, the archetypal critic in public culture and politics. If someone asks difficult questions in a bustling social environment and will not let them be passed over too easily then such a figure may be called *a Socrates*, just as someone else may sit quietly like *a Buddha*.

Socrates initially finds himself when consulting with an oracle at Delphi in Greece. The oracle (in reality probably a priestess) tells him he is the wisest, but Socrates is surprised, for he does not seem to himself to know anything. Or, if he knows, then he does not know that he knows, or what he knows.

This triggers his search for self-knowledge: What may the oracle mean? He asks other Athenians from all walks of life, old and young, rich and poor, what they know and finds that they typically think they know all kinds of things which they do not in fact know. (Usually, just because they know about some things, like carpenters know about carpentry, the Athenians believe that they know about everything on a similar model, e.g., also about pottery, poetry, etc.)

This prompts Socrates to surmise what the trick must be: he is uniquely wise in that only he knows that he does not know. This is his interpretation of the oracle's omen. Now he knows who he is: the paradigmatic skeptic. (*Skepsis* means inquiry in Greek.)

In his own words:[1]

> God orders me to fulfil the philosopher's mission of searching into myself and other men, I were to desert my post through fear of death, or any other fear; that would indeed be strange, and I might justly be arraigned in court for denying the existence of the gods, if I disobeyed the oracle because I was afraid of death...[2]

> O Athenians! I honor and love you; but I shall obey God rather than you; and so long as I breathe and am able, I shall not cease studying philosophy, and exhorting you and warning any one of you I may happen to meet, saying, as I have been accustomed to do: 'O best of men! seeing you are an Athenian, of a city the most powerful and most renowned for wisdom and strength, are you not ashamed of being careful for riches, how you may acquire them in greatest abundance, and for glory, and honor, but care not nor take any thought for wisdom and truth, and for your soul, how it may be made most perfect?'[3]

> And if any one of you should question my assertion, and affirm that he does care for these things, I shall not at once let him go, nor depart, but I shall question him, sift and prove him.

---

[1] Of course these *English* words are not quite Socrates' own *Greek* words, however. They are translations, and they differ from translations made by others. More than this, they are translations of *Plato's* written words, for Socrates himself writes nothing down. Thus in reality we are at quite a distance from the real Socrates and do not know his exact words.

But these complications can also be overemphasized: cf. Lutoslawski for the detailed philological studies of nineteenth century German scholars. They are comical because they lack larger philosophical significance. Every detail is not equally important.

[2] *Apology* 28E-29A.

[3] *Apology* 29D-E.

And if he should appear to me not to possess virtue, but to pretend that he does, I shall reproach him for that he sets the least value on things of the greatest worth, but the highest on things that are worthless.[1]

When I left him, I reasoned thus with myself: I am wiser than this man, for neither of us appears to know anything great and good; but he fancies he knows something, although he knows nothing; whereas I, as I do not know anything, so I do not fancy I do.[2]

Thus I shall act to all whom I meet, both young and old, stranger and citizen [...].

For, if you should put me to death, you will not easily find such another, though it may be ridiculous to say so, altogether attached by the deity to this city as to a powerful and generous horse, somewhat sluggish from his size, and requiring to be roused by a gad-fly; so the deity appears to have united me, being such a person as I am, to the city, that I may rouse you, and persuade and reprove every one of you, nor ever cease besetting you throughout the whole day. Such another man, O Athenians! will not easily be found [...].[3]

But neither did I then think that I ought, for the sake of avoiding danger, to do any thing unworthy of a freeman, nor do I now repent of having so defended myself; but I should much rather choose to die, having so defended myself, than to live in that way. For neither in a trial nor in battle is it right that I or anyone else should employ every possible means whereby he may avoid death; for in battle it is frequently evident that a man might escape death by laying down his arms, and throwing himself on the mercy of his pursuers. And there are many other devices in every danger, by which to avoid death, if a man dares to do and say every thing. But this is not difficult, O Athenians! to escape death; but it is much more difficult to avoid depravity, for it runs swifter than death.[4]

Socrates the gadfly questions the citizens of Athens, who pretend to know but in reality prefer wealth or power to real knowledge. Socrates

---

[1] *Apology* 29E-30A.
[2] *Apology* 21D.
[3] *Apology* 30E-31A.
[4] *Apology* 38E—39A.

will not obey Athens but his God, and he will never quit his questioning ways. He is on a mission.[1]

The Athenians do not like this. They rather like their carpentry, pottery, and poetry, their wealth, etc., but they have no use of this kind of a trouble-maker. Yet Socrates will not budge, and so eventually they have him killed. Enough is enough. Life must go on in its convenient ways, and there is a limit to the questions that the individuals living in the democratic *polis* can comfortably face.

The question this begs is: What is this knowledge that Socrates seeks? How does he measure it? What is its use or point? On what authority is it based? And does Socrates himself also ask things like this? That is, does he also have higher-order questions, questions about right and wrong questions, based on which he can explain and justify his skeptical habits, if need be?

As noted, we need first to look at the things he requires: definitions. Here are a few first samples.[2]

In the *Meno*, Socrates is initially after a definition of virtue (or excellence, Greek: *arete*), and Meno provides him with an unsystematic catalogue of examples. Socrates replies:

> Soc. How fortunate I am, Meno! When I ask you for one virtue, you present me with a swarm of them, which are in your keeping. Suppose that I carry on the figure of the swarm, and

---

[1] Socrates' mission is not *political*, a fact politically minded readers often forget. He says:

> Someone may wonder why I go about in private, giving advice and busying myself with the concerns of others, but do not venture to come forward in public and advise the state. I will tell you the reason of this. You have often heard me speak of an oracle or sign which comes to me, and is the divinity which Meletus ridicules in the indictment. This sign I have had ever since I was a child. The sign is a voice which comes to me and always forbids me to do something which I am going to do, but never commands me to do anything, and this is what stands in the way of my being a politician. And rightly, as I think. For I am certain, O men of Athens, that if I had engaged in politics, I should have perished long ago and done no good either to you or to myself. And don't be offended at my telling you the truth: for the truth is that no man who goes to war with you or any other multitude, honestly struggling against the commission of unrighteousness and wrong in the state, will save his life; he who will really fight for the right, if he would live even for a little while, must have a private station and not a public one. (Apology 31B-D.) This is Socrates' famous inner voice, which always says no and never yes.

More on dialectics and politics in Ch. 4.

[2] I have made these selections with the scientific and dialectical interpretations in mind: the selections from the *Meno* accord better with the former and the others with the latter.

---

ask of you, What is the nature of the bee? and you answer that there are many kinds of bees, and I reply: But do bees differ as bees, because there are many and different kinds of them; or are they not rather to be distinguished by some other quality, as for example beauty, size, or shape? How would you answer me?

Men. I should answer that bees do not differ from one another, as bees.

Soc. And if I went on to say: That is what I desire to know, Meno; tell me what is the quality in which they do not differ, but are all alike;-would you be able to answer?

Men. I should.

Soc. And so of the virtues, however many and different they may be, they have all a common nature which makes them virtues; and on this he who would answer the question, "What is virtue?" would do well to have his eye fixed: Do you understand?

Men. I am beginning to understand; but I do not as yet take hold of the question as I could wish.

Soc. When you say, Meno, that there is one virtue of a man, another of a woman, another of a child, and so on, does this apply only to virtue, or would you say the same of health, and size, and strength? Or is the nature of health always the same, whether in man or woman?

Men. I should say that health is the same, both in man and woman.

Soc. And is not this true of size and strength? If a woman is strong, she will be strong by reason of the same form and of the same strength subsisting in her which there is in the man. I mean to say that strength, as strength, whether of man or woman, is the same. Is there any difference?

Men. I think not.[1]

Socrates wants a uniform formula for virtue. Virtue has a singular form, whether it is encountered in a woman or a man or in whatever situation, just as bees are the same no matter where they happen to be.

A different analogy is not zoological but mathematical:

---

[1] *Meno* 72A-E.

Soc. [...] You will acknowledge, will you not, that there is such a thing as an end, or termination, or extremity?—all which words use in the same sense, although I am aware that Prodicus might draw distinctions about them: but still you, I am sure, would speak of a thing as ended or terminated-that is all which I am saying-not anything very difficult.

Men. Yes, I should; and I believe that I understand your meaning.

Soc. And you would speak of a surface and also of a solid, as for example in geometry.

Men. Yes.

Soc. Well then, you are now in a condition to understand my definition of figure. I define figure to be that in which the solid ends; or, more concisely, the limit of solid.[1]

Socrates means that virtue is definable in the way that a figure is definable, or in the way that bees were above. As noted, this is exemplified at its simplest in $a = b$, where b is an expression which defines and identifies a.

As a third and final example let me bring in another earlier Platonic dialogue, the *Protagoras*. Also here the question is about virtue. What is it? Can it be learned and taught? Protagoras is a 'sophist', that is a professional teacher of speaking skills to future politicians and men of influence. His view is that we humans are formed purely by our cultures, so the only nature we have is our second nature: our cultural climate. Birds can fly, tigers can fight with their sharp claws and jaws, but we humans are left naked in the woods by the Gods, without any special skills — but for our unique ability to learn, our talent for contingent culture. In Protagoras' plastic universe this comes to mean that everything is relative. His definition and standard is that man is the measure of all. There are no absolute truths, but only things we think true. Another Greek philosopher, Xenophanes, summarizes this relativist viewpoint nicely:

The Ethiops say that their gods are flat-nosed and black,

While the Thracians say that theirs have blue eyes and red hair.

Yet if cattle or horses or lions had hands and could draw,

---

[1] *Meno* 75D-76A.

And could sculpt like men, then the horses would draw their gods

Like horses, and cattle like cattle; and each they would shape

Bodies of gods in the likeness, each kind, of their own.

Every animal, like every personality, will think it is right — and in pure reality no one is. No one represents God truly. Socrates objects that if this is a true definition then — by its own lights — it is a false definition,[1] for if it is true that everything is merely relative (and therefore not really true), then so is this very thesis, that everything is merely relative (and therefore not really true). There is no way to speak with authority if one undermines authority.

Scientific Definitions

As suggested in the introduction to this chapter (1), the strategy of many scientifically minded scholars is to analyze Socrates' philosophizing merely as an effort to generalize — in scientific spirit. This is an inductive view of Socrates, which is found already in Aristotle. On it Socrates is only an early and somewhat clumsy scientist.

This position squares well with the dogmas of science-friendly twentieth century analytical philosophers. For them valid generalizations come in only two classes: the logical and the empirical.

- LOGICAL generalizations are tautologous and trivial, like *Bachelors are unmarried, A triangle has three sides, Not-not-p equals p, A chair is a portable seat for one,* etc. These are truths about the meanings of symbols, and they are familiar from everyday life. Only a fool would deny any analytical relation. They are so obvious that their denials are plainly contradictory or nonsensical (as in *I am a married bachelor,* or *I know he is married, but is he a bachelor?*). They could not turn out to be otherwise. The analytical philosopher systematizes conceptual connections like these.
- EMPIRICAL generalizations are scientific as well as contingent. This is the world of empirical facts, which could always surprise us, so it is not trivial — but at the same time it contains nothing inevitable or necessary. It is entirely chancy, and there is nothing logically contradictory about denying any

---

[1] This is actually argued best in Plato's later work, the *Theaetetus.*

of it. It is vaguely familiar from everyday life but is perfected in modern science, especially physics. (For example, *Swans are white, Space is curved.*)

In the words of one eminent popularizer of this view, A.J. Ayer:

The views which are put forward in this treatise derive from the doctrines of Bertrand Russell and Wittgenstein, which are themselves the logical outcome of the empiricism of Berkeley and David Hume. Like Hume, I divide all genuine propositions into two classes: those which, in his terminology, concern 'relations of ideas", and those which concern 'matters of fact'. The former class comprises the a priori propositions of logic and pure mathematics, and these I allow to be necessary and certain only because they are analytic. That is, I maintain that the reason why these propositions cannot be confuted in experience is that they do not make any assertion about the empirical world, but simply record our determination to use symbols in a certain fashion. Propositions concerning empirical matters of fact, on the other hand, I hold to be hypotheses. which can be probable but never certain. And in giving an account of the method of their validation I claim also to have explained the nature of truth.

To test whether a sentence expresses a genuine empirical hypothesis, I adopt what may be called a modified verification principle. For I require of an empirical hypothesis, not indeed that it should be conclusively verifiable, but that some possible sense-experience should be relevant to the determination of its truth or falsehood. If a putative propositipn fails tp satisfy this principle, and is not a tautology, then I hold that it is metaphysical, and that, being metaphysical, it is neither true nor false but literally senseless. It will be found that much of what ordinarily passes for philosophy is metaphysical according to this criterion, and. In particular, that it can not be significantly asserted that there is a non-empirical world of values, or that men have immortal souls, or that there is a transcendent God.

As for the propositions of philosophy themselves, they are held to be linguistically necessary, and so analytic. And with regard to the relationship of pliilosophy and empirical science, it is, shown that the philosopher is not in a position to furnish speculative truths, which would, as it were, compete with the hypotheses of science, nor yet to pass a priori judgements upon the validity of scientific theories, but that his function is to clarify the propositions of science, by exhibiting their logical relationships, and by defining the symbols which occur in them.[1]

On these premises analytically oriented Anglo-American scholars like Vlastos and Owen have an easy time identifying Socrates' philosophical method: if he is to qualify as a rational philosopher in their sense and he is not a scientific experimentalist (he has no laboratory, and he does not travel in the forests to observe animals and plants, etc.) then he had better be an analyst just like them.[2]

Now why exactly would this be wrong?

This is easy to see if we consider the role of Socrates' definitions in his overall philosophy and lifestyle. For if Socrates is only an analyst of commonsensical trivialities, then it hardly makes sense for him to:

- die for his beliefs. For the ordinary trivialities are in place already, so a Socrates of this type would not be a rebel or a reformer. He would be fully at home in Athens.
- say his teachings are divine. For of course the most usual associations are mundane and not divine. They are ordinary habits in the city as it is. They are not higher or supernatural.
- say that Ideas are scales and optimal instances on those scales (see below). Why would he set unusual standards like these? They play no part in the kind of ordinary life which conceptual analysts analyze.
- teach unpopular and even unheard of views, as he does, that all virtues are one, that virtue is knowledge, that to know what it is good is automatically to do it, etc.[3]

One might add that a mere analyst of everyday language would certainly not have inspired a Plato, a Renaissance humanist like Erasmus,

---

[1] Ayer pp. 8-9.

[2] Vlastos does wonder how Socrates can possibly hold that *mere logical consistency or analytical tautologies* can bring him to any of his favorite conclusions, which do not agree with ordinary beliefs. Vlastos does not consider that Socrates may not rely on logical coherence or analyticity alone: that very idea is from Vlastos and people like Ayer, and it is never articulated by Socrates. Thus Vlastos approaches the texts with his own map in his hand.

See Kim for some earlier Continental alternatives: Neokantianism, Heidegger, Nietzsche.

[3] I will not go into these so-called 'Socratic paradoxes' here. For introductory notes on them see Prior.

---

the Enlightenment wit Voltaire, Romantic existentialists like Hamann, Kierkegaard, Nietzsche, and Jaspers, or anti-totalitarians like Arendt and Popper in the aftermath of the Second World War. This entire tradition has celebrated a Socrates of uncompromising idealism and inquiry, and such a aspiration is entirely sidestepped by commonsensical sociologism.[1]

Dialectical Definitions

If Socrates defines things *dialectically* then what does that mean?

In the Introduction I said that dialectical questions are formulated by going all the way: ask *Why?* until you cannot. Hence dialectical reasoning does not produce mere generalizations as does scientific reasoning, but absolutes. For if we trace causes as in a BECAUSE b BECAUSE c BECAUSE d then what we get is not merely a *collection* of causes (a collection which would make up a generalization) but a *hierarchy* of them. In other words, the scientist collects *equal* members of a set so as to get to state a generalization about the set, but that is not what the dialectician does: the dialectician builds a pyramid. The top level is the absolute one and everything below it is only relative or conditional. The scientist is not looking for certainty or absolutes, but the dialectician is.

In this spirit, Socrates seeks the kinds of *absolutes or ultimates* which the Athenians do not even care for, preferring wealth and power etc.

Next I will document evidence for this dialectical view — step by step, section after section.

God in the *Apology*

We may begin with a comparatively *indirect* route to the dialectical view of Socrates. This derives from his curious religion.

We already witnessed Socrates saying that he will obey God rather than the people of Athens — much as he loves them! — and that his special wisdom consists in knowing that he does not know.

Now, per se this already suffices for a dialectical pattern of one kind. For it is self-relational: it is self-critical and self-ironic. Plato's Socrates may maintain that this type of self-irony is in fact superhuman. This is corroborated in Plato's later work, the *Sophist*:

> STRANGER: There is the time-honoured mode which our fathers commonly practised towards their sons, and which is still adopted by many—either of roughly reproving their

---

[1] Despite this the analytical trends continue to dominate research on Socrates at the philosophy departments of Western universities, and the major names now number Irwin, Burnyeat, Benson, and Woodruff.

errors, or of gently advising them; which varieties may be correctly included under the general term of admonition.

THEAETETUS: True.

STRANGER: But whereas some appear to have arrived at the conclusion that all ignorance is involuntary, and that no one who thinks himself wise is willing to learn any of those things in which he is conscious of his own cleverness, and that the admonitory sort of instruction gives much trouble and does little good—

THEAETETUS: There they are quite right.

STRANGER: Accordingly, they set to work to eradicate the spirit of conceit in another way.

THEAETETUS: In what way?

STRANGER: They cross-examine a man's words, when he thinks that he is saying something and is really saying nothing, and easily convict him of inconsistencies in his opinions; these they then collect by the dialectical process, and placing them side by side, show that they contradict one another about the same things, in relation to the same things, and in the same respect. He, seeing this, is angry with himself, and grows gentle towards others, and thus is entirely delivered from great prejudices and harsh notions, in a way which is most amusing to the hearer, and produces the most lasting good effect on the person who is the subject of the operation. For as the physician considers that the body will receive no benefit from taking food until the internal obstacles have been removed, so the purifier of the soul is conscious that his patient will receive no benefit from the application of knowledge until he is refuted, and from refutation learns modesty; he must be purged of his prejudices first and made to think that he knows only what he knows, and no more.

THEAETETUS: That is certainly the best and wisest state of mind.

STRANGER: For all these reasons, Theaetetus, we must admit that refutation is the greatest and chiefest of purifications, and he who has not been refuted, though he be the Great King himself, is in an awful state of impurity; he is uninstructed and deformed in those things in which he who would be truly blessed ought to be fairest and purest.

THEAETETUS: Very true.[1]

Refutations purify the soul, and the health thus attained is moral or religious. It amounts to the chiefest type of purification. (More on this in 1.7.)

As such, However, this lead is too isolated, and we need to look at more numerous aspects of Socrates' philosophy to come to rest content with it dialectical interpretation.

Ideas in the *Hippias Major*

A single early Platonic work, the *Hippias Major*, introduces Plato's two words for the Ideas, *idea* and *eidos*, which mean the same. Both have the familiar double logic. Compare this longish passage to get a sufficient impression:

> Socrates: "Very well," he will say, "and how about a beautiful lyre? Is it not beautiful?" Shall we agree, Hippias?
>
> Hippias: Yes.
>
> Socrates: After this, then, the man will ask, I am sure, judging by his character: "You most excellent man, how about a beautiful pot? Is it, then, not beautiful?"
>
> Hippias: Socrates, who is the fellow? What an uncultivated person, who has the face to mention such worthless things in a dignified discussion!
>
> Socrates: That's the kind of person he is, Hippias, not elegant, but vulgar, thinking of nothing but the truth. But nevertheless the man must be answered, and I will declare my opinion beforehand: if the pot were made by a good potter, were smooth and round and well fired, as are some of the two-handled pots, those that hold six choes, very beautiful ones — if that were the kind of pot he asked about, we must agree that it is beautiful; for how could we say that being beautiful it is not beautiful?
>
> Hippias: We could not at all, Socrates.
>
> Socrates: "Then," he will say, "a beautiful pot also is beautiful, is it not?" Answer.

---

[1] *Sophist* 229E-230E.

Hippias: Well, Socrates, it is like this, I think. This utensil, when well wrought, is beautiful, but absolutely considered it does not deserve to be regarded as beautiful in comparison with a mare and a maiden and all the beautiful things.

Socrates: Very well I understand, Hippias, that the proper reply to him who asks these questions is this: "Sir, you are not aware that the saying of Heraclitus is good, that 'the most beautiful of monkeys is ugly compared with the race of man,' and the most beautiful of pots is ugly compared with the race of maidens, as Hippias the wise man says." Is it not so, Hippias?

Hippias: Certainly, Socrates; you replied rightly.

Socrates: Listen then. For I am sure that after this he will say: "Yes, but, Socrates, if we compare maidens with gods, will not the same thing happen to them that happened to pots when compared with maidens? Will not the most beautiful maiden appear ugly? Or does not Heraclitus, whom you cite, mean just this, that the wisest of men, if compared with a god, will appear a monkey, both in wisdom and in beauty and in every-thing else?" Shall we agree, Hippias, that the most beautiful maiden is ugly if compared with the gods?

Hippias: Yes, for who would deny that, Socrates?

Socrates: If, then, we agree to that, he will laugh and say: "Socrates, do you remember the question you were asked?" "I do," I shall say, "the question was what the absolute beautiful is." "Then," he will say, "when you were asked for the beautiful, do you give as your reply what is, as you yourself say, no more beautiful than ugly?" "So it seems," I shall say; or what do you, my friend, advise me to say?

Hippias: That is what I advise; for, of course, in saying that the human race is not beautiful in comparison with gods, you will be speaking the truth.

Socrates: "But if I had asked you," he will say, "in the beginning what is beautiful and ugly, if you had replied as you now do, would you not have replied correctly? But do you still think that the absolute beautiful, by the addition of which all other things are adorned and made to appear beautiful, when its form is added to any of them — do you think that is a maiden or a mare or a lyre?"

> Hippias: Well, certainly, Socrates, if that is what he is looking for, nothing is easier than to answer and tell him what the beautiful is, by which all other things are adorned and by the addition of which they are made to appear beautiful. So the fellow is very simple-minded and knows nothing about beautiful possessions. For if you reply to him: "This that you ask about, the beautiful, is nothing else but gold," he will be thrown into confusion and will not attempt to confute you. For we all know, I fancy, that wherever this is added, even what before appears ugly will appear beautiful when adorned with gold.[1]

What is the beautiful (*kalon*)?, Socrates asks Hippias, and in the end Hippias reaches his conclusion: it must be gold.

However, Hippias' answer is not credible because he has trouble understanding Socrates' question. The question is after both (i) the most beautiful thing there is and (ii) a general yardstick for what to accept as at all beautiful anywhere. (At (i), the maiden is beautiful only in some comparisons, not in all. At (ii), beauty is 'added' to each beautiful thing.) This is the double logic of the Ideas as in 0.2.

From a modern perspective the oddity is that (i) and (ii) are viewed *together*. After all, a scale for length — like a yard stick — need not be especially long, and money itself is not rich. Might this not be but a logical blunder on Socrates' part? After all, he does write before logic is systematized for the first time by Aristoteles in his *Organon*. On the other hand, what exactly is the weight of Aristotle? He never meets Socrates, and he is utterly wrong about physics, for example. May he not be equally wrong here? May Aristotle not even lead logical reasoning in a wrong direction? I will note in 3.2 that in some ways this is the true story. We cannot delegate the issues to Aristotle.

But then what are we to do?

In terms of *the text itself* the issue is hard to decide. For in principle one could read the passage or the dialogue, and indeed all of Plato's dialogues, in a number of different ways. Perhaps he is not a dialectician in my sense *or* a pre-scientific inductivist: he could also be studied in terms of literary style and narratology. Or is there some concealed structural pattern which keeps recurring? Or should the etymological origin of the word 'idea' decide (the word derives from *idein*: to see)? And which other words recur most frequently with which (cf. Lutoslawski)?

---

[1] *Hippias Major* 288C-289E.

A further decision is whether to be *nice*. Is Socrates not perhaps rather laughable, a public clown as in Aristophanes' comedies? Is indeed much of Western rationalism altogether rather silly, as for instance many post-modernists would have it? This piece of text does not per se determine any answer to such larger and prior questions which loom large in the background.

However, here is the view I would recommend taking: *if* we want to be nice, and *if* our source should make great sense and instruct us about philosophically significant topics, then it is not far-fetched to say that Socrates may have his reasons to conflate (i) and (ii). More than this, if we do not see those reasons now then this may be a shortcoming on *our* part. A reading of this type is respectful. But it is also called for in order to make most of our time: we rank the text above ourselves. (If you open a book, do you want it to be a worthwhile experience? If you go to the park then you do, so why not when opening a book? If you are sure before walking to the park that the experience will be only laughable, why do you go?)

Now let us move on to the next piece of evidence.[1]

Happiness in the *Gorgias*

As noted, some of Socrates' competitors in his day are the *sophists*, who teach affluent youths to speak in public. Unlike Socrates the sophists are rhetoricians, so they teach people to sell ideas or to trick others into believing things. They do not argue or prove like Socrates.

However, the sophists differ from Socrates also in another respect: unlike them he does not expect to get paid. What he expects is only more philosophy! Philosophy is to breed more philosophy. Socrates' craft is thus shaped like a symmetric circle, for he aims to reap what he sows. In contrast the sophists's equation is accidental and uneven, for they teach speaking for money.

This is reflected in an interesting manner in Plato's *Gorgias*. Polus the sophist believes that his skill entitles him to power and profits. For his generalization is that strong individuals who know how to dominate others should be rewarded with riches. But this has Socrates puzzled:

SOCRATES: And ought not the better to have a larger share?

CALLICLES: Not of meats and drinks.

---

[1] I do admit that my own procedure now is inductive (science-like), but only for the time being! It will get more dialectical towards the end of the chapter.

SOCRATES: I understand: then, perhaps, of coats—the skil-fullest weaver ought to have the largest coat, and the greatest number of them, and go about clothed in the best and finest of them?

CALLICLES: Fudge about coats!

SOCRATES: Then the skilfullest and best in making shoes ought to have the advantage in shoes; the shoemaker, clearly, should walk about in the largest shoes, and have the greatest number of them?

CALLICLES: Fudge about shoes! What nonsense are you talking?

SOCRATES: Or, if this is not your meaning, perhaps you would say that the wise and good and true husbandman should actually have a larger share of seeds, and have as much seed as possible for his own land?

CALLICLES: How you go on, always talking in the same way, Socrates!

SOCRATES: Yes, Callicles, and also about the same things.

CALLICLES: Yes, by the Gods, you are literally always talking of cobblers and fullers and cooks and doctors, as if this had to do with our argument.

SOCRATES: But why will you not tell me in what a man must be superior and wiser in order to claim a larger share; will you neither accept a suggestion, nor offer one?[1]

Socrates is saying that the fitting reward for the shoemaker is shoes. The coat-maker gets coats, not shoes. By the same token, the apple-picker would get apples, not money. For whatever is produced is properly attained or owned. If you bake cakes you get cakes. But this means also that the sophist who tricks others should be tricked in turn.

Socrates has not here said anything about an 'idea', but his meaning is formally the same: we are to practice what we preach — so the same x should function both as measure and measured thing. Hence the familiar double logic again sounds entirely fitting, and thus the impression is now a little stronger that its place is not marginal or incidental in Socrates philosophy.

---

[1] *Gorgias* 490D-491A.

But now for the paradox I mentioned, to state the case more conclusively.

The Paradox of Inquiry

Earlier in this chapter, Socrates said in the *Apologia* that he knows that he does not know, and this is of course a paradox. For either one knows or not. If one knows that one does not know some things then one *does* know something else, and then one cannot know truly that one does not know anything at all. If again one is purely ignorant about everything then one must be ignorant also about one's ignorance. These are the two consistent options.[1]

Socrates' response to the oracle's enigmatic pronouncement, However, was to *inquire* into things. He went out into the streets of Athens and questioned everyone until they had him killed. Hence, he did something about his ignorance. He seemed to conquer it.

Now, a different paradox associated with this — the famous *paradox of inquiry*.

Stated bluntly, this paradox is that

- you cannot inquire into x if you do *not* know about x (for how then do you know how to inquire into x?), but that
- you also cannot inquire into x if you *do* know about x (for why would you? It would be like asking your own name).

Hence, you do or you do not, and either way you are doomed. Inquiry is impossible.

If we relate this to Socrates then we seem to have two options. Firstly it is possible that whenever Socrates questions someone — for instance Hippias or Meno — then Socrates only *feigns* ignorance, making believe that he does not know the things he asks about only in order to *teach* about those things in his ironic fashion.

As the reader may well know, ironic instruction of this sort is tremendously effective especially with persons who are full of themselves. The cunning strategy — learned from Socrates' paradigmatic example in Plato's earlier dialogues, for he is *the* reference for this — is then to first flatter the student. Make him proud and puffed up. Next, ask him about the important things you want to teach him — not letting him on of course that in reality you intend to teach and not to learn. After this, all

---

[1] Above I let this paradox live: it was not solved.

you need to do is to — ever so politely — find fault in his answers. (Show they are contradictory.) This you need to keep doing until you purify the student by means of your refutations — quite as in the quotation from the *Sophist* above. The moral lesson is learned by the student once he confesses that actually he does not know, and that knowledge is more difficult to attain than he ever assumed.

Now, it may be that whenever Socrates 'inquires' into things his main object is just this. Perhaps he wants merely to teach the Athenians some manners. They are loud and proud, dominating much of their Mediterranean environment. They deserve to be stung by a gadfly!

However, on this reading Socrates avoids the paradox of inquire by simply *not inquiring*. Hence this is not to solve the paradox but only to stay away from it, and this is not entirely satisfying.

What then is the other option? Socrates could also be be *honestly interested* in finding things out about numerous topics, holding that there are solvable and as yet unsolved questions about knowledge, God, excellence, and so forth, and that his interlocutors, errant as they are about some topics, just might have answers or at least some instructive, inspiring hunches about these higher matters.

On this second reading the paradox of inquiry *would* have bite, however. It would not be avoided. Socrates *would* inquire, and accordingly he would need to have his dogmatic ideals *before* inquiry. Hence, he would have to know the key things before he even begins asking — and still he would actually expect there to be new answers out there waiting for him. Now what coherent sense could that make?

The answer is anticipated in Socrates' original reply to the paradox in Plato's *Meno*:

> MENO: And how will you enquire, Socrates, into that which you do not know? What will you put forth as the subject of enquiry? And if you find what you want, how will you ever know that this is the thing which you did not know?
>
> SOCRATES: I know, Meno, what you mean; but just see what a tiresome dispute you are introducing. You argue that a man cannot enquire either about that which he knows, or about that which he does not know; for if he knows, he has no need to enquire; and if not, he cannot; for he does not know the very subject about which he is to enquire.
>
> MENO: Well, Socrates, and is not the argument sound?
>
> SOCRATES: I think not.
>
> MENO: Why not?

SOCRATES: I will tell you why: I have heard from certain wise men and women who spoke of things divine that—

MENO: What did they say?

SOCRATES: They spoke of a glorious truth, as I conceive.

MENO: What was it? and who were they?

SOCRATES: Some of them were priests and priestesses, who had studied how they might be able to give a reason of their profession: there have been poets also, who spoke of these things by inspiration, like Pindar, and many others who were inspired. And they say— mark, now, and see whether their words are true—they say that the soul of man is immortal, and at one time has an end, which is termed dying, and at another time is born again, but is never destroyed. And the moral is, that a man ought to live always in perfect holiness. 'For in the ninth year Persephone sends the souls of those from whom she has received the penalty of ancient crime back again from beneath into the light of the sun above, and these are they who become noble kings and mighty men and great in wisdom and are called saintly heroes in after ages.' The soul, then, as being immortal, and having been born again many times, and having seen all things that exist, whether in this world or in the world below, has knowledge of them all; and it is no wonder that she should be able to call to remembrance all that she ever knew about virtue, and about everything; for as all nature is akin, and the soul has learned all things; there is no difficulty in her eliciting or as men say learning, out of a single recollection all the rest, if a man is strenuous and does not faint; for all enquiry and all learning is but recollection.[1]

In this passage Socrates first summarizes a paradox and then suggests a solution by reference to *recollection* or *innate ideas*, as they are later known.

For a fuller statement of this view we need now to look to Plato's *Phaedo*.

Enter Plato: the *Phaedo*

As noted the *Phaedo* is by all accounts a Platonic work and no longer Socratic, so even if 'Socrates' appears here he is only Plato's puppet. The central portion of the dialogue is probably this:

---

[1] *Meno* 80D-81D.

"Do you not know, then, that lovers when they see a lyre, or a garment, or any thing else which their favorite is accustomed to use, are thus affected; they both recognize the lyre, and receive in their minds the form of the person to whom the lyre belonged? This is reminiscence: just as anyone, seeing Simmias, is often reminded of Cebes, and so in an infinite number of similar instances."

"An infinite number, indeed, by Jupiter!" said Simmias.

"Is not, then," he said, "something of this sort a kind of reminiscence, especially when one is thus affected with respect to things which, from lapse of time, and not thinking of them, one has now forgotten?"

"Certainly," he replied.

"But what?" he continued. "Does it happen that when one sees a painted horse or a painted lyre one is reminded of a man, and that when one sees a picture of Simmias one is reminded of Cebes?"

"Certainly."

"And does it not also happen that on seeing a picture of Simmias one is reminded of Simmias himself?"

"It does, indeed," he replied.

"Does it not happen, then, according to all this, that reminiscence arises partly from things like, and partly from things unlike?"

"It does."

"But when one is reminded by things like, is it not necessary that one should be thus further affected, so as to perceive whether, as regards likeness, this falls short or not of the thing of which one has been reminded?"

"It is necessary," he replied.

"Consider, then," said Socrates, "if the case is thus. Do we allow that there is such a thing as equality? I do not mean of one log with another, nor one stone with another, nor any thing else of this kind, but something altogether different from all these—abstract equality; do we allow that there is any such thing, or not?"

"By Jupiter! we most assuredly do allow it," replied Simmias.

"And do we know what it is itself?"

"Certainly," he replied.

"Whence have we derived the knowledge of it? Is it not from the things we have just now mentioned, and that from seeing logs, or stones, or other things of the kind, equal, we have from these formed an idea of that which is different from these—for does it not appear to you to be different? Consider the matter thus. Do not stones that are equal, and logs sometimes that are the same, appear at one time equal, and at another not?"

"Certainly."

"But what? Does abstract equality ever appear to you unequal? or equality inequality?"

"Never, Socrates, at any time."

"These equal things, then," he said, "and abstract equality, are not the same?"

"By no means, Socrates, as it appears."[1]

This is best read in R language right away.

The Idea of the Equal is a relation (R) as distinct from its relata, like a and b in aRb, if a and b are such things as logs or stones. But also, the Equal is *itself* equal to something, so RRc (EQUALS EQUALS c). And even more than this, the distance *we* take when we realize this indicates how we are spiritually free from empirical givens or ordinary life. Thus there is a question about a self-relational *Idea* and then there is a question about a superempirical *psyche*.

Let us run through this again but by means of an example. I may say that the number of chairs now on my balcony equals four or that I am identical to the author of this book, but in saying these things I do not believe that I am (a) stating the most perfect equations, or any especially notable examples of equality or identity, or (b) conflating the chairs or myself or this book with the relation of equality or identity itself. Were I do look into (a) then I would compare some key equations, whichever they may be, in science or in metaphysics, or perhaps in certain religious books, but I would certainly not for a moment believe that *chairs* on the balcony or *my personal* identity are the paradigmatic items. At (b) I would be drawn to questions about pure equality or identity, that is — of course

---

[1] *Phaedo* 73D-74C.

— to whatever *they* may equal or be identical with. And they are not a set of chairs, and they are not Tommi: that would be mad to say.

In this way we are confronted with an archetypal topic — a 'Platonic' thought of an Idea, in a standard use of the term. Let us pause briefly to note what *Platonism* in this sense generally means.

In most Plato books the examples first given for Platonism are mathematical: one grasps mathematical truths with one's mind's eye (or in early modern terms a natural light or a reasoning faculty), and one does not empirically sense them — see, hear, taste, smell, or touch. They have a special certainty. Triangles have three sides, for example, and a line is the shortest route between two points: one does not need to study all kinds of triangles or lines to come to appreciate that this will always be so and inevitably. What is more there will never be a picture of a triangle which has no particular size or color — so you cannot draw *the* triangle — that is the perfect and archetypal one. But similarly for the circle, the point, etc. None the less it is *the* triangle that three sides, *the* point that has no extension, etc. Thus the topics of reasoning are like in another world.

Plato (probably following Pythagoras) is certainly impressed by mathematical examples like these, but his main thrust is ethical, aesthetic, religious, and epistemological. How can this be? He takes it that the models which guide these areas of life and thought are the properly archetypal ones, and in fact he says repeatedly and in numerous ways (especially in his *Republic*, Ch. 2 below) that mathematics is not quite *this* archetypal, not as fundamental as what he labels philosophy or dialectic. *Why* he says that exactly, and *how* he may maintain that the highest certainties are like this, has been a subject of philosophical controversy ever since. It is the grand topic for all Plato scholars beginning with his Athenian Academy, the Alexandrian theologians who try to unite Plato's and Aristotle's Athens with the Old Testament's Jerusalem, Renaissance Neoplatonism, German Romantic scholarship, and so on to the present day.

Speaking historically, the variety of main philosophical positions in this — obviously central — arena is surprisingly small. Plotinean mystics abound in Roman antiquity, the Renaissance, and Romanticism, and for them an Idea (or else the Good, the Agathon, which I will come to in Ch. 2) is simply the all, the totality of everything. (The *Parmenides* is the main reference for this view.) The other main class of Platonists says very moderately that an Idea (such as the Equal) is but a universal or concept. This is not to mystify Platonism like a Plotinean but to trivialize it. Why is this so trivial? Yellow is a universal or concept, and car, or hair, shoelace, etc. But are these archetypes? Of course not. However, this type of view is now prevalent in Plato scholarship (believe it or not). How to get more serious? Must one go back to the mystics? In answer to this I already presented aRb and RRc.

Now let us look more closely at the Platonic *psyche.*

Plato says that alongside the Ideas (like the Equal) there need to be certain other things that can reach and think them — and these he has now first called psyches. Thus if we can imagine that the Idea is a thing separate from the mundane situations which we confront, then also we or our psyches are thereby in a sense proved to be separate from the low and mundane run of things. As Plato likes to say, there is an *affinity* between the psyche and the Ideas, and accordingly our thoughtful selves *belong* with the eternal archetypes. We do not know them from this — sensual and bodily — world but we recollect them from times before we were (physically) born! (The Greek word for recollection is *anamnesis.*)

Plato's wish is to use these premises in the *Phaedo* to prove the psyche's *immortality*, and probably the closest he comes to establishing this is in arguing that because the psyche is simple — indivisible into smaller parts — it has to be immortal. In his words:

> "We ought, then," said Socrates, "to ask ourselves some such question as this: to what kind of thing it appertains to be thus affected—namely, to be dispersed—and for what we ought to fear, lest it should be so affected, and for what not. And after this we should consider which of the two the soul is, and in the result should either be confident or fearful for our soul."
>
> "You speak truly," said he.
>
> "Does it not, then, appertain to that which is formed by composition, and is naturally compounded, to be thus affected, to be dissolved in the same manner as that in which it was compounded; and if there is any thing not compounded, does it not appertain to this alone, if to any thing, not to be thus affected?"
>
> "It appears to me to be so," said Cebes.
>
> "Is it not most probable, then, that things which are always the same, and in the same state, are uncompounded, but that things which are constantly changing, and are never in the same state, are compounded?"
>
> "To me it appears so."
>
> "Let us return, then," he said, "to the subjects on which we before discoursed. Whether is essence itself, of which we gave this account that it exists, both in our questions and answers,

always the same, or does it sometimes change? Does equality itself, the beautiful itself, and each several thing which is, ever undergo any change, however small? Or does each of them which exists, being an unmixed essence by itself, continue always the same, and in the same state, and never undergo any variation at all under any circumstances?"

"They must of necessity continue the same and in the same state, Socrates," said Cebes.

"But what shall we say of the many beautiful things, such as men, horses, garments, or other things of the kind, whether equal or beautiful, or of all things synonymous with them? Do they continue the same, or, quite contrary to the former, are they never at any time, so to say, the same, either with respect to themselves or one another?"

"These, on the other hand," replied Cebes, "never continue the same."

"These, then, you can touch, or see, or perceive by the other senses; but those that continue the same, you can not apprehend in any other way than by the exercise of thought; for such things are invisible, and are not seen?"

"You say what is strictly true," replied Cebes.

"We may assume, then, if you please," he continued, "that there are two species of things; the one visible, the other invisible?"

"We may," he said.

"And the invisible always continuing the same, but the visible never the same?"

"This, too," he said, "we may assume."

"Come, then," he asked, "is there anything else belonging to us than, on the one hand, body, and, on the other, soul?"

"Nothing else," he replied.

"To which species, then, shall we say the body is more like, and more nearly allied?"

"It is clear to everyone," he said, "that it is to the visible."

"But what of the soul? Is it visible or invisible?"

"It is not visible to men, Socrates," he replied.

"But we speak of things which are visible, or not so, to the nature of men; or to some other nature, think you?"

"To that of men."

"What, then, shall we say of the soul—that it is visible, or not visible?"

"Not visible."

"Is it, then, invisible?"

"Yes."

"The soul, then, is more like the invisible than the body; and the body, the visible?"

"It must needs be so, Socrates."

"And did we not, some time since, say this too, that the soul, when it employs the body to examine any thing, either by means of the sight or hearing, or any other sense (for to examine any thing by means of the body is to do so by the senses), is then drawn by the body to things that never continue the same, and wanders and is confused, and reels as if intoxicated, through coming into contact with things of this kind?"

"Certainly."

"But when it examines anything by itself, does it approach that which is pure, eternal, immortal, and unchangeable, and, as being allied to it, continue constantly with it, so long as it subsists by itself, and has the power, and does it cease from its wandering, and constantly continue the same with respect to those things, through coming into contact with things of this kind? And is this affection of the soul called wisdom?"

"You speak," he said, "in every respect, well and truly, Socrates."

"To which species of the two, then, both from what was before and now said, does the soul appear to you to be more like and more nearly allied?"

"Every one, I think, would allow, Socrates," he replied, "even the dullest person, from this method of reasoning, that the soul is in every respect more like that which continues constantly the same than that which does not so."[1]

If death is decomposition and x cannot decompose then x cannot die. For compounded things change and perish, and this is what constantly occurs to bodies, which are the objects of experience. Horses come and go, and garments turn back into threads, etc. But the psyche is simple and changeless like the Ideas (misleadingly here translated as 'essences').

---

[1] *Phaedo* 78B-79E.

The psyche is restless until it finds its way to Ideas of Equality and Beauty, but this is how it eventually reaches its peace, stability, and immortality. (The psyche is purified by the Ideas and polluted by the body and the senses, the *Phaedo* says elsewhere.)

Plato's Ideas continue to lead students of philosophy rather directly to the most high-flown regions of theoretical philosophy, but his psyche — as per the *Phaedo* — has a more troubled history in modern times, especially due to Kant's Paralogisms (which I will discuss in 3.4). However, despite this the Platonic psyche should not be viewed as an entirely dead topic because its status is also *ethical:* an *ought* and not only an *is.* The core of Plato's psyche-ethos is that a psyche should purify itself — by philosophizing dialectically. In accordance with this thinking, purity or simplicity is not the psyche's birthright but its achievement. (The *Phaedo* is recurrently of both views: the purity is a given or else it is a trophy.) This permits us to make the following comparisons:

- *Real ruler (fact):* A REAL DICTATOR makes laws which everyone must in fact follow.
- *Imaginary ruler (value):* THE GOLDEN RULE requires you to *imagine* that you rule, i.e. that others in general treat you like you treat them. They need not in fact pay you back in kind: the moral consideration is to consider the prospect that they would. (More on this in the Kant chapter, Ch. 3.)
- *Real reincarnation (fact):* AN IMMORTAL PSYCHE is reincarnated again and again in time, depending on how he acts — so this happens in real fact. If he lives like an ape, he is reborn as an ape, if as saint then as a saint, etc.
- *Imaginary reincarnation (value):* A PLATONIC MORALIST makes laws which do not in fact lead him ever to be reborn but like the Golden-Rule-moralist he is to imagine what *would* follow if he was. He is to live a life he would like to live again.

I am suggesting that (i) relates to (ii) as (iii) relates to (iv) (so i:ii::iii:iv).[1] The difference between the Christian or Confucian moralist on the one hand is and the Platonist on the other is only that the latter generalizes in *intra*subjective *time* and not in *inter*subjective *space.* As in Christianity or Confucianism the point would be to generalize based on a fiction, but the *direction* in which one generalizes is different. (I will address this again in 2.5.)

In Plato's terms this is a comparison between views of *virtue.*

---

[1] This idea is inspired by Magnus, who reads Nietzsche (not Plato) roughly in this manner (cf. my *Plato's Logic*).

A virtue (Greek: *arete*) for the ancient Greeks is not precisely a moral thing, because it is understandable at the same time as a kind of excellence. For example it is normal for them to say that the *arete* of a knife is to be sharp. It performs its function well.

Virtue in this sense is one of Socrates' major topics in Plato's earlier dialogues, so his questions are phrased quite usually in their terms. This is because Socrates does not tend directly to ask about origins or purposes or authorities or contituents — first causes. He tries to make do with the language of his fellow Greeks on the streets. (What is courage (Plato's *Laches*), or temperance (*Charmides*), or how about piety (*Euthyphro*) or justice (*Republic* Book I)?) They all care for virtue and they all want it, so by phrasing his philosophizing in virtue terms Socrates manages to be relevant to the other persons he addresses. (If he asked them what *spin* is then they would not care. He would not be a public critic in a sense that would interest anybody. In modern Western culture a topic such as freedom, rights, or wealth is of common interest. God has become less popular, and virtue now sounds quaint.)

This is how the virtues are defined in the *Phaedo*:

> [...] the courage and temperance of other [non-philosophers], if you will consider them, are really a contradiction.
>
> How so?
>
> Well, he said, you are aware that death is regarded by men in general as a great evil.
>
> Very true, he said.
>
> And do not courageous men face death because they are afraid of yet greater evils?
>
> That is quite true.
>
> Then all but the philosophers are courageous only from fear, and because they are afraid; and yet that a man should be courageous from fear, and because he is a coward, is surely a strange thing.
>
> Very true.
>
> And are not the temperate exactly in the same case? They are temperate because they are intemperate—which might seem to be a contradiction, but is nevertheless the sort of thing which happens with this foolish temperance. For there are pleasures which they are afraid of losing; and in their desire to keep them, they abstain from some pleasures, because they

are overcome by others; and although to be conquered by pleasure is called by men intemperance, to them the conquest of pleasure consists in being conquered by pleasure. And that is what I mean by saying that, in a sense, they are made temperate through intemperance.

Such appears to be the case.

Yet the exchange of one fear or pleasure or pain for another fear or pleasure or pain, and of the greater for the less, as if they were coins, is not the exchange of virtue. O my blessed Simmias, is there not one true coin for which all things ought to be exchanged?—and that is wisdom; and only in exchange for this, and in company with this, is anything truly bought or sold, whether courage or temperance or justice. And is not all true virtue the companion of wisdom, no matter what fears or pleasures or other similar goods or evils may or may not attend her? But the virtue which is made up of these goods, when they are severed from wisdom and exchanged with one another, is a shadow of virtue only, nor is there any freedom or health or truth in her; but in the true exchange there is a purging away of all these things, and temperance, and justice, and courage, and wisdom herself are the purgation of them. The founders of the mysteries would appear to have had a real meaning, and were not talking nonsense when they intimated in a figure long ago that he who passes unsanctified and unini-tiated into the world below will lie in a slough, but that he who arrives there after initiation and purification will dwell with the gods. For 'many,' as they say in the mysteries, 'are the thyrsus-bearers, but few are the mystics,'—meaning, as I interpret the words, 'the true philosophers.' In the number of whom, during my whole life, I have been seeking, according to my ability, to find a place;—whether I have sought in a right way or not, and whether I have succeeded or not, I shall truly know in a little while, if God will, when I myself arrive in the other world—such is my belief.[1]

Here Socrates instructs Cebes that each virtue should be exchanged for *virtue* — not for something else, so the whole field of positive values is to be autonomous. Virtue cannot be a means to something else like pleasure or safety. It cannot have an external yardstick because — like an Idea — it requires autonomy. It must be its own reward. This goes

---

[1] *Phaedo* 68D-69E.

quite well with the reincarnation ethos that was sketched a few pages ago. (One lives in cycles.)

But what does this any of have to do with the *paradox of inquiry?*

This is simple: an Idea like the Equal and the ethos of reincarnation solve the paradox because they are *precisely the kinds of things* which have surface appearances as well as deep structures:

- *THE IDEA OF THE EQUAL:* equality is a relation like = in a = b, but non-tautological relations are progressive and not repetitive, and accordingly the Idea of the Equal lifts itself in the air by the bootstraps: in EQUALS EQUALS c, c does not spell 'EQUALS' again and c rather states what it *is* that equals equals (the product of the equation). This is the identity of identity itself.
- *THE ETHOS OF REINCARNATION:* if a IS REBORN AS b IS REBORN AS c, b reveals the true character of a and c reveals the true character of b. But again, a is not reborn merely as a: a monkey as a monkey, an eagle as an eagle, etc. The reincarnations are not repetitions.[1]

The *changing* shapes of the same individuals solve the paradox of inquiry, and analytical or tautological repetitions do not. The analyst cannot solve the paradox because for him identities are only as in logical analysis: they cannot be news. Unlike the analytically interpreted Socrates, the dialectical Socrates opens a new world for us to study — and this is explored in different ways by numerous later dialecticians.[2]

---

[1] In practice this means that if a monkey is to be reborn as an eagle, it must act like an eagle *while still a monkey!*

[2] Is it now implied, absurdly, that an Idea changes in time, that is first appearing to us in its lower (*unter*) version and then its higher (*über*) version? If not, how else can it be said that the Idea itself solves the paradox of inquiry?

An analogy may be used to clarify this. We humans may need to think of Aphrodite and Poseidon (the normal run of Gods) to get at Zeus (the God of Gods), but this does not mean that Aphrodite or Poseidon changes into Zeus at any time. We change, or our thoughts change, but the Gods are changeless. Similarly, we need EQUALS to climb up to c in EQUALS EQUALS c, but EQUALS does not become c. We state the paradox and suffer from it, wondering what on earth the Equal may equal. But the Idea is only c, so it never suffers. It is the answer, not the question.

CHAPTER 2. PLATO: IDEAS, GOD, UTOPIA

> The Pupil asks: 'At whose wish does the mind sent forth proceed on its errand? At whose command does the first breath go forth? At whose wish do we utter this speech? What god directs the eye, or the ear?'
>
> The Teacher replies: 'It is the ear of the ear, the mind of the mind, the speech of speech, the breath of breath, and the eye of the eye. When freed (from the senses) the wise, on departing from this world, become immortal.'
>
> —Talavakara-Upanishad

In the ancient world Plato's vision is often accepted *in toto*. Centuries after him the Roman author Seneca still maintains that he has nothing essential to discover given that Plato already knew and said it all (see Barnes, "Imperial Plato"). This appears to be a fairly normal view to take throughout Roman antiquity among the educated elite. True, it is not uncontested, for several persons also adhere to diverse religions from Manicheanism and Gnosticism to Judaism and Christianity; however, these are often sects for uneducated persons who do not know of the greats of Greek civilization, and in time their religions are often read in Platonic ways by educated persons anyway — this happens soon enough also to Christianity (people's Platonism, as Nietzsche calls it) —, so there is in general no violent disagreement with Plato's worldview. He dominates the ancient mind. He is the sun around whom they revolve.

However, he is also the center for much of *later Western philosophy*, because he sets so much of the agenda (besides giving the field its name). Are there really Ideas or Gods, or is there only matter in a void? Is there any psyche that is distinct from the body? What is just or moral, and why commit to it? (Why not cheat or be selfish?) What is knowledge, and how is it different in the pure or higher realm which is not merely accidental and empirical but dialectical and rational? In Western history, the faith in the resolvability of such grand questions by and large diminishes with time, and one may map many of the major names in the tradition by their more or less skeptical relations to Plato's utopian program, beginning already with Aristotle. For Aristotle the checklist would be: utopia–no, psychic immortality–no, Ideas–no, but God–yes.

Having said this I need to emphasize that Plato's grandeur is not really his personal property: it is *impersonal and archetypal*. Higher thought itself leads to certain questions and models. Plato acknowledges this in a way in not placing himself in the middle: his star is usually 'Socrates'. However, even this is to personify something that properly has no face. In modern times this is obscured because philosophical questions are often subjectified. The philosophical expression is Kant's when he stages his own philosophy as a Copernican Turn to heliocentrism. In reality it is the very reverse, for it is Plato's Ideas and Gods that are objective and superhuman realities out there, while in Kant they are always only subjective and *in here*, that is inside the human self, as unreal projections and hopes. Compared to Plato we moderns tend to belittle God and the Ideas just as a solipsist could belittle the sun (as his little lamp).[1]

Culturally Plato's distance from us opens wide before our eyes once it is understood that his Ideas and Gods are *objective values*. In modern times we are accustomed to saying that objective reasoning pertains only to means, not to ends. Means are scientific and technological — think of engineering and medical care –, and ends are left to our private discretion. They cannot possibly be proved. By Plato's lights, in turn, our small, disconnected, private, and individual lives look pointless, lacking in any overall, super-individual direction, and science is only a subservient form of knowledge which has nothing to do with authentic objectivity. If we moderns do unite under greater aims then it is typically to defend this small right to privacy over again, thereby only further postponing the question of purpose.[2]

The dialectical cure for this will at first seem painful, because as before it has to solve a paradox. This time the paradox concerns ends or

---

[1] More on this in 3.8.

[2] Compare Appendix C, both quotations.

aims in life: happiness or satisfaction. In Plato's spirit I have labeled this the *utopian paradox*.[1] First I state the paradox from Plato's early work, the *Lysis* (2.1) and from his middle-period work, the *Symposium* (2.2). This paradox, like the other paradox we already examined in Chapter 1 (the paradox of inquiry) should drive rational minds to Platonic conclusions. Its solution is first sketched in the *Symposium* (2.3) but then it is repeated in numerous versions in the *Republic* (2.4-2.6), more vaguely in the *Critias* and the *Timaeus* (2.7), and finally in Plato's last book, the *Laws* (2.8-2.10). Every time the solution is in an autonomous pattern. Humans are bound to put their trust in it if they are to escape from their solitary existential pains.

After this the only thing that remains for this chapter is to summarize how Aristotle and, following him, the Hellenic and medieval philosophers begin to depart from Plato's original dialectical priorities (2.11). Though Plato's utopian school, the Academy, lasts for an entire millennium (until Christian authorities close it), the creative schools of thought sprout up elsewhere. Thus the tracks of the proud and central dialectical tradition are lost. (I do not try to explain this obviously very complex process and only note some main milestones.) It is only with modern German Idealism, especially in Kant and Hegel, that dialectic takes center stage again.

The Utopian Paradox in the *Lysis*

In Plato's *Lysis*, Socrates interrogates Menexenus thus:

> The sick man, as I was just now saying, is the friend of the physician—is he not?
>
> Yes.
>
> And he is the friend of the physician because of disease, and for the sake of health?
>
> Yes.
>
> And disease is an evil?
>
> Certainly.
>
> And what of health? I said. Is that good or evil, or neither? Good, he replied.
>
> And we were saying, I believe, that the body being neither good nor evil, because of disease, that is to say because of evil,

---

[1] It has no commonly acknowledged name, and the scholarly literature on Plato downplays or ignores it.

is the friend of medicine, and medicine is a good: and medicine has entered into this friendship for the sake of health, and health is a good.

True.

And is health a friend, or not a friend?

A friend.

And disease is an enemy?

Yes.

Then that which is neither good nor evil is the friend of the good because of the evil and hateful, and for the sake of the good and the friend?

Clearly.

Then the friend is a friend for the sake of the friend, and because of the enemy?

That is to be inferred.

Then at this point, my boys, let us take heed, and be on our guard against deceptions. I will not again repeat that the friend is the friend of the friend, and the like of the like, which has been declared by us to be an impossibility; but, in order that this new statement may not delude us, let us attentively examine another point, which I will proceed to explain: Medicine, as we were saying, is a friend, or dear to us for the sake of health?

Yes.

And health is also dear?

Certainly.

And if dear, then dear for the sake of something?

Yes.

And surely this object must also be dear, as is implied in our previous admissions?

Yes.

And that something dear involves something else dear?

Yes.

But then, proceeding in this way, shall we not arrive at some first principle of friendship or dearness which is not capable of being referred to any other, for the sake of which, as we maintain, all other things are dear, and, having there arrived, we shall stop?

True.

My fear is that all those other things, which, as we say, are dear for the sake of another, are illusions and deceptions only, but where that first principle is, there is the true ideal of friendship. Let me put the matter thus: Suppose the case of a great treasure (this may be a son, who is more precious to his father than all his other treasures); would not the father, who values his son above all things, value other things also for the sake of his son? I mean, for instance, if he knew that his son had drunk hemlock, and the father thought that wine would save him, he would value the wine?

He would.

And also the vessel which contains the wine?

Certainly.

But does he therefore value the three measures of wine, or the earthen vessel which contains them, equally with his son? Is not this rather the true state of the case? All his anxiety has regard not to the means which are provided for the sake of an object, but to the object for the sake of which they are provided. And although we may often say that gold and silver are highly valued by us, that is not the truth; for there is a further object, whatever it may be, which we value most of all, and for the sake of which gold and all our other possessions are acquired by us. Am I not right?

Yes, certainly.

And may not the same be said of the friend? That which is only dear to us for the sake of something else is improperly said to be dear, but the truly dear is that in which all these so-called dear friendships terminate.

That, he said, appears to be true.

And the truly dear or ultimate principle of friendship is not for the sake of any other or further dear.

True.[1]

---

[1] *Lysis* 218E—219D.

If you reach the aim, then what will you do? The cure will have value only if there is something to cure, but if it has already been cured, then what? If you attain what you want, there is nothing more to want. It is as if you had merely to vanish after that.

Call this the *utopian paradox*.[1]

In the *Gorgias* this is voiced by Callicles, not Socrates:

> SOCRATES: Well, I will tell you another image, which comes out of the same school:—Let me request you to consider how far you would accept this as an account of the two lives of the temperate and intemperate in a figure:—There are two men, both of whom have a number of casks; the one man has his casks sound and full, one of wine, another of honey, and a third of milk, besides others filled with other liquids, and the streams which fill them are few and scanty, and he can only obtain them with a great deal of toil and difficulty; but when his casks are once filled he has no need to feed them anymore, and has no further trouble with them or care about them. The other, in like manner, can procure streams, though not without difficulty; but his vessels are leaky and unsound, and night and day he is compelled to be filling them, and if he pauses for a moment, he is in an agony of pain. Such are their respective lives:—And now would you say that the life of the intemperate is happier than that of the temperate? Do I not convince you that the opposite is the truth?

> CALLICLES: You do not convince me, Socrates, for the one who has filled himself has no longer any pleasure left; and this, as I was just now saying, is the life of a stone: he has neither joy nor sorrow after he is once filled; but the pleasure depends on the superabundance of the influx.

> SOCRATES: But the more you pour in, the greater the waste; and the holes must be large for the liquid to escape.

> CALLICLES: Certainly.

---

[1] Formally this is easy stuff. We have a series or chain from a to b to c, etc., and as is usual for dialectics the question is whether there is an endpoint. The relation (R) to connect these dots may be worded for instance as SERVES THE AIM, or HAS THE FUNCTION. Then a SERVES b SERVES c..., and if z SERVES z then z is a terminus. z should then be something like a classic Idea. The issue is whether there is such a z (i.e. such that zRz). If there is not, then the series will just keep running further and further to the right. Then there would be limitless striving but no happiness at the end. (In Kantian terms, the 'antithesis' would win.)

> SOCRATES: The life which you are now depicting is not that of a dead man, or of a stone, but of a cormorant; you mean that he is to be hungering and eating?
>
> CALLICLES: Yes.
>
> SOCRATES: And he is to be thirsting and drinking?
>
> CALLICLES: Yes, that is what I mean; he is to have all his desires about him, and to be able to live happily in the gratification of them.

If Socrates aims at Stoical apathy then he is not credible or rational — though as we will see below, Buddhists would disagree with this. For them the answer is to rid oneself of desires. Just forget and sleep, be a stone.

But what else can one say? Also Callicles' avenue seems ridiculous — to seek more and more to thirst and hunger for, seek for more of a drive, find more ways to hype everything up — always invent new ways to lack things and be dissatisfied. And is that happiness? Surely the proposal is perverse in a different sense. It is not like being a dead stone, true, but it is artificial. And it is certainly not happiness or satisfaction but unhappiness and dissatisfaction. It is a theory of something else.

But then what? Initially we can seem to be stuck in this either/or. Either we silence ourselves like the stone Buddha. We pretend to be dead and to want nothing, or else we greedily seek things without end like Callicles.

Or — what else is there? What else can Plato show?

The Utopian Paradox in the *Symposium*

The *Symposium* is about *eros*, love. Plato's Socrates begins his part in the discussion by asking whether love is of something or of nothing:

> And here I must explain myself: I do not want you to say that love is the love of a father or the love of a mother-that would be ridiculous; but to answer as you would, if I asked is a father a father of something? to which you would find no difficulty in replying, of a son or daughter: and the answer would be right.
>
> Very true, said Agathon.
>
> And you would say the same of a mother?
>
> He assented.

Yet let me ask you one more question in order to illustrate my meaning: Is not a brother to be regarded essentially as a brother of something?

Certainly, he replied.

That is, of a brother or sister?

Yes, he said.

And now, said Socrates, I will ask about Love:-Is Love of something or of nothing?

Of something, surely, he replied.

Keep in mind what this is, and tell me what I want to know-whether Love desires that of which love is.

Yes, surely.

And does he possess, or does he not possess, that which he loves and desires?

Probably not, I should say.

Nay, replied Socrates, I would have you consider whether "necessarily" is not rather the word. The inference that he who desires something is in want of something, and that he who desires nothing is in want of nothing, is in my judgment, Agathon absolutely and necessarily true. What do you think?

I agree with you, said Agathon.[1]

Eros is of something, so it is a relation. Specifically it is a relation of aiming to possess what one does not already possess:

Would he who is great, desire to be great, or he who is strong, desire to be strong?

That would be inconsistent with our previous admissions.

True. For he who is anything cannot want to be that which he is?

Very true.

And yet, added Socrates, if a man being strong desired to be strong, or being swift desired to be swift, or being healthy

[1] *Symposium* 199C-200B.

desired to be healthy, in that case he might be thought to desire something which he already has or is.[1]

The reader can see that this is much as in the *Lysis*. In the most direct formulation the paradox is this:

- satisfaction (happiness) amounts to wanting x and having x, but
- if one has x then one has no reason to want x any longer,
- therefore satisfaction (happiness) is impossible.

The point is that wanting continues *only until* there is having, and once having comes along then wanting disappears. Thus the one side excludes the other. It is like oil and water, they do not mix. But — they *should* mix, if there were to be happiness or satisfaction. Hence the trouble.

What is the solution? Or is there in fact no happiness?

At first the fictional Socrates of Plato's imagination errs about this. For as his official solution he goes on to say this:

> I give the example in order that we may avoid misconception. For the possessors of these qualities, Agathon, must be supposed to have their respective advantages at the time, whether they choose or not; and who can desire that which he has? Therefore when a person says, I am well and wish to be well, or I am rich and wish to be rich, and I desire simply to have what I have-to him we shall reply: "You, my friend, having wealth and health and strength, want to have the continuance of them; for at this moment, whether you choose or no, you have them. And when you say, I desire that which I have and nothing else, is not your meaning that you want to have what you now have in the future?" He must agree with us-must he not?
>
> He must, replied Agathon.
>
> Then, said Socrates, he desires that what he has at present may be preserved to him in the future, which is equivalent to saying that he desires something which is non-existent to him, and which as yet he has not got.
>
> Very true, he said.

---

[1] *Symposium* 200B-C.

Then he and every one who desires, desires that which he has not already, and which is future and not present, and which he has not, and is not, and of which he is in want;-these are the sort of things which love and desire seek?

Very true, he said.[1]

Where is the error in this? Consider these possibilities:

- Trump owns one skyscraper and wishes to own one skyscraper. In this event Trump already does own the single skyscraper, so he has no need to wish for it. (This is, so to say, a "dead" utopia.)
- Trump owns one skyscraper and wishes to own two. In this situation Trump's wish makes sense but he is not satisfied, so this is not a portrayal of contented wishing nor hence of satisfaction. (In other words, this is not a utopia in the first place, so it is not a "living" utopia either. It is a living place, but not a utopia.)
- Trump has made sure that he will get to keep his one skyscraper as long as he lives. But in this scenario he cannot sensibly wish to keep his skyscraper, because he has already secured that aim. (Here is another dead utopia. Everything has been achieved and only death awaits.)
- Trump has *not* made sure that he will get to keep his one skyscraper as long as he lives. In this scenario there is room for further wishing but there is no satisfaction. (Thus here there is again no utopia at all, and hence also no living utopia. The aims that have been set simply have not been met yet. Notice also that nothing is different if it is *impossible* for Trump to be absolutely sure that he can own his skyscraper for the rest of his life, for then there would again be no utopia.)

Of course, the logic of this situation will not change if we picture one hundred skyscrapers instead of one or two, because the points concern whatever wishes there may happen to be. Also, we can insert whatever we like for the skyscrapers — take millions and billions of dollars, athletic trophies, pop hits — and for Trump and nothing will change.

---

[1] *Symposium* 200C-E.

What this scenario reveals is that the aim of *preserving* something which one has does not take one out of the nihilist's circle. Hence (popular as it is to say the contrary) Socrates' answer is wrong.

Schopenhauer's Indian manner of stating the same paradox is as clear as it is merciless:

> All satisfaction, or what is commonly called happiness, is always really and essentially only *negative*, and never positive. It is not an original gratification coming to us of itself, but must always be the satisfaction of a wish. The wish, *i.e.*, some want, is the condition which precedes every pleasure. But with the satisfaction the wish and therefore the pleasure cease. Thus the satisfaction or the pleasing can never be more than the deliverance from a pain, from a want; for such is not only every actual, open sorrow, but every desire, the importunity of which disturbs our peace, and, indeed, the deadening ennui also that makes life a burden to us. It is, however, so hard to attain or achieve anything; difficulties and troubles without end are opposed to every purpose, and at every step hindrances accumulate. But when finally everything is overcome and attained, nothing can ever be gained but deliverance from some sorrow or desire, so that we find ourselves just in the same position as we occupied before this sorrow or desire appeared. All that is even directly given us is merely the want, *i.e.*, the pain. The satisfaction and the pleasure we can only know indirectly through the remembrance of the preceding suffering and want, which ceases with its appearance. Hence it arises that we are not properly conscious of the blessings and advantages we actually possess, nor do we prize them, but think of them merely as a matter of course, for they gratify us only negatively by restraining suffering. Only when we have lost them do we become sensible of their value; for the want, the privation, the sorrow, is the positive, communicating itself directly to us.[1]

In other words, "all happiness is only of a negative not a positive nature," and "just on this account it cannot be lasting satisfaction and gratification, but merely delivers us from some pain or want which must be followed either by a new pain, or by languor, empty longing, and ennui" (ibid.). Schopenhauer's cynicism is hard and cold: he will not evade the

---

[1] *The World as Will and Idea* § 58.

problem but admits it is true. Life has no aim or purpose, it is all a silly game.[1]

Now for the solution.

The Kalon in the *Symposium*

Here is what Plato says about the Idea of Beauty — the Kalon. (Here Diotima addresses Socrates.)

> "These are the lesser mysteries of love, into which even you, Socrates, may enter; to the greater and more hidden ones which are the crown of these, and to which, if you pursue them in a right spirit, they will lead, I know not whether you will be able to attain. But I will do my utmost to inform you, and do you follow if you can. For he who would proceed aright in this matter should begin in youth to visit beautiful forms; and first, if he be guided by his instructor aright, to love one such form only-out of that he should create fair thoughts; and soon he will of himself perceive that the beauty of one form is akin to the beauty of another; and then if beauty of form in general is his pursuit, how foolish would he be not to recognize that the beauty in every form is and the same! And when he perceives this he will abate his violent love of the one, which he will despise and deem a small thing, and will become a lover of all beautiful forms; in the next stage he will consider that the beauty of the mind is more honourable than the beauty of the outward form. So that if a virtuous soul have but a little come-liness, he will be content to love and tend him, and will search out and bring to the birth thoughts which may improve the young, until he is compelled to contemplate and see the beauty of institutions and laws, and to understand that the beauty of them all is of one family, and that personal beauty is a trifle; and after laws and institutions he will go on to the sciences, that he may see their beauty, being not like a servant in love

---

[1] Actually Schopenhauer has *art* to save him. He says that *active* striving (his term: the will) leads only to strife but *passive* perception (his term: Ideas) does not. The therapeutic change is: instead of trying to change life, look at it as it is. For example, stormy weather is a pain if you have to fight against it from its midst, but no longer if you observe it from the sidelines. Then it becomes beautiful and pleasing. But art shows things like this — as they are, without trying, Schopen-hauer writes.

(This passive way of life is for Schopenhauer *Platonic* because he thinks of the Platonic Ideas as percepts — cf. Berkeley in 3.0.)

with the beauty of one youth or man or institution, himself
a slave mean and narrow-minded, but drawing towards and
contemplating the vast sea of beauty, he will create many fair
and noble thoughts and notions in boundless love of wisdom;
until on that shore he grows and waxes strong, and at last
the vision is revealed to him of a single science, which is the
science of beauty everywhere. To this I will proceed; please to
give me your very best attention:

"He who has been instructed thus far in the things of love,
and who has learned to see the beautiful in due order and
succession, when he comes toward the end will suddenly
perceive a nature of wondrous beauty (and this, Socrates, is
the final cause of all our former toils)-a nature which in the
first place is everlasting, not growing and decaying, or waxing
and waning; secondly, not fair in one point of view and foul
in another, or at one time or in one relation or at one place
fair, at another time or in another relation or at another place
foul, as if fair to some and-foul to others, or in the likeness of
a face or hands or any other part of the bodily frame, or in any
form of speech or knowledge, or existing in any other being,
as for example, in an animal, or in heaven or in earth, or in
any other place; but beauty absolute, separate, simple, and
everlasting, which without diminution and without increase,
or any change, is imparted to the ever-growing and perishing
beauties of all other things. He who from these ascending
under the influence of true love, begins to perceive that beauty,
is not far from the end. And the true order of going, or being led
by another, to the things of love, is to begin from the beauties
of earth and mount upwards for the sake of that other beauty,
using these as steps only, and from one going on to two, and
from two to all fair forms, and from fair forms to fair practices,
and from fair practices to fair notions, until from fair notions
he arrives at the notion of absolute beauty, and at last knows
what the essence of beauty is. This, my dear Socrates," said
the stranger of Mantineia, "is that life above all others which
man should live, in the contemplation of beauty absolute; a
beauty which if you once beheld, you would see not to be after
the measure of gold, and garments, and fair boys and youths,
whose presence now entrances you; and you and many a one
would be content to live seeing them only and conversing
with them without meat or drink, if that were possible-you
only want to look at them and to be with them. But what if
man had eyes to see the true beauty-the divine beauty, I mean,

pure and dear and unalloyed, not clogged with the pollutions of mortality and all the colours and vanities of human life-thither looking, and holding converse with the true beauty simple and divine? Remember how in that communion only, beholding beauty with the eye of the mind, he will be enabled to bring forth, not images of beauty, but realities (for he has hold not of an image but of a reality), and bringing forth and nourishing true virtue to become the friend of God and be immortal, if mortal man may. Would that be an ignoble life?"[1]

The Idea of Beauty, the Kalon, is here presented first as a scale: it is present in things to lesser or greater degrees, such as bodies or persons or laws. Because it is present in so many different places it would be an error to focus on beauty in any particular place at the expense of others. But also, in reality the only truly satisfying beauty is Kalon itself: it is a self-sufficing absolute. If one finds it then this spells ultimate satisfaction.

The thing to cling to is that we thus find the same Idea logic as before. The Kalon is both the scale and the optimum as measured by that scale. It is perfection by its own lights, and all other beauties are only so many stepping stones which lead up to it.

But it is this that *solves the utopian paradox.*

Why? Notice that now the standard and the instance *match each other perfectly* instead of excluding each other like oil and water above. Hence, all that we need to do is translate between two vocabularies, that is from

- wanting and having (the problem terms), to
- scale and instance (the solution terms).

The key question then is of course whether wanting truly amounts to measuring. Can we translate the restless idioms of *eros* into the stable and certain scale of an Idea?

The way to argue for this in Plato's calm and symmetric manner is to say that *eros* (like Schopenhauer's will) is only a helplessly confused and blind drive for more — of something, it knows not what — but that if we have a stable scale or clear a measure like the Kalon, then this gives us eyes. We learn to deliberate, to assess, to correct. Then our blindness is gone. For then we know what to want: the scale gives us directions. We do not run and panic like headless chickens. But having this scale, the only thing that remains is to seek the optimal instance, which in the

---

[1] *Symposium* 209E-212B.

perfect scenario is found in Kalon itself, as Plato says. For in this way we have the exact match: the circle is closed, the sign points to itself.

The reason this is sketchy is not due to the logic of the proposal, which is definite enough. If an Idea is a scale and the best instance on that scale, then the answer is fixed.

What is sketchy however is that nothing in Plato's text actually specifies what beauty *is*. The word 'beauty' (or *kalon*) does not actually say very much at all. (It is a little like 'Hurrah!' for Hume and Ayer, a term for whatever you may like.) But then how are we to actually understand that there is something of the same beauty in bodies as well as souls, artworks and states and philosophies? What do they share? And if we do not know this then where is the symmetric patience and clear reason that we can instance in contrast to the panicking chickens? Until we have the real story we must admit that we have only a thin hope, a sketch.

Probably the most realistic way to fill this void would be by means of a ratio of harmony, which Plato brings up repeatedly in his works (for instance the *Phaedo* and the *Laws*). In this general spirit there is a famous Golden Ratio for architecture which is used in Greece, and I have already mentioned Pythagoras' musical ratios. Next there are meters in poetry, and different color combinations, etc. Now, if we imagine all of this then is it plausible to say that satisfaction or happiness would be attained in an aesthetic utopianism of this sort? Specifically there would have to be

- numerous harmonies, some in music, some in painting, etc. (R, R', R"), and also
- a harmony between those first-level harmonies ((R) S (R') S (R")) such that
- this super-harmony would be in harmony mainly with itself (SSS).

I say this because the Kalon is an Idea: it is self-consistent as in the double logic (thus SSS), and also it is supersensual, so it is inaudible, invisible, etc. (unlike R, R', R").

In the remainder of this chapter I will be showing many times how this is not an isolated thought in Plato: the double logic spreads from the Kalon (the Idea of Beautiful) on to the Agathon (the Idea of the Good, or the Idea of Ideas), to justice (psychic and political), dialectic (upward and downward), and religion as well as cosmology. Consequently, he has *numerous* solutions to the utopian paradox, and this means that it is not specifically beauty that must pan out.

The Agathon in the *Republic*

In Plato's *Republic* the centerpiece is the Good, not the Beautiful: the Agathon, not the Kalon. This is standardly taken to be the Idea of Ideas or the high point of Plato's dialectical philosophy.

What is it? The irony is that as he admits he cannot define it, must as he would like to (506D-E). It is crucial to notice however that he does *not* mean that it is *undefinable*: if he said that he would be a mystic (and among self-professed Platonists there have always been plenty of mystics, beginning with Plotinus). He says he would like to define it, just as he feels that he has defined justice earlier in the *Republic*. Having said this he goes on to present his three famous allegories for the Agathon — the Sun, the Line, and the Cave — because this is the best he can do. It is the Sun allegory that seems to be the most informative of the three:

> But you see that without the addition of some other nature there is no seeing or being seen?
>
> How do you mean?
>
> Sight being, as I conceive, in the eyes, and he who has eyes wanting to see; colour being also present in them, still unless there be a third nature specially adapted to the purpose, the owner of the eyes will see nothing and the colours will be invisible.
>
> Of what nature are you speaking?
>
> Of that which you term light, I replied.
>
> True, he said.
>
> Noble, then, is the bond which links together sight and visibility, and great beyond other bonds by no small difference of nature; for light is their bond, and light is no ignoble thing?
>
> Nay, he said, the reverse of ignoble.
>
> And which, I said, of the gods in heaven would you say was the lord of this element? Whose is that light which makes the eye to see perfectly and the visible to appear?
>
> You mean the sun, as you and all mankind say.
>
> May not the relation of sight to this deity be described as follows?
>
> How?

Neither sight nor the eye in which sight resides is the sun?

No.

Yet of all the organs of sense the eye is the most like the sun?

By far the most like.

And the power which the eye possesses is a sort of effluence which is dispensed from the sun?

Exactly.

Then the sun is not sight, but the author of sight who is recognized by sight?

True, he said.

And this is he whom I call the child of the good, whom the good begat in his own likeness, to be in the visible world, in relation to sight and the things of sight, what the good is in the intellectual world in relation to mind and the things of mind.

Will you be a little more explicit? he said.

Why, you know, I said, that the eyes, when a person directs them towards objects on which the light of day is no longer shining, but the moon and stars only, see dimly, and are nearly blind; they seem to have no clearness of vision in them?

Very true.

But when they are directed towards objects on which the sun shines, they see clearly and there is sight in them?

Certainly.

And the soul is like the eye: when resting upon that on which truth and being shine, the soul perceives and understands, and is radiant with intelligence; but when turned towards the twilight of becoming and perishing, then she has opinion only, and goes blinking about, and is first of one opinion and then of another, and seems to have no intelligence?

Just so.

Now, that which imparts truth to the known and the power of knowing to the knower is what I would have you term the idea of good, and this you will deem to be the cause of science, and of truth in so far as the latter becomes the subject of knowledge; beautiful too, as are both truth and knowledge, you will be right in esteeming this other nature as more beautiful than either; and, as in the previous instance, light and sight may be truly said to be like the sun, and yet not to be the sun, so in this other sphere, science and truth may be deemed to be like the good, but not the good; the good has a place of honour yet higher.[1]

The sun shines on all kinds of things down here on earth, trees and lakes for instance, so it operates as a kind of general illuminator: it makes so many things visible. But it is *also* the brightest object by far (at least to the naked eye), so it instances double logic. The lower role is to light up the world, and the higher role is to illuminate itself the most. This is perfectly analogical with the other Ideas we have already studied, the Kalon and the Equal.

If we replace the figurative language, however, then we must ask how much we learn from this exactly. Is this only to use metaphors to state the same double logic or is there something more in play? There is talk of intelligibility, so we should imagine that the Good is most intelligible and the source of intelligibility anywhere. Plato seems to take this as far as he possibly can:

> You would say, would you not, that the sun is not only the author of visibility in all visible things, but of generation and nourishment and growth, though he himself is not generation?
>
> Certainly.
>
> In like manner the good may be said to be not only the author of knowledge to all things known, but of their being and essence, and yet the good is not essence, but far exceeds essence in dignity and power.
>
> Glaucon said, with a ludicrous earnestness: By the light of heaven, how amazing![2]

What may this mean? Ideas have being — they are the fundamental realities in Plato's universe — but the Idea of Ideas, the Agathon, is somehow *more* than being (the translator's word 'essence' is not right). It is *über*-being, we may surmise as above, an x of x that goes beyond x — but Plato does not explain what he may mean.

---

[1] *Republic* 507D—509A.
[2] *Republic* 509B-C.

Justice in the *Republic*

The main topic of Plato's main work, the *Republic*, is *justice* (Greek: *dikaisyne*). This work ends with the lengthy Myth of Er which states the ethos with which Plato wants to conclude: it is that in the hereafter God will reward or punish us according to our personal decisions, so each of us will reap what he sows (karma).[1] Thus, shocking as this may sound to modern ears, already in ancient times Plato is prepared to place all this weight on individual shoulders — and Plato of all people!, the great philosopher of Ideas, social structures, cosmic patterns, and dialectical progressions! One is surprised that in the end game all these patterns do not matter and each one of us must face God alone.

The only trouble with this concluson is that it is expressed in a myth. For each hearer or reader is free to either accept it or not: after all the story may be false. Only children may believe it. Where is Plato's story for rational and skeptical adults?

Hundreds of pages earlier he begins his *Republic* with this very much in mind. In Book I, the Platonic Socrates' opponent in dialectical debate is the ruthless Thrasymachus, who believes in lying, cheating, and stealing — in whatever means he can use to exercise his own power to rule as a master in his corner of the world. Due to this he is as uninterested as Callicles in the *Gorgias* in any moral rules. He does not care. For him there is only his ego. Compared to this brutish fact, moral rules are only artificial conspiracies of the weak against the strong. The strong by nature deserve to rule. By the lights of Thrasymachus and Callicles Socrates is the worst of all pretenders.

Much of the *Republic*'s text is an argument against just such immoralists. Plato wishes to show that in the real world justice pays. You do not need *myths* for this — there *may be no* hereafter where God looks you in the eyes. Rather, if you play fairly then you will be happier — so you win, here and now. If again you bully others, or if you lie or cheat, then you will pay for this by suffering from unhappiness — in this life, that is even if the Myth of Er is false and there is no God.

How is this supposed to work?

Plato's core argument is that there is such a thing as justice to oneself, or *inner justice*.

---

[1] However, it is notable that Plato views each rebirth as a blessing, which contrasts with Indian philosophies in which the point is to escape from the wheel of recurrent births. (In the Myth of Er, a tyrant like Ardiaeus is only pushed back into inexistence when he wishes to live again.) To him life is not a pain.

A premise for this argument is that as an individual person or self is not so much an egoistic player in a society as a society of his own. This is because each person — each psyche — consists of a variety of impulses and roles. You need justice to function as an organized person.

This is seen best by first comparing a *disorganized* person — a psychic *democracy*:

> Yes, I said, [the democratic man] lives from day to day indulging the appetite of the hour; and sometimes he is lapped in drink and strains of the flute; then he becomes a water-drinker, and tries to get thin; then he takes a turn at gymnastics; sometimes idling and neglecting everything, then once more living the life of a philosopher; often he is busy with politics, and starts to his feet and says and does whatever comes into his head; and, if he is emulous of anyone who is a warrior, off he is in that direction, or of men of business, once more in that. His life has neither law nor order; and this distracted existence he terms joy and bliss and freedom; and so he goes on.
>
> Yes, he replied, he is all liberty and equality.[1]

If your psyche is democratic then you are chaotic, Plato writes. To illustrate this, if on Monday you start your way East, on Tuesday you make a new decision and head South, and then on Wednesday you go West, etc. — then you cancel every decision in time. No day obeys another. But due to this there cannot be any overall direction in your life — because there is no long-term plan.[2]

---

[1] *Republic* 561C—E.

[2] This makes for a marked change compared to the *Phaedo* (Ch. 1). For compared to the *Phaedo*'s psyche in Chapter 1 this new psyche in the *Republic* is *not simple but complex*. The psyche is now no longer seen as an Ur-element which cannot be cut into smaller pieces but as an entire economy. Like a busy beehive it teems with life, and there is a give and take between various impulses and directions.

I do not think there is any real question as to which of the two views of the psyche is *correct*, for they seem to be true of it on different levels. The *Phaedo*'s psyche is the conscious, 'existential' self which will be the topic also of Kant's paralogisms in 3.4, but the *Republic*'s psyche is the ethical self who has numerous types of projects and aims.

However, a delicious question is whether this change in Plato's view (from the *Phaedo* to the *Republic*) *alters his dialectical reasoning.* I will now put this as bluntly as possible.

In the *Phaedo* (in Ch. 1) the simple psyche conformed to the following structure, and this will recur in Kant's second antinomy in 3.4: a IS MADE OF b IS MADE OF c ... z IS MADE OF z, where z would be the simple psyche itself, which cannot be broken down to smaller parts. It would be elementary. In the *Republic*

The remedy is *justice* as Plato defines it:

> For 'every one having his own' is the great object of government;
> and the great object of trade is that every man should do his
> own business. Not that there is much harm in a carpenter
> trying to be a cobbler, or a cobbler transforming himself into a
> carpenter; but great evil may arise from the cobbler leaving his
> last and turning into a guardian or legislator, or when a single
> individual is trainer, warrior, legislator, all in one. And this
> evil is injustice, or every man doing another's business.[1]

Each part of the psyche should focus on its particular task. This is a division of labor, a principle of specialization. The idea seems to be that each part *knows its stuff best*, so it is the authority on how it can flourish: it is after all the expert in its field. Injustice begins only if these limitations are overstepped, for then persons will interfere with specialties they do not properly understand. (Notice that Plato does not view his specialist principle as *democratic*. Democracy is mob rule, he says. It is like sophistry: it can make anything seem like anything else. It is like sales and marketing — that is not at all the same thing as expert rule.)

However, if we had expert rule — in the sense that each expert would rule in its particular area of expertise — then this would per se not result in any co-operation *between* the different experts. Without the urban planner you could have people building houses where there are no streets, for example, and streets where there are no houses! Hence the result would again be alike to a democratic jumble. There needs to be a *general plan*, and if we are to maintain the specialist principle consistently then this should be someone's specialty.

The central thought is expressed in a colorful way in the Hindu myth of the Purusa:

> The Purusa has a thousand heads, a thousand eyes, and a
> thousand feet. He, encompassing the world on all sides...
>
> The Purusa alone is all this universe, what has been, and what
> is to be.[2]

---

we will find that a rationally ordered psyche has the shape of a pyramid, so there is one point at the top but it connects with numerous points at the bottom. Thus there are several lines of ascent, all of which end up at the same exact point. If so then the same dialectical reasoning as before can hold *for each of these lines*, so the model of dialectical reasoning is not in fact altered.

[1] *Republic* 433E-434A.
[2] *Rig Veda* 10.90, 1-2; Edgerton p. 67.

> When they divided the Purusa [...], into how many parts did
> they separate him? What did his mouth become? What his two
> arms? What are declared to be his two thighs, his two feet?
>
> The Brahman (priestly caste) was his mouth, his two arms
> became the Rajanya (warrior caste); his thighs are the Vaisya
> (artisan caste), from his two feet the Sudra (serf caste) was
> produced.[1]

At first the Purusa is everywhere, and then he is divided — into castes or
classes. The priestly caste is the mouth — issuing commands or speeches,
no doubt. The lot of the arms and the legs is to shut up and obey.

Contemporary readers are likely to shudder at this, thinking too
easily that this must be totalitarian. But to remedy this we need only to
recall that the purpose of Plato's utopian city was personal and psychic:
the legs are your legs, the arms your own arms. It is all only about you
obeying you, and each of your parts plays its part. The utopian city is an
imaginary analogue for psychic phenomena which are themselves often
hard to see or to keep track of (*Republic* 368C-369B).

The next thing to process is that the elite cast in Plato's utopian Kallipolis is *philosophical.* Philosophers are his new dictators or monarchs, who
come up with the total visions which the rest of the city should obey.
(This is an aristocracy, or rule by the best: *aristos* means best. The English
translation for Plato's book title is very bad: it should be the *State*, not the
Republic, for it is far from being a republic.)

Now: why philosophers?

Today it would be more conventional to assign the leading role to a
medical doctor or perhaps a fitness trainer. After all, they have empirically testable knowledge that is known to be useful to human beings.
They are now very popular with their cures and services.

What does Plato have against them? He imagines a physically
excellent personality:

> And what happens? If he do nothing else, and holds no converse
> with the Muses, does not even that intelligence which there
> may be in him, having no taste of any sort of learning or
> enquiry or thought or culture, grow feeble and dull and blind,
> his mind never waking up or receiving nourishment, and his
> senses not being purged of their mists?

---

[1] *Rig Veda* 10.90, 11-12; Edgerton p. 68.

True, he said.

And he ends by becoming a hater of philosophy, uncivilized, never using the weapon of persuasion,—he is like a wild beast, all violence and fierceness, and knows no other way of dealing; and he lives in all ignorance and evil conditions, and has no sense of propriety and grace.

That is quite true, he said.

And as there are two principles of human nature, one the spirited and the other the philosophical, some God, as I should say, has given mankind two arts answering to them (and only indirectly to the soul and body), in order that these two principles (like the strings of an instrument) may be relaxed or drawn tighter until they are duly harmonized.

That appears to be the intention.

And he who mingles music with gymnastic in the fairest proportions, and best attempers them to the soul, may be rightly called the true musician and harmonist in a far higher sense than the tuner of the strings.

You are quite right, Socrates.

And such a presiding genius will be always required in our State if the government is to last.

Yes, he will be absolutely necessary.

Such, then, are our principles of nurture and education: Where would be the use of going into further details about the dances of our citizens, or about their hunting and coursing, their gymnastic and equestrian contests? For these all follow the general principle, and having found that, we shall have no difficulty in discovering them.

I dare say that there will be no difficulty.[1]

The perfectly healthy and athletically trained human is like a dangerous weapon in Plato's eyes, lacking the inner priorities or principles to distinguish between proper and improper courses of action. (He is like a professional soldier, or a trained boxer who beats his parents in *Republic* Book I — and this is where I think Thrasymachus and Callicles

---

[1] *Republic* 411D-412B.

get off the bus.[1]) But the higher training such a character lacks is exactly dialectical and philosophical, for if he is to decipher what is authoritative then he is inevitably to reflect on first principles — just as our dialecticians have always been doing in this book. (That is their very definition!)

From a Platonic and idealistic point of view, too much of the current health culture is obsessed with the body. We usually do not need all these special products, cures, and services if we lead simple and healthy lives. They distract us from the hard questions about priorities. (It is again as if we were bodies without heads!)

A less obvious function of the rational part is to *unify* the soul or city:

> Shall we try to find a common basis by asking of ourselves what ought to be the chief aim of the legislator in making laws and in the organization of a State,—what is the greatest good, and what is the greatest evil, and then consider whether our previous description has the stamp of the good or of the evil?
>
> By all means.
>
> Can there be any greater evil than discord and distraction and plurality where unity ought to reign? or any greater good than the bond of unity?
>
> There cannot.
>
> And there is unity where there is community of pleasures and pains—where all the citizens are glad or grieved on the same occasions of joy and sorrow?
>
> No doubt.
>
> Yes; and where there is no common but only private feeling a State is disorganized—when you have one half of the world triumphing and the other plunged in grief at the same events happening to the city or the citizens?
>
> Certainly.
>
> Such differences commonly originate in a disagreement about the use of the terms 'mine' and 'not mine,' 'his' and 'not his.'

---

[1] If the psyche must be a coherent city ruled by a philosopher then we have already established the need of inner justice. This inner justice turns into outer justice — fairness to others and not only to oneself — as soon as it is shown further that the philosophizing must be social, which issue I have to exclude here to reduce complexity (cf. my *Dialectical Thinking* Ch. 2 and *Socrates' Crieria* Ch. 6 as well as Habermas).

Exactly so.

And is not that the best-ordered State in which the greatest number of persons apply the terms 'mine' and 'not mine' in the same way to the same thing?

Quite true.

Or that again which most nearly approaches to the condition of the individual—as in the body, when but a finger of one of us is hurt, the whole frame, drawn towards the soul as a centre and forming one kingdom under the ruling power therein, feels the hurt and sympathizes all together with the part affected, and we say that the man has a pain in his finger; and the same expression is used about any other part of the body, which has a sensation of pain at suffering or of pleasure at the alleviation of suffering.

Very true, he replied; and I agree with you that in the best-ordered State there is the nearest approach to this common feeling which you describe.

Then when any one of the citizens experiences any good or evil, the whole State will make his case their own, and will either rejoice or sorrow with him?

Yes, he said, that is what will happen in a well-ordered State.[1]

Each part of the psyche is to suffer with each other part, and one may imagine that this requires certain soft skills by the elite. For the general order needs to be presented in universally plausible and attractive terms, and everyone (or every part) must seem like a fully natural element in it. In real states, this is perhaps achieved by means of traditional narratives, national hymns and public rituals of various kinds: these flatter the common folk while simultaneously bringing them together. Plato's version of this is that his utopian elite needs in effect to manipulate the lower orders (414B-415D).[2] (The role of traditions will be more prominent later on, in the *Laws'* utopia of Magnesia.)

---

[1] *Republic* 462A-E.

[2] This is one of the many places in the Republic where Plato gets carried away by the psyche-polis analogy, in effect designing a social utopia without any regard for its relevance to the psyche. For instance, he defends eugenics and communism (among the elite).

Usually scholars read Plato's *Republic* politically *and* psychologically. The most sympathetic interpretation is Reeve's and the least sympathetic is Popper's (*Open Society*). For Plato's place in ancient utopianism seem Ferguson and for his influential role in modern utopianism see Manuel & Manuel.

However, there are two key problems with strategies of this kind. First, *inside the individual psyche* this would amount to a kind of self-manipulation, and it may well be doubted whether any individual actually wishes to subscribe to this in concrete practice. (Who would willingly mislead and manipulate himself?) Second, it is not plausible to assume that histories, hymns, and rituals are manufactured by means of dialectical reasoning (i.e. the special skill of the philosophical elite). The unity of the Platonic psyche seems instead to require sincere and transparent reasoning more than anything — not myths or lies. In many contexts it will probably depend on easily recalled simplifications, like slogans or rules which can be more carefully assessed only in special circumstances — only on your philosophical Sundays, for example. However, it is credible to say that such *in nuce* meanings (and not only the foundational arguments) are naturally produced precisely by dialecticians, that is even if sentimental hymns or myths are not.

Now if we take stock, there is a psyche which is structured like a city, so it has numerous parts. It is ruled by a philosophical part, and this is what makes it inwardly just. The philosophical part sets the agenda for the whole, but — thus it seemed — it needs to convince the other parts freely and openly, so it cannot manipulate them.

Two main questions seem to remain. The first is: What is the relation of the philosophical part to *itself*? The master part is master over the other parts — OK — but is it also its own master? If yes, then what does that mean?

Plato evades the issue:

> There is something ridiculous in the expression 'master of himself;' for the master is also the servant and the servant the master; and in all these modes of speaking the same person is denoted.

> Certainly.

> The meaning is, I believe, that in the human soul there is a better and also a worse principle; and when the better has the worse under control, then a man is said to be master of himself; and this is a term of praise: but when, owing to evil education or association, the better principle, which is also the smaller, is overwhelmed by the greater mass of the worse—in this case he is blamed and is called the slave of self and unprincipled.

> Yes, there is reason in that.[1]

---

[1] *Republic* 430E-431B.

In this passage, no one controls the master — so the master is not his own master. Rather the master is a given: here is the master, now obey. But then — and this is our final question — why should this master be obeyed? What is it that he will find? We do need a foundation if we are to obey — as always!

Plato fills this gap by letting the master turn *upward:*

> In heaven, I replied, there is laid up a pattern of it, methinks, which he who desires may behold, and beholding, may set his own house in order. But whether such an one exists, or ever will exist in fact, is no matter; for he will live after the manner of that city, having nothing to do with any other.[1]

Thus the rational part must look down on the other parts and up to the perfectionistic model — but never sideways to itself. It must reason in two rather different ways:

- *DOWNWARD REASONING:* if the psyche's rational part organizes the entire psyche's activities, delegating tasks to the other parts in the light of its master plan, then it takes its master plan for granted and merely uses it to order inferior things. Here is what the psyche should read, and this is what is to be eaten, this much exercise, such and such company kept, this pace for savings, this much rest.

- *UPWARD REASONING:* if the psyche studies and polishes its master plan then it had better speculate about Ideas again. After all, the psyche's master plan in life is not derived from the lower parts. It is attained from a superior realm (the *daimon*).

This is analogous to the dual role of the Ideas in previous sections: they are general scales or standards (downward role) and the best uses of those scales or standards (upward role). But as before, the utopian paradox is solved only if the scale is specified, for otherwise *eros* remains blind. If it is blind, it will rush from one thing to the next quite like a headless chicken — or indeed like Plato's democratic personality above! So what is the scale, exactly? This is again left open for later generations.

---

[1] *Republic* 592B.

Dialectic in the *Republic*

An analogical duality is mirrored in the *Republic*'s official pronounce-ments about *dialectics* or *dialecticians*.

The dialogue says both

- that dialecticians are persons who typically view things synoptically as unified and complex wholes (*downward* function), and
- that dialecticians characteristically isolate pure Ideas or blue-prints from their copies or various uses (*upward* function).

Thus the dialectician looks *both* down and up, that is, down to all kinds of objects and types of thought and life, but also up to the perfect Ideas in the light of which he knows to interpret and refashion both himself and the things below him.

Let us look at the upward aspect first.

Here is how the *Republic* introduces dialectics:

> ...all these things are only the prelude, and you surely do not suppose that a mere mathematician is also a dialectician? 'Certainly not. I have hardly ever known a mathematician who could reason.' And yet, Glaucon, is not true reasoning that hymn of dialectic which is the music of the intellectual world, and which was by us compared to the effort of sight, when from beholding the shadows on the wall we arrived at last at the images which gave the shadows? Even so the dialectical faculty withdrawing from sense arrives by the pure intellect at the contemplation of the idea of good, and never rests but at the very end of the intellectual world. And the royal road out of the cave into the light, and the blinking of the eyes at the sun and turning to contemplate the shadows of reality, not the shadows of an image only—this progress and gradual acquisition of a new faculty of sight by the help of the math-ematical sciences, is the elevation of the soul to the contem-plation of the highest ideal of being.
>
> 'So far, I agree with you. But now, leaving the prelude, let us proceed to the hymn. What, then, is the nature of dialectic, and what are the paths which lead thither?' Dear Glaucon, you cannot follow me here. There can be no revelation of the absolute truth to one who has not been disciplined in the

previous sciences. But that there is a science of absolute truth, which is attained in some way very different from those now practised, I am confident. For all other arts or sciences are relative to human needs and opinions; and the mathematical sciences are but a dream or hypothesis of true being, and never analyse their own principles. Dialectic alone rises to the principle which is above hypotheses, converting and gently leading the eye of the soul out of the barbarous slough of ignorance into the light of the upper world, with the help of the sciences which we have been describing—sciences, as they are often termed, although they require some other name, implying greater clearness than opinion and less clearness than science, and this in our previous sketch was understanding. And so we get four names—two for intellect, and two for opinion,— reason or mind, understanding, faith, perception of shadows— which make a proportion— being : becoming : : intellect : opinion—and science : belief : : understanding : perception of shadows. Dialectic may be further described as that science which defines and explains the essence or being of each nature, which distinguishes and abstracts the good, and is ready to do battle against all opponents in the cause of good. To him who is not a dialectician life is but a sleepy dream; and many a man is in his grave before his is well waked up. And would you have the future rulers of your ideal State intelligent beings, or stupid as posts? 'Certainly not the latter.' Then you must train them in dialectic, which will teach them to ask and answer questions, and is the coping-stone of the sciences.[1]

Sciences such as arithmetic, geometry, and astronomy make for but a prelude to dialectic, which is the hymn proper. The difference between the sciences and dialectic is that only dialectic goes beyond hypotheses and scrutinizes its own principles. Hence it identifies its foundations. Due to this, dialectics leads one as it were to wake up from a dream. Scientists are asleep.

But how can this actually be done? What exactly does a dialectician know and how?

And do you also agree, I said, in describing the dialectician as one who attains a conception of the essence of each thing? And he who does not possess and is therefore unable to impart this

---

[1] *Republic* 531B-534B.

conception, in whatever degree he fails, may in that degree also be said to fail in intelligence? Will you admit so much?

Yes, he said; how can I deny it?

And you would say the same of the conception of the good? Until the person is able to abstract and define rationally the idea of good, and unless he can run the gauntlet of all objections, and is ready to disprove them, not by appeals to opinion, but to absolute truth, never faltering at any step of the argument—unless he can do all this, you would say that he knows neither the idea of good nor any other good; he apprehends only a shadow, if anything at all, which is given by opinion and not by science;—dreaming and slumbering in this life, before he is well awake here, he arrives at the world below, and has his final quietus.

In all that I should most certainly agree with you.

And surely you would not have the children of your ideal State, whom you are nurturing and educating—if the ideal ever becomes a reality—you would not allow the future rulers to be like posts (Literally 'lines,' probably the starting-point of a race-course.), having no reason in them, and yet to be set in authority over the highest matters?

Certainly not.

Then you will make a law that they shall have such an education as will enable them to attain the greatest skill in asking and answering questions?

Yes, he said, you and I together will make it.

Dialectic, then, as you will agree, is the coping-stone of the sciences, and is set over them; no other science can be placed higher—the nature of knowledge can no further go?

I agree, he said.[1]

The dialectician can distinguish each thing by means of a definition. But again we need to consider that *sorts* of definitions Plato intends. One contention is that dialectics is supersensual:

> The lovers of sounds and sights, I said, delight in beautiful tones and colors and shapes and in everything that art fashions

---

[1] *Republic* 534B–535A.

out of these, but their thought is incapable of apprehending and taking delight in the nature of the beautiful in itself.

Why, yes, he said, that is so.

And on the other hand, will not those be few who would be able to approach beauty itself and contemplate it in and by itself?

They would, indeed.

He, then, who believes in beautiful things, but neither believes in beauty itself nor is able to follow when someone tries to guide him to the knowledge of it—do you think that his life is a dream or a waking? Just consider. Is not the dream state, whether the man is asleep or awake, just this: the mistaking of resemblance for identity?

I should certainly call that dreaming, he said.

Well, then, take the opposite case: the man whose thought recognizes a beauty in itself, and is able to distinguish that self-beautiful and the things that participate in it, and neither supposes the participants to be it nor it the participants—is his life, in your opinion, a waking or a dream state?

He is very much awake, he replied.

Could we not rightly, then, call the mental state of the one as knowing, knowledge, and that of the other as opining, opinion?

Assuredly.

Can we find any way of soothing him and gently winning him over, without telling him too plainly that he is not in his right mind?

We must try, he said.[1]

What is beautiful in itself is not empirical — it has no sound or color. It is beyond time and space — it is pure, eternal, archetypal. But therefore its definition should also be superempirical. We cannot refer to colors and sounds in Platonic definitions. (This is as before with the *Symposium* and the *Phaedo*.)

---

[1] *Republic* 476B-E.

But what resources does this leave us? To say we cannot use empirical contents is not to say what we can use. One lead is that dialecticians refute *objections:*

> Until the person is able to abstract and define rationally the idea of good, and unless he can run the gauntlet of all objections, and is ready to disprove them, not by appeals to opinion, but to absolute truth, never faltering at any step of the argument—unless he can do all this, you would say that he knows neither the idea of good nor any other good; he apprehends only a shadow, if anything at all, which is given by opinion and not by science;—dreaming and slumbering in this life, before he is well awake here, he arrives at the world below, and has his final quietus.
>
> In all that I should most certainly agree with you.
>
> And surely you would not have the children of your ideal State, whom you are nurturing and educating—if the ideal ever becomes a reality—you would not allow the future rulers to be like posts (Literally 'lines,' probably the starting-point of a race-course.), having no reason in them, and yet to be set in authority over the highest matters?
>
> Certainly not.
>
> Then you will make a law that they shall have such an education as will enable them to attain the greatest skill in asking and answering questions?
>
> Yes, he said, you and I together will make it.
>
> Dialectic, then, as you will agree, is the coping-stone of the sciences, and is set over them; no other science can be placed higher—the nature of knowledge can no further go?
>
> I agree, he said.[1]

In consequence, science is relative or conditional, whereas dialectic is absolute or unconditional (as in this book's Introduction). Ultimately the dialectician needs to make do only with *Ideas in relation to Ideas* — no hypotheses anymore of any kind:

---

[1] *Republic* 534B-E.

And when I speak of the other division of the intelligible, you will understand me to speak of that other sort of knowledge which reason herself attains by the power of dialectic, using the hypotheses not as first principles, but only as hypotheses— that is to say, as steps and points of departure into a world which is above hypotheses, in order that she may soar beyond them to the first principle of the whole; and clinging to this and then to that which depends on this, by successive steps she descends again without the aid of any sensible object, from ideas, through ideas, and in ideas she ends.

I understand you, he replied; not perfectly, for you seem to me to be describing a task which is really tremendous; but, at any rate, I understand you to say that knowledge and being, which the science of dialectic contemplates, are clearer than the notions of the arts, as they are termed, which proceed from hypotheses only: these are also contemplated by the understanding, and not by the senses: yet, because they start from hypotheses and do not ascend to a principle, those who contemplate them appear to you not to exercise the higher reason upon them, although when a first principle is added to them they are cognizable by the higher reason. And the habit which is concerned with geometry and the cognate sciences I suppose that you would term understanding and not reason, as being intermediate between opinion and reason.

You have quite conceived my meaning, I said [...].[1]

Of course, Plato's version of this has now been sketchy, not rigorous. However, as far as anyone seems to know he is utterly original in this (like in many other places), so he seems to be giving only the first sketch, as it were pointing the direction for later persons and movements to follow.

Now let us turn to the *downward* dialectic in Plato's *Republic*:

---

[1] *Republic* 514B-D. (In this quotation the Good is present only implicitly.)

The Victorian translator, Benjamin Jowett, here uses English terms which are now antiquated, like 'understanding' and 'higher reason' — and which accord nicely with Kant's dichotomy between (the largely dialectical) *Vernunft* and the (largely mechanical) *Verstand*, which dichotomy I mentioned already in the Introduction. Coleridge is to my knowledge its first popularizer in the English speaking world, followed closely by Carlyle, Green, Emerson, and many others.

> Yes, I said; and the capacity for such knowledge is the great criterion of dialectical talent: the comprehensive mind is always the dialectical.
>
> I agree with you, he said.
>
> These, I said, are the points which you must consider; and those who have most of this comprehension, and who are most steadfast in their learning, and in their military and other appointed duties, when they have arrived at the age of thirty have to be chosen by you out of the select class, and elevated to higher honour; and you will have to prove them by the help of dialectic, in order to learn which of them is able to give up the use of sight and the other senses, and in company with truth to attain absolute being [...].[1]

Persons have dialectical talent if they can view things synoptically as wholes, not merely in isolation (or as pure absolutes, as in upward dialectics above!). The same is echoed here:

> The sciences which they have hitherto learned in fragments will now be brought into relation with each other and with true being; for the power of combining them is the test of speculative and dialectical ability. And afterwards at thirty a further selection shall be made of those who are able to withdraw from the world of sense into the abstraction of ideas.

Curiously, the naturally gifted dialecticians are first selected due to their synoptic abilities — but what they ultimately aim is the very reverse of synoptic. They first combine things and then they separate them.

What sense does this make? Actually, it makes good *dialectical* sense. (We need to read dialectical texts dialectically!) For if a thing is or seems contradictory on the surface, it may still be interpreted in a way which renders it coherent. We need to shift between different *levels* of thinking. Plato himself demonstrates this with relative predicates. He writes:

> When speaking of uninviting objects, I mean those which do not pass from one sensation to the opposite; inviting objects are those which do; in this latter case the sense coming upon the object, whether at a distance or near, gives no more vivid idea of anything in particular than of its opposite. An

---

[1] *Republic* 537C-D.

illustration will make my meaning clearer:—here are three fingers—a little finger, a second finger, and a middle finger.

Very good.

You may suppose that they are seen quite close: And here comes the point.

What is it?

Each of them equally appears a finger, whether seen in the middle or at the extremity, whether white or black, or thick or thin—it makes no difference; a finger is a finger all the same. In these cases a man is not compelled to ask of thought the question what is a finger? for the sight never intimates to the mind that a finger is other than a finger.

True.

And therefore, I said, as we might expect, there is nothing here which invites or excites intelligence.

There is not, he said.

But is this equally true of the greatness and smallness of the fingers? Can sight adequately perceive them? and is no difference made by the circumstance that one of the fingers is in the middle and another at the extremity? And in like manner does the touch adequately perceive the qualities of thickness or thinness, of softness or hardness? And so of the other senses; do they give perfect intimations of such matters? Is not their mode of operation on this wise—the sense which is concerned with the quality of hardness is necessarily concerned also with the quality of softness, and only intimates to the soul that the same thing is felt to be both hard and soft?

You are quite right, he said.[1]

This is to distinguish between two classes of objects for thought: the stimulating and the not stimulating (the inviting and the uninviting). What is the difference between these classes? In Plato's example, a thing is or is not a finger — that is only a black and white affair, because — clearly — being a finger is only a one-term predicate: x *is a finger*. But relatives are not as obvious, for if x *is small* then this is really to compare x with some y, as in x *is smaller than* y. This is a two-term predicate, in other words a relation! But this leads to a *contradiction* of sorts if x is also

---

[1] *Republic* 523B-524A.

larger than some other thing, v. (Then we have v IS SMALLER THAN x IS SMALLER THAN y. Formally: vRxRy.) The 'contradiction' is that x is large and small: large compared to v but small compared to y (precisely as in 0.3). However, if we state the logic thus in a relational series then there is of course no contradiction, and the appearance of a contradiction arises only if one deals only in one-term predicates. But *this* is to shift between 'levels' of thought and language! We do not simply say, True! or False!, but: Based on what? And how is the material organized? And to do this we need both — the low relatives and the high absolutes. This is how dialectical reasoning operates.

Stated differently, dialectics then we should conclude similarly that dialectical reasoning is a two-way street. The same road goes up and down (as Epictetus says): it all depends on which way you happen to go. If you go upward, you will be reaching for the Ideas, and ultimately for the Agathon. But as soon as you look down, you will get tangled in contradictions or relatives — and that is when you will need your synoptic and comparative skills. As a dialectician you will need to move both ways.

It may surprise some readers that Plato extends this kind of thinking also to *numbers* (and this short passage is one pioneering impulse in a branch later known now as philosophy of mathematics):

> This was what I meant when I spoke of impressions which invited the intellect, or the reverse—those which are simultaneous with opposite impressions, invite thought; those which are not simultaneous do not.
>
> I understand, he said, and agree with you.
>
> And to which class do unity and number belong?
>
> I do not know, he replied.
>
> Think a little and you will see that what has preceded will supply the answer; for if simple unity could be adequately perceived by the sight or by any other sense, then, as we were saying in the case of the finger, there would be nothing to attract towards being; but when there is some contradiction always present, and one is the reverse of one and involves the conception of plurality, then thought begins to be aroused within us, and the soul perplexed and wanting to arrive at a decision asks 'What is absolute unity?' This is the way in which the study of the one has a power of drawing and converting the mind to the contemplation of true being.

> And surely, he said, this occurs notably in the case of one; for
> we see the same thing to be both one and infinite in multitude?
>
> Yes, I said; and this being true of one must be equally true of
> all number?
>
> Certainly.
>
> And all arithmetic and calculation have to do with number?
>
> Yes.[1]

Viewed thus, numbers are not simply givens. A calculator runs through them quickly and in impressive volumes, but it never faces the bottom-line issue: What are numbers, really? As before Plato sees problems or conflicts as food for thought — that is for real, dialectical thought. A calculator or a computer is not like this. It is not after problems and foundations. It is for efficiency. It is happy if things are predefined. It does not want to ask or ponder.

What then is the philosophical question about numbers? On one level it is this: one tree contains many branches, one branch has many leaves. Now what is one, what is many? What to *count* as one and what to count as many? It depends on how you individuate things. But the purer question is: What is 1? (What are numbers?) It is not a tree, of course. It is not a finger which you can count. It is not a word only ('one' in English) or a sign ('1', or 'I' for the Romans), of course. But what is left? How do you explain it? The pocket calculator could not care less: Just give me things to count! Plato cares, but he leaves this matter open for later generations.[2]

A tension between the upward and downward directions of dialectical reasoning still remains if we ask which to *prioritize*. This conflict is brought to a head when Plato considers the political obligations of his ideal philosophers. For their inner drive is to live simply on the blessed isles, contemplating and studying the perfect Ideas, but social obligations await them in the city below:

---

[1] *Republic* 524D-525A.

[2] *Platonists* of various stripes abound in the philosophy of mathematics, including Frege and Russell. In Plato scholarship the Tübingen School is known for its emphasis on Plato's view of numbers.

In my view this is interesting stuff, but it cannot be central. The main point with Plato and with philosophy in general must be to figure out absolutes like Ideas or Gods, not mere numbers. (What is your scale or standard? And what is your scale or standard for that? The extreme questions need to come first.)

Yes, I said; and there is another thing which is likely, or rather a necessary inference from what has preceded, that neither the uneducated and uninformed of the truth, nor yet those who never make an end of their education, will be able ministers of State; not the former, because they have no single aim of duty which is the rule of all their actions, private as well as public; nor the latter, because they will not act at all except upon compulsion, fancying that they are already dwelling apart in the islands of the blest.

Very true, he replied.

Then, I said, the business of us who are the founders of the State will be to compel the best minds to attain that knowledge which we have already shown to be the greatest of all—they must continue to ascend until they arrive at the good; but when they have ascended and seen enough we must not allow them to do as they do now.

What do you mean?

I mean that they remain in the upper world: but this must not be allowed; they must be made to descend again among the prisoners in the den, and partake of their labours and honours, whether they are worth having or not.

But is not this unjust? he said; ought we to give them a worse life, when they might have a better?

You have again forgotten, my friend, I said, the intention of the legislator, who did not aim at making any one class in the State happy above the rest; the happiness was to be in the whole State, and he held the citizens together by persuasion and necessity, making them benefactors of the State, and therefore benefactors of one another; to this end he created them, not to please themselves, but to be his instruments in binding up the State.

True, he said, I had forgotten.

Observe, Glaucon, that there will be no injustice in compelling our philosophers to have a care and providence of others; we shall explain to them that in other States, men of their class are not obliged to share in the toils of politics: and this is reasonable, for they grow up at their own sweet will, and the government would rather not have them. Being self-taught, they cannot be expected to show any gratitude for a culture which they have never received. But we have brought you into the world to be rulers of the hive, kings of yourselves and of the other citizens, and have educated you far better and more perfectly than they have been educated, and you are better able to share in the double duty. Wherefore each of you, when his turn comes, must go down to the general underground abode, and get the habit of seeing in the dark. When you have acquired the habit, you will see ten thousand times better than the inhabitants of the den, and you will know what the several images are, and what they represent, because you have seen the beautiful and just and good in their truth. And thus our State, which is also yours, will be a reality, and not a dream only, and will be administered in a spirit unlike that of other States, in which men fight with one another about shadows only and are distracted in the struggle for power, which in their eyes is a great good. Whereas the truth is that the State in which the rulers are most reluctant to govern is always the best and most quietly governed, and the State in which they are most eager, the worst.[1]

Plato obviously knows that the dialectical speculators are apolitical persons who would prefer to philosophize freely without any social obligations. They must be forced down to the city, he has now said, because the well-being of the entire city is the priority. However, if the elevated speculators are viewed from below then they seem irresponsible. Who is right? The answer seems to be that in fairness the question should not even arise, for it is not a good idea to elect dialecticians as *political* authorities. After all, what do dialectical skills have to do with politics? The polis was brought up only as an illustrative analogue for the psyche. In reality Plato seems to be of many minds about this.

Now I turn to his later works.

Atlantis in the *Timaeus* and the *Critias*

Plato's second utopia, Atlantis, is a mythical island which is supposed to have existed on the Eastern Atlantic. Its descriptions in Plato's *Timaeus* and the *Critias* are not philosophically deep. They repeat some of the associations about a communist elite of dialectical philosophers and peaceful concord, but beyond this we get only story-like descriptions of city planning and public decorations in gold, silver, and bronze. The city's

---

[1] *Republic* 519B-520D.

circular design (with a network of canals) may have some significance in the light of Plato's other cycles in these and other books. The central temple is devoted to a God (Poseidon). The social order is virtuous and not materialistic, and eventually Atlantis perishes because of the rise of an all-too-human vanity. The *Critias*, which tells this tale, has been partly lost. The text we have ends thus:

> For many generations, as long as the divine nature lasted in them, they were obedient to the laws, and well-affectioned towards the god, whose seed they were; for they possessed true and in every way great spirits, uniting gentleness with wisdom in the various chances of life, and in their intercourse with one another. They despised everything but virtue, caring little for their present state of life, and thinking lightly of the possession of gold and other property, which seemed only a burden to them; neither were they intoxicated by luxury; nor did wealth deprive them of their self-control; but they were sober, and saw clearly that all these goods are increased by virtue and friendship with one another, whereas by too great regard and respect for them, they are lost and friendship with them. By such reflections and by the continuance in them of a divine nature, the qualities which we have described grew and increased among them; but when the divine portion began to fade away, and became diluted too often and too much with the mortal admixture, and the human nature got the upper hand, they then, being unable to bear their fortune, behaved unseemly, and to him who had an eye to see grew visibly debased, for they were losing the fairest of their precious gifts; but to those who had no eye to see the true happiness, they appeared glorious and blessed at the very time when they were full of avarice and unrighteous power. Zeus, the god of gods, who rules according to law, and is able to see into such things, perceiving that an honourable race was in a woeful plight, and wanting to inflict punishment on them, that they might be chastened and improve, collected all the gods into their most holy habitation, which, being placed in the centre of the world, beholds all created things. And when he had called them together, he spake as follows [...].[1]

---

[1] *Critias* 120E-121C.

As the divine portion fades away, the high principles fall. The God of Gods (Zeus) sees to it that all the Gods in unison destroy Atlantis once and for all. Without the divine principles the city does not deserve to exist.

The *Timaeus* begins with mythical descriptions of both the Kallipolis and Atlantis, but the dialectical question one may fruitfully ask about this work concerns the divine models these utopias are meant to follow. Why should human cities or personalities care to become Godlike as Plato requires? Why should such a paradigm qualify as obvious?

This issue takes us to Plato's creation myth, which Christian authorities follow in the medieval period because Plato's myth is in some ways analogical to the Bible's *Genesis* (by contrast Aristotle's world is eternal). God is like a gigantic craftsman, Plato writes in the *Timaeus*, so He is in some ways similar to a human. Somehow He originally finds himself in a world of material chaos, but luckily He also has access to the perfect Ideas. His craftsman-like activity then consists of shaping the chaotic, material world in the light of the Ideas, so his role is like that of an intermediate between the low world of sensual bodies and the higher sphere of the Ideas.

> HERMOCRATES: [...] Then now let me explain to you the order of our entertainment; first, Timaeus, who is a natural philosopher, will speak of the origin of the world, going down to the creation of man, and then I shall receive the men whom he has created, and some of whom will have been educated by you, and introduce them to you as the lost Athenian citizens of whom the Egyptian record spoke. As the law of Solon prescribes, we will bring them into court and acknowledge their claims to citizenship. 'I see,' replied Socrates, 'that I shall be well entertained; and do you, Timaeus, offer up a prayer and begin.'
>
> TIMAEUS: All men who have any right feeling, at the beginning of any enterprise, call upon the Gods; and he who is about to speak of the origin of the universe has a special need of their aid. May my words be acceptable to them, and may I speak in the manner which will be most intelligible to you and will best express my own meaning!
>
> First, I must distinguish between that which always is and never becomes and which is apprehended by reason and reflection, and that which always becomes and never is and is

conceived by opinion with the help of sense. All that becomes and is created is the work of a cause, and that is fair which the artificer makes after an eternal pattern, but whatever is fashioned after a created pattern is not fair. Is the world created or uncreated?—that is the first question. Created, I reply, being visible and tangible and having a body, and therefore sensible; and if sensible, then created; and if created, made by a cause, and the cause is the ineffable father of all things, who had before him an eternal archetype. For to imagine that the archetype was created would be blasphemy, seeing that the world is the noblest of creations, and God is the best of causes. And the world being thus created according to the eternal pattern is the copy of something; and we may assume that words are akin to the matter of which they speak. What is spoken of the unchanging or intelligible must be certain and true; but what is spoken of the created image can only be probable; being is to becoming what truth is to belief. And amid the variety of opinions which have arisen about God and the nature of the world we must be content to take probability for our rule, considering that I, who am the speaker, and you, who are the judges, are only men; to probability we may attain but no further.

SOCRATES: Excellent, Timaeus, I like your manner of approaching the subject—proceed.

TIMAEUS: Why did the Creator make the world?...He was good, and therefore not jealous, and being free from jealousy he desired that all things should be like himself. Wherefore he set in order the visible world, which he found in disorder. Now he who is the best could only create the fairest; and reflecting that of visible things the intelligent is superior to the unintelligent, he put intelligence in soul and soul in body, and framed the universe to be the best and fairest work in the order of nature, and the world became a living soul through the providence of God.[1]

Here we first see Plato's usual *dualism*: on the one side there are perfectly knowable and changeless archetypes or Ideas (the higher world), and then on the other side there are sensible, material objects in flux, knowledge of which is always at most probable (the lower world). God steps in *between* these two worlds and alters the lower half so that

---

[1] *Timaeus* 27A-30B.

it comes to resemble the higher half to some extent — but only to some extent. For the low world does continue to change despite its refashioning, and accordingly it remains partly irrational or arational even after God's intervention. Due to this, all that Plato can ever offer concerning it is only a likely story — a myth, not a proper theory.

This is another opportunity for Plato's imagination to soar:

> TIMAEUS: [...] In the likeness of what animal was the world made?—that is the third question...The form of the perfect animal was a whole, and contained all intelligible beings, and the visible animal, made after the pattern of this, included all visible creatures.
>
> Are there many worlds or one only?—that is the fourth question...One only. For if in the original there had been more than one they would have been the parts of a third, which would have been the true pattern of the world; and therefore there is, and will ever be, but one created world. Now that which is created is of necessity corporeal and visible and tangible,—visible and therefore made of fire,—tangible and therefore solid and made of earth. But two terms must be united by a third, which is a mean between them; and had the earth been a surface only, one mean would have sufficed, but two means are required to unite solid bodies. And as the world was composed of solids, between the elements of fire and earth God placed two other elements of air and water, and arranged them in a continuous proportion—
>
> fire : air : : air : water, and air : water : : water : earth,
>
> and so put together a visible and palpable heaven, having harmony and friendship in the union of the four elements; and being at unity with itself it was indissoluble except by the hand of the framer. Each of the elements was taken into the universe whole and entire; for he considered that the animal should be perfect and one, leaving no remnants out of which another animal could be created, and should also be free from old age and disease, which are produced by the action of external forces. And as he was to contain all things, he was made in the all-containing form of a sphere, round as from a lathe and every way equidistant from the centre, as was natural and suitable to him. He was finished and smooth, having neither eyes nor ears, for there was nothing without him which he could see or hear; and he had no need to carry

food to his mouth, nor was there air for him to breathe; and he did not require hands, for there was nothing of which he could take hold, nor feet, with which to walk. All that he did was done rationally in and by himself, and he moved in a circle turning within himself, which is the most intellectual of motions; but the other six motions were wanting to him; wherefore the universe had no feet or legs.

And so the thought of God made a God in the image of a perfect body, having intercourse with himself and needing no other, but in every part harmonious and self-contained and truly blessed. The soul was first made by him—the elder to rule the younger; not in the order in which our wayward fancy has led us to describe them, but the soul first and afterwards the body. God took of the unchangeable and indivisible and also of the divisible and corporeal, and out of the two he made a third nature, essence, which was in a mean between them, and partook of the same and the other, the intractable nature of the other being compressed into the same. Having made a compound of all the three, he proceeded to divide the entire mass into portions related to one another in the ratios of 1, 2, 3, 4, 9, 8, 27, and proceeded to fill up the double and triple intervals [...].[1]

God makes the world into a single circular whole, a strange 'animal' — handless, legless, eyeless, earless! — which consumes what it produces, revolving around its own belly. Next Plato pieces it into units according to mathematical proportions. By the standards of modern science Plato's myth is fanciful, of course, but some of his structural innovations are deeply insightful. (To this day Plato like Pythagoras is viewed as a precursor to mathematical or realistic philosophies of sciences, and later in the tradition we have, e.g., Galileo and Kant, see Ch. 3. Compare Losee.[2])

---

[1] *Timaeus* 30C-35C.

[2] Plato's geometrical theory of the elements runs thus:

From the triangle of which the hypotenuse is twice the lesser side the three first regular solids are formed—first, the equilateral pyramid or tetrahedron; secondly, the octahedron; thirdly, the icosahedron; and from the isosceles triangle is formed the cube. And there is a fifth figure (which is made out of twelve pentagons), the dodecahedron—this God used as a model for the twelvefold division of the Zodiac.

Let us now assign the geometrical forms to their respective elements. The cube is the most stable of them because resting on a quadrangular plane surface, and composed of isosceles triangles. To the earth then, which is the most stable of bodies and the most easily modelled of them, may be assigned the form of a

The origin of *time* is equally mythical and vaguely intelligible:

> When the Father who begat the world saw the image which
> he had made of the Eternal Gods moving and living, he
> rejoiced; and in his joy resolved, since the archetype was
> eternal, to make the creature eternal as far as this was possible.
> Wherefore he made an image of eternity which is time, having
> an uniform motion according to number, parted into months
> and days and years, and also having greater divisions of past,
> present, and future. These all apply to becoming in time, and
> have no meaning in relation to the eternal nature, which ever
> is and never was or will be; for the unchangeable is never older
> or younger, and when we say that he 'was' or 'will be,' we are
> mistaken, for these words are applicable only to becoming,
> and not to true being; and equally wrong are we in saying
> that what has become IS become and that what becomes IS
> becoming, and that the non-existent IS non-existent...These
> are the forms of time which imitate eternity and move in a
> circle measured by number.[1]

In the world of Ideas there is no time, for everything only always *is*.
But thoughts of time and verbal expressions of time — what *will be*, what
has been — pop up once God has first organized the world. Now it begins
to move.

Finally — to complete the cycle — God also made us humans, whom
He provided with a remarkable ability to learn to become like Him, their
creator:

> Sight is the source of the greatest benefits to us; for if our eyes
> had never seen the sun, stars, and heavens, the words which we
> have spoken would not have been uttered. The sight of them

---

cube; and the remaining forms to the other elements,—to fire the pyramid, to
air the octahedron, and to water the icosahedron,—according to their degrees
of lightness or heaviness or power, or want of power, of penetration. The single
particles of any of the elements are not seen by reason of their smallness; they only
become visible when collected. The ratios of their motions, numbers, and other
properties, are ordered by the God, who harmonized them as far as necessity
permitted.
A single point or a pair of points is of course not yet a shape or area, but with a
triangle we have the first and simplest tool for a mathematical interpretation
of a portion of the physical world — namely fire. Plato is of course wrong to
identify fire with triangles or earth with squares, but his historical achievement
is to even *try* to reason thus. The world should make sense! (It should reduce to
ratios.) This he says though he also resorts to mythology.

[1] *Timaeus* 37C-38A.

and their revolutions has given us the knowledge of number and time, the power of enquiry, and philosophy, which is the great blessing of human life; not to speak of the lesser benefits which even the vulgar can appreciate. God gave us the faculty of sight that we might behold the order of the heavens and create a corresponding order in our own erring minds. To the like end the gifts of speech and hearing were bestowed upon us; not for the sake of irrational pleasure, but in order that we might harmonize the courses of the soul by sympathy with the harmony of sound, and cure ourselves of our irregular and graceless ways.[1]

We have eyes — not so that we may forage and multiply or adapt and survive in a natural environment as the modern Darwinist would say — but so that we may see the world and be impressed with its beautiful regularity! For this will drive us to know about God, and on this basis we will learn to be Godlike. In other words, a 'book' of nature — not a written document like the Bible or Plato's own corpus of texts — has been given to us to read so that we may learn our higher lesson. Like little gods we should seek and manufacture an Idea-like order in the material world around us. This is fundamental Plato. Similarly, speech and writing are not only playthings for irrational fun: they are to be used to make sense of all this that is around us.

Also these ideas are influential in history (though by our time they may sound rather strange). Later in antiquity Plato's view is taken over by the Stoics, who study divine nature to learn how to lose themselves in it. Even in modern times Copernicus is said to hit upon his idea of heliocentrism due to Plato's Sun Allegory (thus Popper), and Newton is an ardent believer in the divinity of nature. Indeed why else would one study physical reality with any hope that it is fundamentally orderly? (Why would one assume that it all makes sense if it is not a rational creation?) But this trust is lost by the time of quantum physics and its associated uncertainties, and in our day it is more common to think of science in strictly secular terms. Natural knowledge is now not divine but useful.[2]

---

[1] *Timaeus* 47A-C.

[2] Despite this it remains popular say that we have inalienable human dignity due to human 'nature'. Of course there is no such dignity in the light of modern science.

God in the *Laws*

Plato's last and longest work, the *Laws*, makes no mention of dialectics, it praises theology instead of philosophy and God instead of the Ideas, and its hero is not Socrates but 'the Athenian' — However, all the hall-marks of Plato's usual philosophizing are there, so in reality only the names change and beyond such superficial aspects everything stays the same.

The main argument of the work runs thus. God (*theos*) is the perfect model for the human soul (Greek: *psyche*), for a yet further social utopia (Magnesia), and for the physical cosmos.

Again it is pertinent to ask what is it about God that is worth all this emulating. The main, structural descriptions of God in the *Laws* are two. The first of them contrasts self-movers from other-movers:

> [Athenian Stranger] Let us assume that there is a motion able to move other things, but not to move itself;—that is one kind; and there is another kind which can move itself as well as other things, working in composition and decomposition, by increase and diminution and generation and destruction—that is also one of the many kinds of motion.[1] [...]
>
> [Cleinias] What do you mean?
>
> [Ath.] I mean this: when one thing changes another, and that another, of such will there be any primary changing element? How can a thing which is moved by another ever be the beginning of change? Impossible. But when the self-moved changes other, and that again other, and thus thousands upon tens of thousands of bodies are set in motion, must not the beginning of all this motion be the change of the self-moving principle?
>
> [Cle.] Very true, and I quite agree.
>
> [Ath.] Or, to put the question in another way, making answer to ourselves:—If, as most of these philosophers have the audacity to affirm, all things were at rest in one mass, which of the above-mentioned principles of motion would first spring up among them?
>
> [Cle.] Clearly the self-moving; for there could be no change in them arising out of any external cause; the change must first take place in themselves.

> [Ath.] Then we must say that self-motion being the origin of all motions, and the first which arises among things at rest as well as among things in motion, is the eldest and mightiest principle of change, and that which is changed by another and yet moves other is second.
>
> [Cle.] Quite true.[1]

If a chain of movers has a beginning somewhere, then what may that beginning be like? Is it a self-mover or a thing moved by another thing? Obviously the former, Plato answers.

This accords nicely with the format that has been used in this book: a MOVES a MOVES b MOVES c... Besides this structure, the *Laws* features the familiar dialogical manner of philosophizing. These are reasons enough to say that the *Laws* is a dialectical and philosophical piece even if the word 'dialectic' or its cognates is never brought up in the text.

However, this tells us only that a is a self-mover: nothing more specific has so far been offered. How are we to imagine the intrinsic nature of self-motion?

One lead is the second key passage I referred to above. This outlines *ten types of motion*:

> [Ath.] Come, then, and if ever we are to call upon the Gods, let us call upon them now in all seriousness to come to the demonstration of their own existence. And so holding fast to the rope we will venture upon the depths of the argument. When questions of this sort are asked of me, my safest answer would appear to be as follows: — Some one says to me, "O Stranger, are all things at rest and nothing in motion, or is the exact opposite of this true, or are some things in motion and others at rest?-To this I shall reply that some things are in motion and others at rest. "And do not things which move a place, and are not the things which are at rest at rest in a place?" Certainly. "And some move or rest in one place and some in more places than one?" You mean to say, we shall rejoin, that those things which rest at the centre move in one place, just as the circumference goes round of globes which are said to be at rest? "Yes." And we observe that, in the revolution, the motion which carries round the larger and the lesser circle at the same time is proportionally distributed

---

[1] *Laws* 894E-895B.

to greater and smaller, and is greater and smaller in a certain proportion. Here is a wonder which might be thought an impossibility, that the same motion should impart swiftness and slowness in due proportion to larger and lesser circles. "Very true." And when you speak of bodies moving in many places, you seem to me to mean those which move from one place to another, and sometimes have one centre of motion and sometimes more than one because they turn upon their axis; and whenever they meet anything, if it be stationary, they are divided by it; but if they get in the midst between bodies which are approaching and moving towards the same spot from opposite directions, they unite with them. "I admit the truth of what you are saying." Also when they unite they grow, and when they are divided they waste away-that is, supposing the constitution of each to remain, or if that fails, then there is a second reason of their dissolution. "And when are all things created and how?" Clearly, they are created when the first principle receives increase and attains to the second dimension, and from this arrives at the one which is neighbour to this, and after reaching the third becomes perceptible to sense. Everything which is thus changing and moving is in process of generation; only when at rest has it real existence, but when passing into another state it is destroyed utterly. Have we not mentioned all motions that there are, and comprehended them under their kinds and numbered them with the exception, my friends, of two?

[Cle.] Which are they?

[Ath.] Just the two, with which our present enquiry is concerned.

[Cle.] Speak plainer.

[Ath.] I suppose that our enquiry has reference to the soul?

[Cle.] Very true.

[Ath.] Let us assume that there is a motion able to move other things, but not to move itself;-that is one kind; and there is another kind which can move itself as well as other things, working in composition and decomposition, by increase and diminution and generation and destruction-that is also one of the many kinds of motion.

[Cle.] Granted.

[Ath.] And we will assume that which moves other, and is changed by other, to be the ninth, and that which changes itself and others, and is co-incident with every action and every passion, and is the true principle of change and motion in all that is-that we shall be inclined to call the tenth.

[Cle.] Certainly.

[Ath.] And which of these ten motions ought we to prefer as being the mightiest and most efficient?

[Cle.] I must say that the motion which is able to move itself is ten thousand times superior to all the others.

[Ath.] Very good; but may I make one or two corrections in what I have been saying?

[Cle.] What are they?

[Ath.] When I spoke of the tenth sort of motion, that was not quite correct.

[Cle.] What was the error?

[Ath.] According to the true order, the tenth was really the first in generation and power; then follows the second, which was strangely enough termed the ninth by us.

[Cle.] What do you mean?

[Ath.] I mean this: when one thing changes another, and that another, of such will there be any primary changing element? How can a thing which is moved by another ever be the beginning of change? Impossible. But when the self-moved changes other, and that again other, and thus thousands upon tens of thousands of bodies are set in motion, must not the beginning of all this motion be the change of the self-moving principle?

[Cle.] Very true, and I quite agree.[1]

Thus a self-mover is intelligible as the high point in a hierarchy of movers, and all types of motion are presented in circular shapes. The circular motions seem to be more or less perfect depending on the degree of their autonomy, and the most autonomous point — as it were the Archimedean point — in Plato's universe is God.

Plato offers a neat illustration for this in terms of *puppets* (*Laws* 644D-645C). Only God is a puppeteer proper, so God alone is fully active.

---

[1] *Laws* 893A-895A.

Compared to Him we are all mere puppets. But then there is also a question of degree, for we can be more or less puppeteers and more or less puppets: we can become more or less Godlike.

In more literal terms this is to say that we may learn to *rule over ourselves*. Plato arrives at this pattern by first considering hostile relations between states and families:

[Ath.] [...] You seem to imagine that a well governed state ought to be so ordered as to conquer all other states in war: am I right in supposing this to be your meaning?

[Cle.] Certainly; and our Lacedaemonian friend, if I am not mistaken, will agree with me.

[Meg.] Why, my good friend, how could any Lacedaemonian say anything else?

[Ath.] And is what you say applicable only to states, or also to villages?

[Cle.] To both alike.

[Ath.] The case is the same?

[Cle.] Yes.

[Ath.] And in the village will there be the same war of family against family, and of individual against individual?

[Cle.] The same.

[Ath.] And should each man conceive himself to be his own enemy: — what shall we say?

[Cle.] O Athenian Stranger-inhabitant of Attica I will not call you, for you seem to deserve rather to be named after the goddess herself, because you go back to first principles you have thrown a light upon the argument, and will now be better able to understand what I was just saying-that all men are publicly one another's enemies, and each man privately his own.

([Ath.] My good sir, what do you mean?) —

[Cle.].... Moreover, there is a victory and defeat-the first and best of victories, the lowest and worst of defeats-which each man gains or sustains at the hands, not of another, but of himself; this shows that there is a war against ourselves going on within every one of us.

[Ath.] Let us now reverse the order of the argument: Seeing that every individual is either his own superior or his own inferior, may we say that there is the same principle in the house, the village, and the state?

[Cle.] You mean that in each of them there is a principle of superiority or inferiority to self?

[Ath.] Yes.

[Cle.] You are quite right in asking the question, for there certainly is such a principle, and above all in states; and the state in which the better citizens win a victory over the mob and over the inferior classes may be truly said to be better than itself, and may be justly praised, where such a victory is gained, or censured in the opposite case.

[Ath.] Whether the better is ever really conquered by the worse, is a question which requires more discussion, and may be therefore left for the present. But I now quite understand your meaning when you say that citizens who are of the same race and live in the same cities may unjustly conspire, and having the superiority in numbers may overcome and enslave the few just; and when they prevail, the state may be truly called its own inferior and therefore bad; and when they are defeated, its own superior and therefore good.

[Cle.] Your remark, Stranger, is a paradox, and yet we cannot possibly deny it.[1]

If the Lacedaemonians make a general principle out of war then this principle will rule not only between states but also between families and persons, and even inside persons. Persons can be their own enemies, as it were in inner civil war. But if the parts which fight inside them are not equals, then either is inferior and the other superior. In the self-ruled person the superior part rules over the inferior part (quite as in the *Republic*, see above). Self-rule requires such a hierarchical principle, not one of hostility but also not merely one of egalitarian concord.

This raises a question which can be state in terms of puppets again: the great puppeteer, God, pulls our strings, and we are puppets (only more or less). But does the great puppeteer pull his own strings too?

The preceding quote implies that if the puppeteer has parts then one part of God may be the puppeteer — a kind of homunculus ruling God from within. But does this not only push the question further? Is there

---

[1] *Laws* 626A-627D.

a still smaller miniature dictator inside the miniature dictator? How can this series end? What happens inside God?

Plato does not seem to see the problem. For in the following passage his distrust or merely human powers leads him to idolize God so blindly that he can not assess His inner character. Plato writes:

> [Ath.] [...] There is a tradition of the happy life of mankind in days when all things were spontaneous and abundant. And of this the reason is said to have been as follows: — Cronos knew what we ourselves were declaring, that no human nature invested with supreme power is able to order human affairs and not overflow with insolence and wrong. Which reflection led him to appoint not men but demigods, who are of a higher and more divine race, to be the kings and rulers of our cities; he did as we do with flocks of sheep and other tame animals. For we do not appoint oxen to be the lords of oxen, or goats of goats; but we ourselves are a superior race, and rule over them. In like manner God, in his love of mankind, placed over us the demons, who are a superior race, and they with great case and pleasure to themselves, and no less to us, taking care us and giving us peace and reverence and order and justice never failing, made the tribes of men happy and united. And this tradition, which is true, declares that cities of which some mortal man and not God is the ruler, have no escape from evils and toils.[1]

Oxen should not rule among oxen, nor goats among goats. Similarly, humans must serve a higher standard, that of demigods or demons (*daimons*), or ultimately that of God. But the question begged is what or who rules God.

As the reader may be able to guess by now, my personal response would be to go back to a MOVES a again and to insist that there is nothing wrong with that. If a IS SUPERIOR TO a then this may mean merely that a is autonomous: a COMMANDS a, or a FORMULATES PRINCIPLES FOR a (as in Kant, see Ch. 3 below). (The relation need not spell anything as physical as IS LARGER IN SIZE THAN or IS FASTER THAN, which would make aRa incoherent.) God can be theorized coherently in this fashion. (God as a person probably cannot be a rational foundation, meanwhile, because the authority of his His person seems

---

[1] *Laws* 713C-713E.

to require formats like the above. Nothing can be proved only by an *autós epha — ipse dixit.*)

To conclude this we need to circle back to our original question. What does any of this have to do with *utopias* or the *utopian paradox*?

The *Laws* is actually not concerned officially and essentially with this paradox in particular, but its cyclical model bears on the question rather naturally. For the *Laws* teaches in effect that

- the beginning is the end,
- the origin is the purpose.

For *theos* comes first in the chain of movers, but *theos* is also the final lesson for the human soul to learn from theology!

If we multiply this circle in the wider world then we find a whole series of circles in the text of the *Laws:*

- each civilization rises and falls in time, and the *Laws* says that many are washed away in a deluge. Egypt's monuments remain though its high culture has perished, and in the *Laws* they are ancient objects of wonder to the Greeks much as the Greeks are to us (the distance in time is about as long).
- each generation is born in dependency to the previous generation and only gradually learns to become independent — after which point it generates the next generation. (The child relies on the parent, but the child grows into an independent adult and as a self-mover he produces offspring, which are again at first dependent, etc.)
- seasons of the year change, days and nights take turns, the sun, moon, and stars continue on their paths.

In these terms there appears to be a general *wheel of life* in Greece just as there is in Indian philosophy: once we attain what at least seems like satisfaction, the wheel only spins again, and in the longer time span the result seems illusory (*maya*). However, in Plato's universe there is also a constant you can trust — God — and I already noted that he does not see endless rebirths as a pain.

Atheism in the *Laws*

Scientifically minded readers will be interested to hear how Plato plans to deal with atheists so I will document this briefly.

In the *Laws*, Magnesia is described in detail. Its priorities are as above, and this means that all free citizens of this community devote most of their time to an examined life. Plato holds that astronomy and mathematics will be useful as introductions or supplements to the philosophical or theological dialectic proper, and he has reason to say this given that his theology now is formally circular or cyclical and he is accustomed to observing similar cycles in the heavens.

However, being Plato, he well realizes that the astronomical facts are not by *themselves* divine. Accordingly, there is the logical possibility of atheism: "the possibility that there are earth and stones only, which can have no care at all of human affairs, and [...] all religion is a cooking up of words and a make-believe" (*Laws* 886E). In other words:

> [Ath.] In the first place, my dear friend, these people would say that the Gods exist not by nature, but by art, and by the laws of states, which are different in different places, according to the agreement of those who make them; and that the honourable is one thing by nature and another thing by law, and that the principles of justice have no existence at all in nature, but that mankind are always disputing about them and altering them; and that the alterations which are made by art and by law have no basis in nature, but are of authority for the moment and at the time at which they are made. — These, my friends, are the sayings of wise men, poets and prose writers, which find a way into the minds of youth. They are told by them that the highest right is might, and in this way the young fall into impieties, under the idea that the Gods are not such as the law bids them imagine; and hence arise factions, these philosophers inviting them to lead a true life according to nature, that is, to live in real dominion over others, and not in legal subjection to them.
>
> [Cle.] What a dreadful picture, Stranger, have you given, and how great is the injury which is thus inflicted on young men to the ruin both of states and families![1]

The atheists are presented as lovers of power (*Might makes right*) and as humanistic relativists (like Protagoras, see Plato's *Theaetetus* and *Protagoras*). No truly binding laws exist at all, they say, for humans merely

---

[1] *Laws* 889D-890B.

invent them. Meanwhile reality is only a cold piece of rock, so it is utterly indifferent to human plans.[1]

However, Plato knows that the proper utopian response to such thoughts is to reason, not to punish — and in general civilized reason is to rule in the light of his theology, not brutish force. (This utopia is a giant school! The rulers are teachers.)

> [Ath.] True, Cleinias; but then what should the lawgiver do when this evil is of long standing? should he only rise up in the state and threaten all mankind, proclaiming that if they will not say and think that the Gods are such as the law ordains (and this may be extended generally to the honourable, the just, and to all the highest things, and to all that relates to virtue and vice), and if they will not make their actions conform to the copy which the law gives them, then he who refuses to obey the law shall die, or suffer stripes and bonds, or privation of citizenship, or in some cases be punished by loss of property and exile? Should he not rather, when he is making laws for men, at the same time infuse the spirit of persuasion into his words, and mitigate the severity of them as far as he can?
>
> [Cle.] Why, Stranger, if such persuasion be at all possible, then a legislator who has anything in him ought never to weary of persuading men; he ought to leave nothing unsaid in support of the ancient opinion that there are Gods, and of all those other truths which you were just now mentioning; he ought to support the law and also art, and acknowledge that both alike exist by nature, and no less than nature, if they are the creations of mind in accordance with right reason, you appear to me to maintain, and I am disposed to agree with you in thinking.[2]

Also drama, choirs, gymnastics, poetry, music, etc. are prescribed in the utopian curriculum. It is all about learning by liberal methods and numerous channels to appreciate what is divinely regular and to emulate it in one's own thoughts and life. The body and the psyche are to accord

---

[1] Notice that these perspectives are entirely familiar to Plato, so they are not modern discoveries. In general Plato is an idealist not because he cannot imagine anything else — he knows his cynics and hard power players — but because he *consciously aims and builds* upward anyway. It is a battle even in his day.
[2] *Laws* 890B-D.

with the music of the cosmos!, for, much as in the *Timaeus* before, all sides of life are to cohere at least vaguely with the highest principles.

Plato realizes that this has begin in human infancy:

> [Ath.] Pleasure and pain I maintain to be the first perceptions of children, and I say that they are the forms under which virtue and vice are originally present to them. As to wisdom and true and fixed opinions, happy is the man who acquires them, even when declining in years; and we may say that he who possesses them, and the blessings which are contained in them, is a perfect man. Now I mean by education that training which is given by suitable habits to the first instincts of virtue in children;-when pleasure, and friendship, and pain, and hatred, are rightly implanted in souls not yet capable of under-standing the nature of them, and who find them, after they have attained reason, to be in harmony with her. This harmony of the soul, taken as a whole, is virtue; but the particular training in respect of pleasure and pain, which leads you always to hate what you ought to hate, and love what you ought to love from the beginning of life to the end, may be separated off; and, in my view, will be rightly called education.
>
> [Cle.] I think, Stranger, that you are quite right in all that you have said and are saying about education.
>
> [Ath.] I am glad to hear that you agree with me; for, indeed, the discipline of pleasure and pain which, when rightly ordered, is a principle of education, has been often relaxed and corrupted in human life. And the Gods, pitying the toils which our race is born to undergo, have appointed holy festivals, wherein men alternate rest with labour; and have given them the Muses and Apollo, the leader of the Muses, and Dionysus, to be companions in their revels, that they may improve their education by taking part in the festivals of the Gods, and with their help. I should like to know whether a common saying is in our opinion true to nature or not. For men say that the young of all creatures cannot be quiet in their bodies or in their voices; they are always wanting to move and cry out; some leaping and skipping, and overflowing with sport-iveness and delight at something, others uttering all sorts of cries. But, whereas the animals have no perception of order or disorder in their movements, that is, of rhythm or harmony, as they are called, to us, the Gods, who, as we say, have been appointed to be our companions in the dance, have given the

pleasurable sense of harmony and rhythm; and so they stir us into life, and we follow them, joining hands together in dances and songs; and these they call choruses, which is a term naturally expressive of cheerfulness. Shall we begin, then, with the acknowledgment that education is first given through Apollo and the Muses? What do you say?

[Cle.] I assent.

[Ath.] And the uneducated is he who has not been trained in the chorus, and the educated is he who has been well trained?

[Cle.] Certainly.

[Ath.] And the chorus is made up of two parts, dance and song?

[Cle.] True.

[Ath.] Then he who is well educated will be able to sing and dance well?

[Cle.] I suppose that he will.

[Ath.] Let us see; what are we saying?

[Cle.] What?

[Ath.] He sings well and dances well; now must we add that he sings what is good and dances what is good?

[Cle.] Let us make the addition.

[Ath.] We will suppose that he knows the good to be good, and the bad to be bad, and makes use of them accordingly: which now is the better trained in dancing and music-he who is able to move his body and to use his voice in what is understood to be the right manner, but has no delight in good or hatred of evil; or he who is incorrect in gesture and voice, but is right in his sense of pleasure and pain, and welcomes what is good, and is offended at what is evil?[1]

Animals are not sensitive to the harmonies, so they do not begin to dance to the beat of the drum and the melodious song. But humans can begin their utopian education already when young. Plato surmises that young children will be receptive to performances especially by a puppet theater: this is where they will be addressed on their level. But he also

---

[1] *Laws* 652A-654C.

pictures regular, collective gymnastics in his school society, largely in the manner of twentieth-century totalitarian societies. Typically he mixes a kind of military rigor with an idealistic trust in humanistic education: he is always inevitably on both of these sides, however disturbing we modern readers may find this.[1]

Slavery in the *Laws*

A further question may be raised about labor in Magnesia. For if the Magnesians lead this idealistic a lifestyle — speculating and dancing away every day — then who does all their dirty work? Who washes their laundry? Where do they get food?

The answer is shocking: slaves. They are not reasoned with, but commanded and forced in technocratic fashion. However, I will not dwell on this factor here, for this is not automatically to discredit Plato's utopianism entirely. After all, as Marx will say in Ch. 4, humans have invented machines for the chores which used to require demeaning toil in the past. Before oxen, humans pulled carts, and then it was steam engines, etc. If so, no humans may need to do the dirty work. (This need not be a gap in Plato's utopian argument.)

Aristotle, Hellenism, Scholasticism

After Plato's death his Athenian school, the Academy, continues to exist for nearly a millennium until it is finally shut down by Christian authorities in the year 529. However, the Academy does not flourish in others' hands as it does in Plato's: they are usually too prone to follow his example to do anything new. (It is too often as with Pythagoras and his Pythagoreans: *autós epha* — *ipse dixit.*)

The innovative philosopher of the next generation is by common consensus Aristotle, whose thought is typically more prosaic than Plato's. The cliché is as in Raphael's Renaissance painting, *The School of Athens*, where Plato and Aristotle stand as equals in the middle and all the other Greek philosophers surround them. Plato is shown pointing up to

---

[1] I am suggesting that in reality Plato is both the first great dialectician and one of the early technocrats. Philosophically it is unappealing to consider a mixture of this sort, but the more one studies the history, the more usual and natural it comes to seem. E.g., Newton is the clockwork scientist — but he is religious. Hegel is such a vehement opponent of the Romantics — but in many ways he is one of them. Socrates looks much like the sophists, Kant's Enlightenment has much in common with the French *philosophes*, and this book which opposes AI is written by a person who also admires it.

the sky and Aristotle down to the ground, and every human personality is said to belong to one of these two kinds.

This is simplistic but by and large it is also true, at least about Plato and Aristotle. With Aristotle, there are no more utopias, Ideas, or immortal psyches. His very method is less idealistic and more empirical — and of course in human affairs this is needed too. In politics this contrast appears with special clarity, for Plato's *Republic* compares four or five constitutions as idealized types (timocracy, oligarchy, etc.) and Aristotle compares no fewer than 158 different constitutions which he actually finds in Greek city states around the Mediterranean. Plato is the rationalist with the archetypes, but Aristotle is the comparative and empirical scientist. (Plato's distinctions are radical, but they have comparatively little to do with the real historical world. Aristotle's map again is built from what actually happens, but in the light of pure reason, it is a mess — not a map.)

Despite this, Aristotle also retains much of Plato. In his universe, God remains. Aristotle cannot eliminate Him from his cosmos, and his cosmological argument for the existence of God is that a chain of movers must build on a first mover, God. Thus there is the familiar dialectical picture: we have a chain of movers, and then the first link in the series, the one who pulls the entire chain, is *theos*, God. But unlike Plato's self-mover, Aristotle's *theos* is the unmoved mover — there is no self-mover. He is this as a thinker about Himself (aRa if a = *theos*, R = THINKS ABOUT) or else as a thinker about thought (RRR if R = THINKING).[1] More than this,

---

[1] However, Aristotle's vocabulary is not like this. The following is a selection from his *Metaphysics* Book XII part 7:

> [...] thinking in itself deals with that which is best in itself, and that which is thinking in the fullest sense with that which is best in the fullest sense. And thought thinks on itself because it shares the nature of the object of thought; for it becomes an object of thought in coming into contact with and thinking its objects, so that thought and object of thought are the same. For that which is capable of receiving the object of thought, i.e., the essence, is thought. But it is active when it possesses this object. Therefore the possession rather than the receptivity is the divine element which thought seems to contain, and the act of contemplation is what is most pleasant and best. If, then, God is always in that good state in which we sometimes are, this compels our wonder; and if in a better this compels it yet more. And God is in a better state. And life also belongs to God; for the actuality of thought is life, and God is that actuality; and God's self-dependent actuality is life most good and eternal. We say therefore that God is a living being, eternal, most good, so that life and duration continuous and eternal belong to God; for this is God.

Aristotle sketches his God in terms of the dichotomies he normally utilizes in his philosophy, like actual/possible, active/passive, essential/accidental, but we also see here a distinction between a thought and its object and a reference to fullness. In these symbols, God realizes His essence actively in thinking of thought or of God. There are plenty of philosophy books in which scholars attempt to reason in Aristotle's terms, but my choice has been to sidestep them.

Aristotle's God is the *telos*, the aim or goal of all life: the optimum towards which everything else strives, the best it can. His physics and his ethics, politics, view of metaphors, etc., all testify to this. Everything wants to be God or Godlike: this is how Aristotle explains regularity. Hence, empiricist though he is, he attains his structures from a first philosophy which quite resembles Plato's.[1]

The last complication, however, is that Aristotle does not view even his theology as a *dialectical* piece of reasoning. His view of dialectics is far more belittling. Usually, dialectic is only about debates between hypothetical positions, he says. You play the devil's advocate and maintain a viewpoint coherently against objections — and that is all there is to dialectic. There is nothing in Aristotle's definition of dialectics about foundations: it is all hypothetical. *If* a is said, *then* b is to be said. But should a be said? That is something the Aristotelian dialectician cannot even begin to assess, and this is the blind spot in Aristotle's dialectics. At the same time as he shrinks dialectics in this manner, Aristotle exaggerates the potentials of empirical science — but this topic I will have to leave aside here (cf. Irwin).

Aristotle's mild dialectic affects Hellenic and medieval minds all the way to Kant's eighteenth century[2] — the rebirth of *pure reason.*

Relational idioms enable one to be more systematic (because a single relation suffices to relate several terms) and more focused (because one can relate the same relation or its relatum to itself). Aristotle is forced to shift between terminologies because his logic cannot deal in complex systems. On the contrast between modern relational logic and Aristotle's simplistic logic — a straightjacket of a logic — see 3.2 and especially the quotation from Carnap.

[1] In Chapter 3, I will note briefly how Aristotelian physics is refuted in modern times and how his biological observations are not similarly undermined. This is because physics drops all talk of aims or goals in nature by the time of Galileo, but biological organisms continue even now to be explained by functions. The elephant's trunk enables it to drink, e.g., Aristotle collects thousands of pieces of evidence to this effect, but it does not quite lead him all the way to Darwinian evolution.

[2] Here I need to simplify in this way. The real story however is again more complex: identifiably 'dialectical' authors in the medieval and Renaissance periods are very numerous, and though they seem to have little effect on Kant they influence Schelling and Hegel. Bruno and Böhme are perhaps the most obvious examples.

CHAPTER 3. KANT: AUTONOMY AND THE ANTINOMIES

> The noble man seeks what he wants in himself; the
> inferior man seeks it from others.

— Confucius

Immanuel Kant (1724–1804) steps on the historical stage in an age which is dominated by Enlightenment ideas about scientific progress and human liberty. In the French Revolution both the king and queen and the church authorities are ousted from power, but the people who then come to rule are not idealists. Rather, the French *philosophes* normally picture man as an animal or a machine, without any free will or independent soul. There is no higher knowledge, they write in their pamphlets. Everyone is just as ordinary. This is equality. Morality boils down to utility, beauty to pleasure. We are not holy. But the crux is that even supposed nobles or priests are not holy either, so the *philosophes* oppose hierarchy on the grounds that everyone is as low. With the old order of pretentious hierarchies and unscientific mythology out of the way, henceforth planned societies are to be organized as mechanical clock-works. Thus the great liberation is like an animal liberation movement, and what is unleashed is mainly a light-minded drive to physicality or compara-tively mindless pleasure. (Hence it is not only the king and queen who are decapitated, but all of France!)

To this background, Kant's tendency is well introduced by looking at his popular essay on the *Enlightenment* (3.1). Despite the title of this famous essay, Kant does not here actually argue like the *philosophes* from whom he gets his term. He considers himself an advocate of the Enlightenment in a different sense: he says that humans need to live as self-critical and inquisitive beings who refuse to depend heavily on outer authorities. We should not delegate serious questions to experts but assess them ourselves. What is un-French about this? Broadly, this is *positive* not negative freedom. The negative freedom of the *philosophes* entails the right to free speech and religion, suffrage and private property. In contrast, the positive liberty of Kant and the German Idealists who come after him involves many further duties beyond this, and all these duties are self-imposed. (Cf. Confucius in the chapter's epigraph.)

Which these are is explained in a rudimentary way in Kant's *moral philosophy* (3.2). The *philosophes* said usually that morality is only about pleasure or utility, but Kant argues that it is about duty and autonomy. Thus to be kind is not to cause pleasure to others, but rather to formulate general laws or principles which one thinks all should obey. This difference is immense, for in principle the *philosophes* make sense of morality in natural and animal terms, but with Kant the focus is in our ability to think freely. In one sense this contrast is brought to a head in the problem of free will. Like the British empiricists before them, the *philosophes* tend to say that real freedom is compatible with a scientific world view because there are no causally free choices. (According to compatibilists, you are free in doing what you like but what you like or do need not be purely self-caused.) Crucially for the unscientific status of idealism or dialectics, Kant emphasizes that his view of morality and liberty is not metaphysically compatible with science, because without a free will self-imposed laws cannot really be self-imposed. The individual must design his out of nothing, from within. (To be sure, Kant does maintain that also scientific knowledge requires spontaneously generated structures which cannot be proved empirically, so there is for him something of a parallel between having a free will and *doing* science — as contrasted with the findings of science –, but as I will note this is increasingly an outdated view because the scope of logical computation has grown exponentially since Kant and many of the structures may now be mechanized.)

Kant's most complete departure from the French *philosophes* occurs when he begins to rely on higher versus lower reasoning, *Vernunft* versus *Verstand.* This takes us to his *antinomies* (3.3-3.6). These are dialectical arguments in which ultimate reality can always be interpreted in contradictory ways, but Kant's larger point is that the ultimate interpretations are *not* optional or contradictory as ideals (3.7).[1] The thing to note is the contrast between the *is* and the *ought*. We run into anomalies about the *is* but not about the *ought*. This is to say that pure reasoning is really about rational *ideals*. It is not a physical system out there in the world, but an imaginary optimum. (This has merely been *projected* to outer reality all along by speculative metaphysicians and theologians. Their patterns are not wrong, but they mislocate them.) As rational creatures we *must* seek for conclusive answers, that is even though we must also admit that such ideals correspond to nothing that is ever discovered empirically or scientifically.[2] But Kant is not saying that we should be happy with such illusions merely in themselves. Rather, as an ideal each Idea or archetype tells us what to think and do, and though we can never match it exactly, it can always be matched more closely than before. The end result is that we are always compelled by laws of our own making to look beyond mere physical reality. We must run for the *horizon*, as Kant likes to say. (This is *idealism* in one sense of the word. It is Kant's special brand. Berkeley's brand is very different.[3])

---

[1] Here I must in honesty note that Kant himself uses the word 'dialectic' (or *Dialektik*) only for the negative and destructive half of this picture, that is not for the positive and creative half. Despite this I will use 'dialectic' for both halves, as Plato and Hegel usually do. Kant's own word for higher reasoning is *Vernunft*, as remarked, see Introduction.

[2] Actually Kant says that Ideas are *noumena*, not *phenomena*: things you see with your eyes closed, in a manner of speaking. For they are 'things in themselves', outside our perceptual capabilities. However, this is easily confusing if it is combined with the *ought* vs. *is* message, so I will downplay it here.

[3] *The word 'idealism'* has numerous uses and this can at first be a little confusing. Obviously this word derives from 'Idea', which in turn comes from the Greek word for seeing: However, this should not lead anyone astray because the Ideas in Plato and Kant are not visual but abstract. They are not seen with the eye. They are not heard either, or touched. Rather, they are grasped in thought (and also willed as principles, wondered about in questions or aesthetic objects, et cetera). However, and as we will soon see, more specifically Ideas in Kant as in Plato are extremes in relational series, so they are absolutes, ultimates, or archetypes. Kant writes:
> A conception formed from notions, which transcends the possibility of experience, is an idea, or a conception of reason. To one who has accustomed himself to these distinctions, it must be quite intolerable to hear the representation of the colour red called an idea. It ought not even to be called a notion or conception of understanding. *Critique of Pure Reason* A320/B377. Cf. also: I understand by idea a necessary conception of reason, to which no corresponding object can be discovered in the world of sense. *Critique of Pure Reason* A327/B383.)

A different use of the word 'idealism' stems from George Berkeley (1685–1753): an 'idea' (without capitals) in his sense accords with the philosophies of Locke and Descartes. It is only as in everyday life and ordinary speech, as when we say, 'I have an idea, let's go see a movie'. These are mere mental associations, not archetypes or absolutes. In accordance with this usage, Berkeley's 'idealism' is that there is there is derives from no real world outside our mental associations. If so then real life is not distinct from a dream, hallucinations are inseparable from

Where exactly is the difference between Kant and Plato (3.8)? Also Kant welcomes the Ideas, but they have no business being real. They are values: ideals. That is one shift. A second shift is from objective idealism to subjective: in Plato the Ideas like Gods are out there, totally independent form human soul or mind. Not so for Kant: his world has been disenchanted by modern natural science. The real world out there is but a giant Newtonian clockwork. The free live by their own inner requirements. Kant's thinking leads to the Romantic revolution in culture (3.9): it is not so much the world that counts as how we see it. This is totally foreign to both Plato and to the empiricists.

What Is Enlightenment?

We may begin this chapter moderately by looking at one of the popular articles which Kant published in old age. Here is a famous passage from it which describes the meaning of Enlightenment in human affairs:

> Enlightenment is man's emergence from his self-imposed nonage. Nonage is the inability to use one's own understanding without another's guidance. This nonage is self-imposed if its cause lies not in lack of understanding but in indecision and lack of courage to use one's own mind without another's guidance. *Dare to know!* (*Sapere aude.*) "Have the courage to use your own understanding," is therefore the motto of the enlightenment.

> Laziness and cowardice are the reasons why such a large part of mankind gladly remain minors all their lives, long after nature has freed them from external guidance. They are the reasons why it is so easy for others to set themselves up as guardians. It is so comfortable to be a minor. If I have a book that thinks for me, a pastor who acts as my conscience, a physician who prescribes my diet, and so on--then I have no need to exert myself. I have no need to think, if only I can pay; others will take care of that disagreeable business for me.[1]

> To be mature is to be free is to think for oneself, and to be immature is merely to trust others. One cannot trust a politician or an expert, and one needs to research every-

---

other perceptions. This is emphatically not the kind of idealism advocated or even discussed in this book. (Kant opposes this type of idealism in his *Critique of Pure Reason* but I will not go into that because it has little to do with dialectics.)
[1] This is from Kant's *Answering the Question: What Is Enlightenment?*

thing openly and thoroughly oneself. Each individual is to research all the different branches!

Thus Kant's view of maturity or liberty does not boil down to mere tolerance (*Live and let live*). It is also certainly not sufficient to work hard and earn a living to cover one's own expenses and hence to live independently in a material or economic sense. No, for only the examined life is worth living, as Socrates said. 'Nonage' is immaturity, a kind of voluntary submission or slavery. (Kant chooses strong words.)

Strikingly, though Kant's essay aims to state the meaning of 'Enlightenment', he does not say things that are familiar from previous paradigms on this subject. For though the French *philosophes* publish their multi-volume encyclopedia to cover all existing branches of human knowledge from astronomy and botany all the way to music, political science, and zoology, and though especially Voltaire champions unlimited freedom of speech in the public sphere on whatever topic, they emphatically do not picture such widely ranging inquisitive activities as normal preconditions for the liberties of all human individuals. Rather, their conviction is typically that liberty boils down only to social tolerance. Two centuries later this still popular perspective is summarized aptly by the Oxford philosopher Isaiah Berlin:

> I am normally said to be free to the degree to which no man or body of men interferes with my activity. Political liberty in this sense is simply the area within which a man can act unobstructed by others. If I am prevented by others from doing what I could otherwise do, I am to that degree unfree; and if this area is contracted by other men beyond a certain minimum, I can be described as being coerced, or, it may be, enslaved. Coercion is not, however, a term that covers every form of inability. If I say that I am unable to jump more than ten feet in the air, or cannot read because I am blind, or cannot understand the darker pages of Hegel, it would be eccentric to say that I am to that degree enslaved or coerced. Coercion implies the deliberate interference of other human beings within the area in which I could otherwise act. You lack political liberty or freedom only if you are prevented from attaining a goal by human beings.[1]

---

[1] Isaiah Berlin, "Two Concepts of Liberty" (1958).

Liberty or freedom on this negative view is only a function of social permission: if no one else stops you, you are free. As Berlin explains, this position has been advocated by progressives as well as conservatives, and its exact scope has varied in their minds:

> Philosophers with an optimistic view of human nature and a belief in the possibility of harmonising human interests, such as Locke or Adam Smith or, in some moods, Mill, believed that social harmony and progress were compatible with reserving a large area for private life over which neither the State nor any other authority must be allowed to trespass. Hobbes, and those who agreed with him, especially conservative or reactionary thinkers, argued that if men were to be prevented from destroying one another and making social life a jungle or a wilderness, greater safeguards must be instituted to keep them in their places; he wished correspondingly to increase the area of centralised control and decrease that of the individual. But both sides agreed that some portion of human existence must remain independent of the sphere of social control. To invade that preserve, however small, would be despotism. The most eloquent of all defenders of freedom and privacy, Benjamin Constant, who had not forgotten the Jacobin dictatorship, declared that at the very least the liberty of religion, opinion, expression, property must be guaranteed against arbitrary invasion. Jefferson, Burke, Paine, Mill compiled different catalogues of individual liberties, but the argument for keeping authority at bay is always substantially the same. We must preserve a minimum area of personal freedom if we are not to 'degrade or deny our nature'.[1]

Berlin, like Jefferson, Locke, and the rest is saying that we are free in a 'negative' sense which does not require Kant's 'positive' sense: we are free if only others to not interfere with our doings. We do not actually have to be self-movers or have free wills. (Forget the idealists' systems of self-imposed duties!)

This negative view is called 'compatibilism' in the academic literature on free will because it makes freedom compatible with scientific or physical determinism, that is with the view that every event or action is *causally determined* by some prior even or action, implying that no will is ever free or spontaneous. (In terms of relations, this is again a familiar

---

[1] Ibid.

issue about chains which terminate or do not, as we will see in 3.4. For if there is a first link in a chain of movers then that link will be spontaneous or free. If on the other hand the series never begins at any point then every link is only pulled by some prior link, further back in beginningless time.)

A major reason why so many Enlightenment *philosophes* are negative libertarians and not positive libertarians is the then recent emergence of the physics of Isaac Newton. Newton's laws seem to be so certain and so general to his contemporaries that many theologians of the period are driven to *deism*: the view that the universe is a mechanical clockwork which always obeys Newton's laws though that the clockwork is created and designed by God. (God sets up this machine of a world — and then he stays out of it. This is deism.) Thus in a sense the only truly or positively free being in the universe for deists is God, the creator of the universal system. (He is the puppeteer and everyone else is a little puppet, in Plato's terms.) Newton for instance is not free, for he merely learns to read the book of nature — a book he does not write. Also Newton's many students only learn to read nature's book (from him). They cannot write anything into this book. It is closed. It is God's own book forever.

In our day we know, of course, that Newton's laws are simplistic. Now there is no short catalogue of laws which determine the course of the world, for physics since Planck and Einstein is driven to numerous regions and questions which do not appear to obey the same laws. With Planck physicists consider the smallest particles and with Einstein they consider the largest, but no one seems to know how both extremes could be studied in the same way (cf. Greene). On a different level, astronomists now commonly suppose that 95 percent of the universe remains completely unknown (consisting of a mysterious 'dark energy' and 'dark matter'). Thus there is no general and secure science of the kind that the French *philosophes* presuppose and confidently sell to the public. If there is one great clockwork, what is it? With Newton this still seems clear but in our time it is obscured.

A different complication takes us outside the bounds of science. *If* we knew the physical laws that govern all of nature then this would still not obligate any free or reasoning being to obey those laws, Kant says, for such laws would be functions merely of *Verstand* and not *Vernunft*. The difference is this: they would not be valid per se, or intrinsically, unconditionally. They would be only such laws as physical nature *happens* to obey. It is the *Stoics* who go along with nature, and we may compare them briefly here. In modern philosophy the major name for this is Spinoza, who also influences many German Romantics after Kant. The Stoics say the free conform to nature. Go with the tide! (For example, if a downhill skier falls, he is well advised to *not* resist the pressures when tumbling down. He would only break his limbs if he tried that, for the powers opposed to him would be too great for him. Do no resist!) Due to this, the key to Stoical freedom is knowledge, for if you know nature's laws then you know what to conform to. Knowledge saves you and quiets you down (to *apathia*) because it tells you what you must accept. As long as you are ignorant, you will be wrong and frustrated, blaming people and things for things they could not help doing or being. To top it all off, God for the Stoics is only another name for nature (*Deus sive natura*). Thus again, nature is God's 'book', not the Bible.

Now, if we compare Kant with the Stoics then the central contrast is that between *Vernunft* and *Verstand*. If you go by low laws, you will be submissive and passive, quite as in negative liberty or compatibilism. For then nature or science will make all your key decisions for you! Clearly that would be nonage all over again. If you are to be active and truly free your actions must be *in*compatible with low, natural laws. A free will of this kind is not caused by any prior event, but only by itself. (It is as if Baron Münchhausen lifted himself in the air by the bootstraps.) It is a *first* cause in a chain, so it occurs *ex nihilo* — out of nothing.

The question this begs is how any purely free will might make its decisions. How is it at all possible? Are there no criteria for making choices? And how are these outside physical reality? Or can a purely free will have no standards? Is it a miracle?

Autonomy in a World of Science

Kant writes:

> The will is a kind of causality belonging to living beings in so far as they are rational, and freedom would be this property of such causality that it can be efficient, independently of foreign causes determining it; just as physical necessity is the property that the causality of all irrational beings has of being determined to activity by the influence of foreign causes.

> The preceding definition of freedom is negative and therefore unfruitful for the discovery of its essence, but it leads to a positive conception which is so much the more full and fruitful.

Since the conception of causality involves that of laws, according to which, by something that we call cause, some-thing else, namely the effect, must be produced; hence, although freedom is not a property of the will depending on physical laws, yet it is not for that reason lawless; on the contrary it must be a causality acting according to immutable laws, but of a peculiar kind; otherwise a free will would be an absurdity. Physical necessity is a heteronomy of the efficient causes, for every effect is possible only according to this law, that something else determines the efficient cause to exert its causality. What else then can freedom of the will be but autonomy, that is, the property of the will to be a law to itself? But the proposition: "The will is in every action a law to itself," only expresses the principle: "To act on no other maxim than that which can also have as an object itself as a universal law." Now this is precisely the formula of the categorical imperative and is the principle of morality, so that a free will and a will subject to moral laws are one and the same.[1]

The hallmark of true liberty is its autonomy: self-legislation. To be free is to create a general law which one is not only prepared to live by but which one would wish everyone to follow. (The point however is not to *tell* them to follow it, for as autonomous individuals they are to make laws of their own — of course. The only general law is thus that there must be autonomy for all.)

Notice how this is to use the familiar dialectical pattern aRa above.[2] For the ethic now under consideration says that if you are for lying then you are to be lied to. Hence if a LIES TO b then it is only just and proper if b LIES TO a: the same thing comes back, so the effect is that a LIES TO a (which is aRa if LIES TO = R). If we want to be more nuanced about this we may also write (aRb S bRa) if R = LIES TO and S = IT IS JUST THAT. In any case, you reap just what you sow.

But based on this the notion of a *first cause* should make some sense! It is not really a miracle, and nor is it arbitrary, because it is aRa in the series aRaRbRc... This is not obscure in principle. The first cause self-consistent: that is what distinguishes it. Therefore, as soon as we step outside negative liberty and compatibilism, and also outside Stoicism or Spinozism, it is not really irrational wonders or nonsense that we come

---

[1] This is from his *Foundations of the Metaphysics of Morals*, Section III.
[2] Not that Kant calls this '*dialectical*'. As noted he uses that word for the antin-omies, which I will come to soon below.

to. Rather, we have a higher law, and this is not a law of science. It is *Vernunft*, not *Verstand.*

But how can there ever in fact be first causes like these? Only to say aRa or *Vernunft* sounds so dry and empty.

Kant has a cunning strategy for this. The little circle becomes dynamic and realistic due to what he calls *heteronomy*. For Kant teaches that if someone is autonomous, he must fight against just the opposite force inside himself, and this is heteronomy. This is easiest to see from examples:

- If you are to be freely honest then you must be *able also to lie*, for otherwise the difference is not up to you.
- If you are to be courageous, you can make the decisive choice only if you are *prone to fear*.
- The freely kind must be *naturally cruel.*
- Autonomously rational beings can *not* have an innate propensity to reason!

In every case freedom has to originate in an inner contest between opposed forces or drives, namely on the one hand our lower or animal selves and on the other our higher or free and reasoning selves. (One may visualize this as a conflict between directions, so that if a series aRbRc... ends in zRz, then zRz is pure freedom but one is always pulled backwards to the left. If one were to merely run with easy to the endpoint on the right hand side, without any trouble or tension, then the element of heteronomy would be missing. The line would be too straight.[1])

The dynamic aspect that is thus introduced into freedom may be summarized by saying that one always only *becomes* free and never *is*: there is liberation if one overcomes one's lower self, but as soon as one has succeeded in this, one will have to go through another round of the same contest all over again or one is not free. Therefore one can never *remain* free for long. (One is like a wrestler who qualifies as a wrestler only when he wrestles. If he stops he is something else or nothing.)

The *anti-scienftic or nonnatural* aspect in this is now easy to pin down. This is because for Kant it is the lower, animal self that is scientifically explained, but never the higher. The low self has 'inclinations': it is hungry, selfish, impatient, etc. It is an animal, and science knows its stuff regarding animals. But science knows nothing whatever about the higher self or the patterns of *Vernunft*. It will act as if they were never

---

[1] Also this kind of thing is at times called 'dialectical'. (Compare relativity in the Introduction.)

there — and so it must, for its methods are such. It has its own kind of radar — and there is no radar for everything.

Now let us look a little more closely to Kant's view of *science.*

His position originates as a rebellion against the empiricist method of Bacon, Locke, and Hume. They say that scientific laws are generalizations from experience. The Kantian objection to this is primarily against its *passivity.* There can be no science merely by reporting events, he says, for too much in science depends on its systematization. He famously states:

> Reason must approach nature with the view, indeed, of receiving information from it, not, however, in the character of a pupil, who listens to all that his master chooses to tell him, but in that of a judge, who compels the witnesses to reply to those questions which he himself thinks fit to propose.[1]

The scientist must approach nature not merely as a passive recipient who reports all the things which may happen to come his way if he only stands still — but as an *active questioner.* He must take the initiative and set up the right kinds of experiment. He must be constructive.[2]

---

[1] *Critique of Pure Reason* Bxiv.

[2] What are such questions and how are they chosen? Shanahan outlines the history of questions driving physics (pp. 18-19):

> Consider the very different starting points for Aristotelian and Galileian dynamics. Aristotle formulated his physics of motion by generalizing from a commonsense explanation of a moving object: A cart being pulled by a horse. The cart continues to move just insofar as the horse continues to pull it along. Two factors are at work: The external agency (the horse) keeping the body in motion, and resistance (the weight of the cart) tending to bring the motion to a stop. Aristotle realized that this explanation could be generalized for any moving body. Explaining the motion of any body means recognizing that a body moves at the rate appropriate to an object of its weight, when subjected to just that particular balance of force and resistance. In order for an object to remaining motion, a force must be continually exerted. Relax the force being exerted, and the object in motion will eventually come to rest. Being "at rest" is the natural state of any natural substance, and requires no special explanation. Being "in motion" requires special explanation. Complete rest, or steady motion under a balance of actions and resistances, is the natural motion of an object. Anything that can be shown to exemplify this balance will thereby be explained.
>
> As is well known, the science of motion underwent a dramatic revolution in the seventeenth century in which the ideal of natural order at the heart of Aristotelian physics was abandoned and replaced by another, quite different conception. The most radical step was taken by Galileo, who argued that rest and motion are equally "natural" for bodies, with neither in need of explanation. Only changes in motion, for example, acceleration, require special explanation. [Original in italics.] (Continued)

This is reflected in the scientist's choice of *language*. To see how, notice first that there is no possibility of a neutral report concerning even the simplest of objects or situations. If I were to merely state what is in my small garden, honestly or candidly, without any assumptions, preferences, background theories, or conceptual categories, then I would certainly need to remain silent, for there would be nothing to report. What after all would be the point of the report? What kinds of things should be said in it, what is the demand to which I should react? I could not say how *many* things are in the garden in any neutral way: after all, that depends on what to count as a thing. There are perhaps a million of grass blades, thousands of leaves, but one fence around the whole thing, and one garden. How many things? This depends on what to count. What is a thing, this time around? In other words, what is my report about? The reference to 'things' or to numbers unassisted by categories, classes, or descriptions does not make any sense. I *first* need relevant descriptions or types and *then* I can tell you about things, but the naked things I cannot report.[1]

What goes for numbers goes also for *qualities*. How exactly should one describe these complex shades of green that I am now seeing? 'Green' already is true of them, but is it true enough? What level of precision do you need? Would 'color' be enough, or 'light'?

Also the kind of motion which may be presupposed as a supposedly natural given — which requires no explanation! — changes as we turn the pages of history. In Aristotle it does not exist, as Shanahan says, for rest was the natural state. In Galileo it is circular, in Newton it is a Euclidian straight line, and in Einstein it is different once again (ibid. p. 19). However, these pure and neutral movements are never observed, so they are always only background idealizations made by scientists. This is to say that the science itself gets started only if these background considerations are made first. They are the questions that need to get left out for science to operate. But are they obvious? Of course not. They are decisions. What justifies them is only the smoothness of the results: Einstein's formulas predict things more generally and exactly than Newton's, which beat Galileo's, which beat Aristotle's. Everything else must be left out.

[1] This is in keeping with *logicism*, which is perhaps the predominant philosophy of mathematics since the late nineteenth century. It says numbers are class concepts, so that the number 1 means the same as that x belongs in a class C and if some y belongs in C too then x = y. This is in effect to say that only one thing belongs in C — but without saying anything about *one*, which would make the definition circular. Now there is no circle because class-membership is used to define numbers. For 2 the procedure is analogical: x and y belong to class D and if some z belongs to D then x = z or y = z. (This definition said nothing about *two*, so it is not circular.) Thus we always need to characterize a thing first, and only based on this can we count it as one of something, two of something, etc. (Hence logical groupings and decisions about identity and difference come first, and arithmetic is only a convenient short-hand for such processes.) On logicism see Carnap, in Ayer, ed.

Crucially for Kant's position, the garden itself does not decide any of this for us. The choice of language is *ours*. It is something separate from nature.

As noted the Kantian way to generalize about this is that all empirical cogitation is in fact *constructive*: active. It is not reflective in the way that a quiet pond reflects the clouds in the sky. It moves. It is not a passive mirror. We look at the world, yes, but we cannot look at it from nowhere, or from everywhere at once. We are always positioned in relation to it, and the position is never purely neutral. On a fundamental level this is to say that things need to be read *as* other things: this here is purple and not some unidentifiably precise shade or it, and this purple thing here is a 'plum'. That is how it tastes. I categorize it.

But now, once we have confessed this much, it is no step at all to *study* of our chosen categories. What justifies each choice? Kant's *table of twelve conceptual categories* is his famous response to this. However, it is not in general as neutral as he believes, and for that reason I will not present it in much detail. Suffice it to say that he inherits his term 'category' from Aristotle and attempts to improve on Aristotle's catalogue of categories in systematizing it into an orderly table.[1] In contrast with Kant, Aristotle only lists his categories, and the number of categories on his list varies by publication. Kant seeks more uniformity, arguing that his particular system is present and presupposed in all cognition. It is not analytic (cf. Ch. 1) but 'synthetic': not a set of logical truths but a kind of intuitive human knowledge about the outside world. It consists of spacial, temporal, causal, and modal relationships which we usually have difficulties articulating or even noticing. (It is like a pair of glasses that every human needs to wear in order to make sense of the world, that is in order to give it enough structure to find it intelligible in the first place. You do not tend to see the glasses you wear but all the while they are there. You do not get them by looking: they are always presupposed beforehand.) But this demand of rigid systematicity also leads Kant's table to become *too* stiff — too stiff for the historical changes in science. This point can be made by looking backward or forward in time from Kant.

---

[1] A second difference between Aristotle's and Kant's categories is that Aristotle thinks his derive directly from reality — so he is a 'realist' in philosophical jargon. In contrast Kant is a 'constructivist'. (This is his Copernican Turn, as he calls it.) The meaning of this is as in the preceding pages: Kant sees that categories are imposed on nature. Aristotle believes naively that they are in nature — that natural objects or events come prepackaged.

(Plato by contrast does not deal in categories but in Ideas. Categories are *Verstand* things and Ideas are *Vernunft* things, and categories interpret experience and Ideas transcend experience. Kant is unique in covering *both* the higher and lower worlds.)

Backward. Kline describes Galileo Galilei's Renaissance revolution in physics thus:

> The Aristotelians said that a ball falls because it has weight and it falls to the earth because it, like every object, seeks its natural place, and the natural place of heavy objects is the center of the earth. The natural place of a light body, such as fire, is in the heavens, and hence fire rises. These principles are qualitative. By contrast let us consider the statement that the speed (in feet per second) with which a ball falls is 32 times the number of seconds it has been falling. This statement can be expressed more briefly in symbols. If we denote by v the speed of the body and by t the number the number of seconds it has been falling, then the above assertion amounts to $v = 32t$.[1]

Before Galileo, the medieval Aristotelians describe natural events in terms of qualities or adjectives, but Galileo shifts to quantitative formulas. Thus he does not want to hear that a thing is heavy, for example. He needs to know how heavy it is, in numbers. He needs the measurements in standardized units of something or other. Next, he will use language of this type to utter his findings: $v = 32t$. Now his predictions turn out to work precisely, and we can measure what happens. But in formal tems Galileo's revolution carries weight to this day, for even in Einstein's equation for energy this basic model is only repeated though the numbers are of course different: $E = mc^2$. (m is mass as in Newton and c is the speed of light, 299792458 meters per second.) What grows from Galileo to Newton to Einstein is the range and the precision. Galileo looks at falling objects, Newton looks at the entire solar system, but Einstein expands further to space, etc. However, in the future this may again change, and there may be a future Galileo who redefines the game.

Forward. In general, conceptual changes after Kant are a well known topic for historians and philosophers of science, but one tendency that is relevant to this book is the exponential growth in mechanical computation which derives from the field of logic. The eminent Vienna Circle philosopher Rudolf Carnap explains the shift accessibly in his "The Old and the New Logic" (from 1930):

> The new logic is distinguished from the old not only by the form in which it is presented but chiefly also by the increase of its range. [...] The only form of statements (sentences) in

---

[1] Kline p. 287.

the old logic was the predicative form 'Socrates is a man,' 'All (or some) Greeks are men'. A predicate-concept or property is attributed to a subject-concept. Leibniz had already put forward the demand that logic should consider sentences of relational form. In a relational sentence such as, for example, 'a is greater than b,' a relation is attributed to two or more objects, (or, as it might be put to several subject-concepts). Leibniz's idea of a theory of relations has been worked out by the new logic. The old logic conceived relational sentences as sentences of predicative form. However, many inferences involving relational sentences thereby become impossible. To be sure, one can interpret the sentence 'a is greater than b' in such a way that the predicate 'greater than b' is attributed to the subject a. But the predicate then becomes a unity, one cannot extract b by any rule of inference. Consequently, the sentence 'is is smaller than a' cannot be inferred from this sentence. In the new logic, this inference takes place in the following way. The relation 'smaller than' is defined as the 'converse' of the relation 'greater than'. The inference in question then rests on the universal proposition. If a relation holds between x and y, its converse holds between y and x. [...]

Relational statements are especially indispensable for the mathematical sciences. Let us consider as an example the geometrical concept of the three place relation 'between' (on an open straight line). The geometrical axioms 'If a lies between b and c, b does not lie between c and a' can be expressed only in the new logic. According to the predicative view, in the first case we would have the predicates lying between b and c and 'lying between c and a'. If these are left unanalyzed, there is no way of showing how the first is transformed into the second. If one takes the objects b and c out of the predicate, the statement 'a lies between b and c' no longer serves to characterize only one object, but three. It is therefore a three place relational statement.

The relations 'greater than' and 'between' are of such a kind that the order of their terms cannot be altered at will. The determination of any order in any domain rests essentially on relations of this kind. If among a class of persons it is known which of any pair is the taller, this class of persons is thereby serially ordered. It might be held that this could also be done by means of predicative ascriptions—namely, by attributing a definite measure as a property to each person. But in that case it would again have to be assumed that with respect to any two of these quantities, it was known which was greater. Thus without an ordering relation no series can be constructed. This shows the indispensability of the theory of relations for all those sciences which deal with series and orderings: arithmetic (number series), geometry (point series), physics (all scales of measurement from those of space and time and the various state magnitudes).[1]

Obviously the result of this revolution in logic is that entire *series and systems* can be articulated rigorously. Logical operations are not restricted to consider only isolated dots one at a time, as they were with one-term predicates like x IS YELLOW. Here the only term is x. In y IS MARRIED TO z we have two terms, y and z, and this is already a relational expression. In general, a great deal *more can be done* mechanically or logically than earlier philosophers or scientists ever realized.[2]

Compared to this, Kant still thinks that his intuitive and humane ('synthetic') categories are required to construct order in the world — because for him the domain of analytical or logical, mechanical relations is still so much more limited — which in turn is because his logic is not yet relational. It is only about one-term predicates (with Aristotle).

The lesson now is that machines have learned to do many of the things that Kant still pictures as human constructions. Hence he is a quaint humanist about science, that is about a thing which per se has zero to do with humanity or vague intuitions and everything to do merely with effective computability or predictability and empirical control. *Now* we know that we need no human mind to organize the data, for the scope of logical computation has grown exponentially. At the same time the autonomous human individual is of course increasingly alienated: the physical world is a stranger place than any early modern or ancient scientist or philosopher could ever have imagined. (And very probably in the future this will be even more so, so that a Carnap will seem quaint and humane by the standards of future robotics.) Thus the abyss between freedom and science is only greater than Kant knows.

[1] pp. 137-138.
[2] In Carnap's passage relations stand mainly for series, like a IS GREATER THAN b IS GREATER THAN c IS GREATER THAN d, or a > b > c > d, which is a version of aRbRcRd given that > is one type of relation and 'R' is the generic symbol for a relation. In Carnap's passage, *converseness* then means that a > b is identical to b < a, and *betweenness* is the role of b or c in a > b > c > d or a < b < c < d. (*Transitivity* is also often brought up in introductory discussion of relational logic, e.g., if a > b and b > c then a > c.)

Now let us turn to the official heartland of Kantian dialectics: the *antinomies.*

The First Antinomy: Largest Wholes

As noted previously, even small children can generate dialectical questions: they ask *Why?*, and if you answer they only ask *Why?* again.

The most popular version of this is perhaps to wonder whether space has outer limits and whether time can ever begin or end. This is the core of Kant's first antinomy. Formally it is a series:

- aRbRcRd... which either ends or does not end at some last point z.

If its topic is space then...:

- R = IS CONTAINED IN, so if the series ends with z then z contains the rest of the series: all of a, b, c, etc.

I could as well write IS IN, for example. (The exact wording should not be thought to color this series in any way, for it is just your generic spatial series of increasingly greater sizes.[1]) This series can be formed by asking questions in Socrates' spirit. Try asking *Where is...?* over and over again. If a is in b, where is b? In c, but where is c? d, etc., until eventually everything is in z. For example:

- Pumpernickel City is in Oklahoma is in the USA is in... the Milky Way is in..., and then eventually there is a terminus z for this series or else there is not.

This much is easy even for a child. But where is the serious lesson about higher, dialectical reasoning?

To see what Kant wants to get at we need to add another piece:

- a THESIS says that the series ends in some z, so space has an outer limit somewhere, and

---

[1] I will ignore time.

Also I will ignore Kant's personality and his historical conditions (unlike Al-Azm), for such detours would lead us away from the timeless questions that the antinomies are rationally understood to be. For example, if we read Kant's antinomies in the light of Newton then they will no longer quite hold in an age of Einstein. All pure reasoning proper must be timeless and faceless like the barest archetype.

- *an ANTITHESIS* says that the series has no limit or terminus, so space is infinite.

Kant uses these same terms, 'thesis' and 'antithesis', for all four of his antinomies in his main work, the *Critique of Pure Reason*. (He presents seven further antinomies in his later works but they are not structured in exactly the same way.)

Kant himself pictures the thesis and antithesis as parties in a legal dispute in court. (He will later say that *Vernunft* is the judge, or rather its *own* judge, given that it is *Vernunft itself* which generates the theses and the antitheses! See below.) The thesis is usually Platonic, he says, and the antithesis is Epicurean. This is to say that the thesis is rationalistic, or such as to rely on pure reasoning alone, whereas the antithesis represents a kind of unleashed empiricism: not the kind of empiricism which is content to experiment with detailed and individual circumstances but the kind of empiricism which flies far beyond any possible experiment that can ever be conducted and pronounces about absolutes just as unhypothetically as the rationalist. (This wilder type of empiricism is hyperbolic, not factual.)

Now we can state the first lesson which Kant wants to draw from the antinomies.

It is that in each antinomy the truth is a thing we cannot know. The question is impossible to solve either way, so we cannot know whether there is a limit z or not. Neither can be ruled in or out, for both options can be consistently argued and neither can be empirically tested. More radically he says that the problem is only apparent, a *Scheinproblem* as his later scientistic followers will generally call metaphysical questions. It is sophistical and rhetorical, and not a real problem at all. It is children's games! It is not serious adult business.

But if antinomous questions like this one are only children's games, where is the serious adult business? Is it in science and commerce? Is this what Kant is suggesting? We are still left asking.

If he did suggest that then he could side with Voltaire, whose best-selling eighteenth century novel *Candide* narrates the adventures of Candide, a silly German prince who is blinded by his idealistic and rationalistic standards (drawn from Leibniz's philosophy). In the meantime, the real-world meaning of everything is continually less than perfect. The human lot is chaotic and comical. Candide the idealist lacks humility. He should observe and not think so much. The best thing is to focus on cultivating one's garden, Voltaire says as his *Candide* ends. Retreat to a small world of *Verstand* and be quiet!

But this is not Kant's message at all. According to him, adult reasoning does not conform to the accidental ways of the world. It is not opportunistic (or 'pragmatic' as many people now say, in traditionally American spirit) but principled. I will come to this shortly.

Now I have so far only hinted *why* Kant is so sure that the above limit question about z is beyond our capabilities.

His main answers to this are two, as noted. Firstly he states that only much tamer questions can ever be solved by empirical science. These are the relative questions of *Verstand* as opposed to the extreme issues of *Vernunft*. Thus we can discover empirically that some b is inside c but never that some z is *not* inside anything further or that *everything* is inside z. Science requires conditional and controlled settings, and all the extreme issues of pure reason will be much too bold for its reach.

Second, Kant points out that we can feel the pull of *both* options, the thesis and the antithesis. We may bolster this with modalities: the thesis *must* be true by its own lights, but it *can* not be true by the antithesis' lights, and vice versa. In any case, both are not true. They rule each other out: there is a limit or there is not.[1]

Kant's view is thus in a way that our generative capabilities are not too small but *too large:* we can create *too many* models. Perhaps we can ignore this over-productive ability happily if we are raised in traditional societies where free thought is not encouraged or even publicly allowed. Then the real potentials are concealed artificially by force. But if we are lucky enough to avoid such artificial limitations then the wild world of Kant's antinomies opens up before us.

---

[1] This is not *exactly* true especially with regard to the third antinomy below, see 3.5, because then Kant says that *both are true,* the thesis and the antithesis. (Kant also says this about the fourth antinomy, but in such an implausible way that I will not address that in this book.)

A different complication I am here ignoring is that Kant's theses and antitheses are usually *not self-confirming* but such as to primarily *refute each other.* Thus the first thesis is supposed to be true mainly because the first antithesis is false, or self-contradictory, and likewise the first antithesis is supposed to compel because the first antithesis leads to a dead end. (Similarly for the second, third, and fourth pairs.) In the history of ideas this is manifest in the way Leibniz and the Newtonians mainly attack each other instead of defending themselves. (In my personal view, this is a major fault in the antinomian picture. It is not honest and clean! This is so even though it is common for logicians to proceed thus, i.e., to prove that p by supposing that not-p and then deducing from that that not-not-p. This is indirect, artificial, and dishonest compared to a self-commentary on a higher level.)

A different generalization (also not highlighted by Kant) is that our shortcomings are actually *on the empirical side alone*. For we cannot experiment with absolutes, as noted, and we can do this only with relatives. But this is simultaneously the reason why the antithesis is not properly empiricist at all. It is only like an over-bold extrapolation, as by a potter in Socrates in Ch. 1, a potter who holds his skill in pottery up as the model for all skills and knowledge types, like a small dictator basing on his parochial little knowledge base. But by contrast the rationalist is not extrapolating all. He is only playing a game he in fact does know how to play already. For of course any reasoning being wants compelling and conclusive absolutes, because this will satisfy the needs of reasoning. Who would ever reason for the sake of mere anomalies? Of course the point in reasoning is to find stable laws and complete conclusions. (Questions need answers!)

Let us briefly consider the role of the first antinomy in modern *science*. What is its place, according to eminent scientists today? Have they refuted Kant?

The reality is rather that they ignore his anomalies. They are not considered internal to science. None the less scientists or at least the loud popularizers of scientific findings sense that they are entitled (by science) to pronounce conclusively about the topics of the antinomies.

Here is a description of the Big Bang by a major physics professor:

> According to the big bang model of cosmology, the whole of the universe violently emerged from a singular cosmic explosion, some 14 or so billion years ago. Today, as originally discovered by Hubble, we can see that the 'debris' of this explosion, in the form of billions of galaxies, is still streaming outward. The universe is expanding. We do not know whether this cosmic growth will continue forever or if there will come a time when the expansion slows to a halt and then reverses itself, leading to a cosmic implosion. Astronomers and astrophysicists are trying to settle this question experimentally, since the answer turns on something that in principle can be measured: the average density of matter in the universe.[1]

The *empirical evidence* that astronomers have for their Big Bang theory is just this: the universe has recently been observed to be expanding. The measured density is decreasing. The whole idea of a first Big Bang

---

[1] Greene p. 234.

is only an *extrapolation* from this, so there is no *direct* evidence of it. It is a supposition, a theory. (A scientist like Greene knows this, but it does not disturb him: he does not see, or has not heard, that this will lead to an antinomy.)

If the same thing happens backwards then:

> All galaxies and stars will start to approach one other slowly, and then as time goes by, their speed of approach will increase until they rush together at blinding speed. [...] [Thus] *every-thing* is crushed together to the size of a single galaxy, and then to the size of a single star, a planet, and down to the size of an orange, a pea, a grain of sand, and further, according to general relativity, to the size of a molecule, an atom, and in a final inexorable crunch to *no size at all*. According to conventional theory, the universe began with a bang from an initial state of zero size, and if it has enough mass, it will end with a crunch to a similar state of ultimate cosmic compression.[1]

Einstein's physical laws combined with observations made since Hubble drive astronomers to this conclusion, so of course they are not merely guessing. There are plenty of scientifically established regularities on their side.

The trouble is only that even a small child can see through them. For this is only another opportunity to ask why. *Where did the first nut come from? What was before it and what was around it? (Nothing? But surely there is no such thing as nothing.)* There is nothing in Greene's description that would compel one to accept any conclusive answer. (Very likely he has never even heard of any 'antinomy'.[2])

But can future science not get around this somehow? If Kant is right it never can, for science is compelled to rely on empirical evidence, which is always relative.

Why is it so clear that empirical tests will have to be *relative?*

Let us consider that again. Science studies each given thing x by relating it to some ulterior thing y. If x and y are experienced many enough times as occurring in constant conjunction, then the scientist will eventually consider it warranted to conclude that x and y are causally related.

---

[1] Greene p. 235, italics in original.
[2] My guess is that Greene and many other scientists hold that all we know about the universe is through science and that the question about the origins of the universe also belongs to science. The trouble with this is only that certain kinds of questions elude science because of its methods. As noted, methods are assessed in philosophy, which is not a science.

(This is the scientist's induction: the kind of generalization that the scientist always aims to make. The empirical data should be sufficient to support the generalization. There are no other questions to ponder.)

However, if we take it that the scientist has found that x 'causes' y in this manner, then what happens? (For example: y = the universe, x = the Big Bang.) There is nothing to science but to ask next what causes x, and if that is v, then the question is asked again and the answer will be u, etc.,, without end.

This follows because the cause must be ulterior as before — these are the presuppositions of science — so the cause can only be discovered eventually to be something prior every time. (It is as with the donkey and the carrot.)

It may help to name these variables:

- y = the universe,
- x = the Big Bang,
- v = the Little Nut (let us call it),
- u = the First Hole (say),
- t = the Great Cloud (say),

... etc. Whatever happens in future science the scientific question about a prior ulterior cause will inevitably pop up over again.

Whatever beginning or end you locate, the questioning will only begin again. But on the other hand if you only keep asking you will still always want and seek for a conclusive answer anyway. Hence there no way out and no rest.

Does this mean that all science is false? Far from it! It means only that science is limited to relative and conditional questions, as before. It is out of its depth with absolutes. If it is extended — as by thoughtless and ill informed popularizers — to absolute or unconditional issues then it becomes laughable, for then it will inevitably use methods that are totally out of place. Accordingly, there is no scientific world-view: there is a scientific practice, and there is scientific organization and efficiency. It is afloat in nothing.[1]

---

[1] To illustrate this contrast, compare a *legal system* which consists not only of a set of laws but also of a constitution on which those laws are based. Now, science is like an opportunistic legal system without any constitution! It is mobile, quick, adaptive, efficient, sure, but it has no interest in foundations. (Cf. Quine and Popper on science.)

Is Kant saying, then, that there will be some type of *speculative insight* (by 'higher' reason) about the origins of the universe, which insight we should trust even without any empirical or scientific evidence?

No. He says, as we will soon find out more fully, that reasoning has very little to do with the physical world, and that all the higher ideals — all longings for absolutes — are only *projected* to the physical world in his antinomies. They do not belong there, because they are values: ideals. If we reason properly then we say how one *ought* to think, not what ordinary or mostly *is* thought, or what happens in the world at large. Nature cannot be our dictator, for the freedom to reason comes first. (What the Big Bang scientists fail so utterly to grasp is the radical distance between pure reasoning and empirical facts. With Kant, they are further apart than any practicing scientist realizes. There are, as it were, on one side the barest facts and on the other hand the orderly and idealized things which we want to see in the facts.[1])

But then what is the situation with the antinomies really? We do not have scientific knowledge *or* special and miraculous intuitions about the limits of space and time — alright. Now what?

Kant writes:

> In neither case—the regressus in infinitum, nor the regressus in indefinitum, is the series of conditions to be considered as actually infinite in the object itself. This might be true of things in themselves, but it cannot be asserted of phenomena, which, as conditions of each other, are only given in the empirical regress itself. Hence, the question no longer is, "What is the quantity of this series of conditions in itself—is it finite or infinite?" for it is nothing in itself; but, "How is the empirical regress to be commenced, and how far ought we to proceed with it?"[2]

There *is no such thing* as an absolute fact. (Rather there are *relative* facts and then there are absolute *values*.) Such a thing is but a dream which

---

[1] Kant actually stresses that reality as it truly is, independently of our relations to it, is unknowable. It is his *Ding an sich*: the thing in itself.

This faith in an external and neutral reality 'out there' is undermined by all the major authors of German Idealism after Kant, Fichte and Hegel especially. They try to make reality seem more mental or spiritual, but unlike Kant they know little about hard science.

[2] *Critique of Pure Reason* A512/B540.

arises only if one takes *Vernunft* and clumsily tries to place it in the physical universe — where it simply does not belong.

If we picture the universe in our minds then we believe that either model *must* be true, and even if we can never discover it — there either is a finite picture or an infinite one: thesis or antithesis. But Kant maintains that this is meaningless, for there is no fact about this.

Reflect: this business about models which may or may not match the world comes from us, not from the world. But it should not sound so strange to say that at least at times our models may simply be in the wrong language for the world. (The world operates in concrete events and facts, but as free and reasoning beings we operate in principles and rules. Nature just ticks like a clock, indifferently. It does not ask for any rules.)

The Second Antinomy: Smallest Parts

A very similar story is told in Kant's *second* antinomy, even though its topic is the very opposite of the first.

Now we ask not what is largest but what is smallest. Is any part ultimately partless? Compare this series:

- a CONSISTS OF b CONSISTS OF c CONSISTS OF d... y CONSISTS OF z.[1]

The questioning that shapes this kind of a series is like this: What is a made of? What are the ingredients that make up b? What elements is c built from? (A cake is made of sugar and other ingredients, but what is sugar made of?, etc.)

Again we need to imagine that there are numerous symbols and styles for stating this, and that regardless of this variety the uniform point is always to go for parts of parts of parts — etc. Thus there is again a generic question which does not depend on any special word choices, for instance by Kant. The timeless issue is what concerns us, and a particular Prussian personality named Kant does not. (Though of course we may *separately* study his peculiar biography. The interest and method of that study would be different.)

---

[1] Of course in many cases this would really have a *tree-shape* so that a consists of b and c, b consists of d and e and c consists of f and g, etc., for many things are not made of only one kind of element.

This is one of the many dialectical formats that are easier to draw than to write (left to right). A more complete book of dialectics might well be a picture book!

And then what? What do we learn? As before the realistic reply we learn from Kant is that there is no right reply. There are only pretended and traditional 'answers' which are not rational answers at all. Hence we may expect that Kant will not go along with atomists like Democritus or Leucippus but nor will be side with their opponents. For the entire debate is refuted. It is only another *Scheinproblem* — a problem only for the deluded.

But what is illusory this time?

At first sight there are only the kinds of problems one would expect in the light of the first antinomy, for also now there is no empirical test for positive findings about ultimate atoms, and once more both the thesis and the antithesis can be consistently argued. But if we dig a little deeper into Kant then the story contains something more besides, because one of the fundamental elements on the thesis' side is the *human soul*. Perhaps you and I are endpoints to the series! If that is true then we are simples, and by the argument of Plato's *Phaedo* we are immortal. In Kant's time, this type of argument is reinvigorated by Moses Mendelssohn, who in his book *Phaedo* takes his main cues from Plato's work of the same name (though he is in major respects a Leibnizian).

In response to this view Kant states four *paralogisms* in his *Critique of Pure Reason*, each of which is meant to show that the soul or psyche cannot be simple or immortal (thereby discrediting the thesis side of the second antinomy):

- *FIRST PARALOGISM (substantiality):* You think of things, say about different countries, and then from this you conclude that you exist as a thinker just as the countries exist. The error is to leap from the subject to the object. In reality thought is no object: it is about different things, but it is not by itself an independent thing. In Kant's metaphor it is the *vehicle*: it is not a place you go but a thing you use to go places. It is not a topic, a place. (*Topos* in Greek means both.)

- *SECOND PARALOGISM (simplicity):* You again think about things, for instance about different countries, and you notice that though the countries change in your mind, the thinking is somehow continuous and unified. This leads you to say that it is simple — indivisible. But again there is an erroneous leap because the thinking is no object. It unifies, it is not unified. (It cannot turn around and face itself: the seer is unseen, the thinker is unthinkable.)

- *THIRD PARALOGISM (personality):* Here you are thinking about different countries again, and you sense that because your thinking is coherent in time no matter what countries you think of, so that you recall many past thoughts too and find that all of them fit together in your present mind, you must therefore be one person, one thinker, who exists through time. But the error is again the same. You never actually locate any pure 'I'. Objects get in the way. You are condemned to deal in a world of things.

- *FOURTH PARALOGISM (ideality):* Now the point is that you know about countries only in a rather mediated and insecure sense and that your access to your own thoughts is immediate and secure. Hence you sense that you must be something quite different from those physical countries out there: you are a spiritual thing. But again the trouble is the same: you have no territory of your own. There is no inner country, so the thoughts you access are only thoughts about external and real countries again.

All of this is to say that Plato's *Phaedo* (cf. Ch. 1) is all wrong in seeking a simple psyche, even if its simplicity did establish its immortality. For a psyche does not in fact find itself to be a simple *object*: it is rather a *simplifying subject*, that is a thing which unifies whatever it considers. ("The logical exposition of thought in general is mistaken for a metaphysical determination of the object." *Critique of Pure Reason* B409.)

Notice how this is *quintessential Kant*: things (objects) do not determine theories, we (subjects) do. Reasoning is a human activity, not a thing, not a fact observed in nature. Reality is out there, yes, so there is no Berkeleyan 'idealism', but its intelligibility presupposes a structure which we must choose or create. Hence there is plenty of voluntarism even if it is not total: whatever you project outward is by and large what you will find. The initial choice is always yours.

To this background Kant's position on the I, self, person, or mind may be a bit surprising. He writes: "'I think' ... is readily perceived that this thought is as it were the vehicle of all conceptions in general..."[1] Every sentence or thought is prefixed by a self: *I think* that it is a pretty summer day, *I think* 29-2 = 27, etc. Notice that the I or self is now the speaker and not the thing stated like numbers or the weather. (Accordingly there are no ownerless thoughts flying around — no faceless Platonic archetypes.)

---

[1] *Critique of Pure Reason* A341/B399.

In Kant's language:

> We can, however, lay at the foundation of this science nothing
> but the simple and in itself perfectly contentless represen-
> tation "I" which cannot even be called a conception, but
> merely a consciousness which accompanies all conceptions.
> By this "I," or "He," or "It," who or which thinks, nothing more
> is represented than a transcendental subject of thought = x,
> which is cognized only by means of the thoughts that are its
> predicates, and of which, apart from these, we cannot form
> the least conception. Hence in a perpetual circle, inasmuch
> as we must always employ it, in order to frame any judgement
> respecting it. And this inconvenience we find it impossible
> to rid ourselves of, because consciousness in itself is not so
> much a representation distinguishing a particular object, as a
> form of representation in general, in so far as it may be termed
> cognition; for in and by cognition alone do I think anything.[1]

Unlike the Socratic (cf. Ch. 1), the Kantian self does *not* know itself. It
can only look *outward*, not inward. It shapes and unifies outer facts.

Notice that Kant is *not* saying that there is no self, or that there is only
an outer world and no inner world. The self is real, but it is condemned
to view only other things instead of itself.

Is this to defend the *antithesis* against the thesis? No! It is rather to
shift from the great questions of *Vernunft* to the more prosaic world of
Verstand. For the materials the Kantian I organizes seem to operate by
means precisely of the categories. But this makes the situation look a
little curious, for now it is as if Kant wrote only about a lower self and
not of a higher self or daimon at all!

Here is one way to reflect about the difference. If Kant is right, your
self is *equally* in play every time you think or say something (or judge, as
he likes to say). This means that there is no *hierarchy*. In contrast with
this, for Socrates or Plato the psyche proper is not present in all kinds of
ordinary thoughts or sentences but only in the highest issues of principle.
This is clearly one implication of Socrates' one-man protest movement in
the *Apology* (see Ch. 1): he said after all that the Athenians should think
of the first questions first, leaving pettier concerns aside. But in Plato's
Phaedo we have the same lesson in another way, for there Socrates (or
'Socrates') does not sense that his psyche is in play before he is in the

---

[1] *Critique of Pure Reason* A345-346/B404.

middle of a dialogue with fellow Platonists about immortality, the Ideas, the virtues, or reincarnation. He is purified in this way, he says, and before he is purified he is somehow mixed up.

From here we can return to the paralogisms. Do they refute Socrates' and Plato's higher and purified self or only a kind of lower everyday consciousness? The answer is easily stated: the latter. Thus the paralogisms may be true — against the lower self — and the Kantian lower I may be real — but then there may simultaneously be some higher self or higher I which is simple and even immortal. We do not know this based on the paralogisms.

The Third Antinomy: Creation or Free Will

Kant's third antinomy is causal, and this takes us directly to the problem of free will and determinism. For if everything is only a link in a closed causal chain then determinism is true and there is no free will, and conversely if there is free will then the chains must begin out of the blue in many places: every time someone is free. This contest is made obvious in R language:

- aRbRcRc... xRyRz, plus
- R=IS CAUSED BY, imply that
- a IS CAUSED BY b IS CAUSED BY c... x IS CAUSED BY y IS CAUSED BY z.

But if z is to be free z must be self-caused as in

- z IS CAUSED BY z

Hence the format is zRz — and there is no self-caused (or freely willed) z of this kind if the antithesis is true, for after all it states that the chain has no beginning or end. (a IS CAUSED BY b IS CAUSED BY c... x IS CAUSED BY y IS CAUSED BY z.) In that case every time there is R there is something *different* to its left than to its right, so nothing IS CAUSED BY itself (as in zRz).

Thus we see how Kant's third antinomy is exactly a debate between free will (its thesis) and determinism (its antithesis).

Kant bolsters this duality by arguing that any generalized conception of causality is only a dogma. Such a principle is not possible to discover inductively:

> That everything that happens has a cause, cannot be concluded
> from the general conception of that which happens; on the
> contrary the principle of causality instructs us as to the mode
> of obtaining from that which happens a determinate empirical
> conception.[1]

If scientists maintain, roughly as determinists in the manner of the
antithesis of Kant's third antinomy, that every event has a cause in a prior
event, then this generalization only describes their presupposition. It is
not a scientific discovery but one of the fictions science needs in order
to begin to operate as scientists in the first place. If scientists are usually
naïve about this and do hold that science has proved a generalized law of
causality or determinism, then this is explained by the fact that science
does not study its own presuppositions: it studies nature, and it does
not study the norms of science. (The norms of science are studied in the
philosophy of science, but this is not a science. The philosophy of science
is not about nature but about science.)

But next, there are *two types* of causation, Kant teaches: "There are only
two modes of causality cogitable—the causality of nature or of freedom."[2]
Here is their difference:

> That reason possesses the faculty of causality, or that at
> least we are compelled so to represent it, is evident from the
> imperatives, which in the sphere of the practical we impose
> on many of our executive powers. The words I ought express
> a species of necessity, and imply a connection with grounds
> which nature does not and cannot present to the mind of man.
> Understanding knows nothing in nature but that which is, or
> has been, or will be. It would be absurd to say that anything
> in nature ought to be other than it is in the relations of time in
> which it stands; indeed, the ought, when we consider merely
> the course of nature, has neither application nor meaning. The
> question, "What ought to happen in the sphere of nature?" is
> just as absurd as the question, "What ought to be the prop-
> erties of a circle?" All that we are entitled to ask is, "What
> takes place in nature?" or, in the latter case, "What are the
> properties of a circle?" [...] Reason will not follow the order of
> things presented by experience, but, with perfect spontaneity,
> rearranges them according to ideas, with which it compels

[1] *Critique of Pure Reason* A301/B357.
[2] *Critique of Pure Reason* A530/558.

empirical conditions to agree. It declares, in the name of these ideas, certain actions to be necessary which nevertheless have not taken place and which perhaps never will take place; and yet presupposes that it possesses the faculty of causality in relation to these actions.[1]

In the realm of freedom we deal in reasons, not merely in causes, and the reasons must build on ideals as to how one ought to reason or act. In the lower realm of things, of objects or non-subjects, there are no oughts, for things merely happen. One cannot persuade a tree to change. One can force it and reshape it, but this is not how one would approach a free individual. It is not to reason with the tree.

On the scientitic worldview there is usually said to be but *one* type of causation, and then freedom is missing. This may accord rather well with the scientist's own activities if he operates as a straight-forward empiricist and seldom idealizes or compares alternatives. However, the gap between the two types of causation begins to appear if we philosophize dialectically:

It is especially remarkable that the practical conception of freedom is based upon the transcendental idea, and that the question of the possibility of the former is difficult only as it involves the consideration of the truth of the latter. Freedom, in the practical sense, is the independence of the will of coercion by sensuous impulses. A will is sensuous, in so far as it is pathologically affected (by sensuous impulses); it is termed animal (arbitrium brutum), when it is pathologically necessitated. The human will is certainly an arbitrium sensitivum, not brutum, but liberum; because sensuousness does not necessitate its action, a faculty existing in man of self-determination, independently of all sensuous coercion. [...] The question of the possibility of freedom does indeed concern psychology; but, as it rests upon dialectical arguments of pure reason, its solution must engage the attention of transcendental philosophy.[2]

---

[1] *Critique of Pure Reason* in A547-548/575-576.

[2] *Critique of Pure Reason* A533-34/561-562. Kant actually argues that both free will and determinism may be true and real, and about the same events, if they merely concern the same events on different levels or in different vocabularies. If you look at things scientifically, you will be forced to a more or less deterministic view of things, but if you look at them morally or intentionally (viewing the events as *actions* performed by *persons* for *reasons*) then the same events will instance free will. (Continued)

Sensual conditions may drive us to actions in specific environments — you may be accustomed to 'reading' particular situations in a game of football or chess, say. Then if a happens, you rather automatically do b. Similarly, if there is a red light in traffic then you know right away what to do: you are accustomed to this. These are the rules you often live by in daily life.

However, things are less automatic if questions are asked, and the extreme ones arise in dialectics. In such settings it is as difficult as it is undesirable to operate automatically. Reflection is called for, and reflection on reflection. But now freedom begins to appear.

To this background it is again surprising that Kant's reflected view is in some ways closer to *Verstand* than *Vernunft*:

> The rule of right and wrong must help us to the knowledge of what is right or wrong in all possible cases; otherwise, the idea of obligation or duty would be utterly null, for we cannot have any obligation to that which we cannot know. On the other hand, in our investigations of the phenomena of nature, much must remain uncertain, and many questions continue insoluble; because what we know of nature is far from being sufficient to explain all the phenomena that are presented to our observation.[1]

Whatever *duties* we have must be familiar and accessible to us, Kant means, for we are free to do our duties come what may. (If we are not free to x, then we cannot have a duty to x. *Ought* implies *can*, he says.)

But why does Kant connect free will with *moral duties*? This we saw already in 3.2: a free will is moral because it is autonomous. This is because — to put this in different terms than before — if you are autonomous (free) then you legislate for yourself, and then you must step back from your particular life conditions. For example, as an autonomous creature I cannot make a traffic law which says that *Tommi* always gets to go first and others yield, because to be autonomous I need to be a reasoning being, and so I must write my laws in a kind of reason language. (The law L I am for is *L*, not *L-for-me*.) But this already leads me to consider situations

---

Many have not been satisfied with this position of Kant's, myself included. It is better to say that the empirical regularities studied by science are not strictly causal at all. For causes proper we need more than constant conjunction: we need contact and force, as Hume says (for further discussion compare my *Plato's Logic*, section 3.11).

[1] *Critique of Pure Reason* A476-477/B504-505.

of *other persons* — not only of myself. Roughly in this spirit, Kant seems to think that as a rational planner one must step up to play the part of a representative of reason, not only a representative of oneself individually.

Is Kant right? (Or, how right is he? What do you say?)

He has now said that freedom must be universally accessible to everyone in all situations, but again a more complex and stratified possibility suggests itself:

- I am perfectly free as a self-mover, like a in a MOVES a MOVES b MOVES c, and
- in this same chain b and c are not free like a is for they are not *self*-moved, but
- b is freer than c, because is more like a or closer to a.

Against Kant we here have a hierarchy instead of equality. Freedom is not a black-and-white affair like 1/0. Rather it comes in degrees. We may represent this as in a > b > c, but more than this we need philosophical arguments to explain this hierarchy. (For what does it *mean* for there to be more or less freedom in different places?) In his *Laws* Plato argued that theos = a, the theologian = b, and the non-theologian = c, for the movements of the psyche were more or less wise or Godlike, and this is certainly one way to flesh out the matter. Spinoza would tell a different story about the freedom hierarchy, saying like the ancient Stoics before him that one is free to the extent that one knows the inevitable course of nature, for that is the extent to which one will know how to adapt to nature. (In Plato God soars *above* nature, in Spinoza God *is* nature.) Hegel takes up Spinoza's story but he tells it in his own way: one is to go along with the tide of history, not of nature.[1]

The Fourth Antinomy: God or Necessary Being

In the fourth antinomy of the *Critique of Pure Reason* the modern reader needs in a sense to begin backwards. For Kant's question about God will make sense only if we first learn to *suffer* from the generalized sense of contingency which most of us are so accustomed to. In our day it is all too usual to accept life's contingency without much ado: you were born in this historical period, not a hundred or a thousand years earlier or later, but why? The catalogue of chance events and life factors seems to be

---

[1] So who is correct? The solution is I think to distinguish between *higher and lower* freedom just as the preceding section distinguished between higher and lower selfhood. Thus Kant is right, but not only Kant.

endless. Are their conditions as chaotic? And how about the conditions of the conditions? By modern, Humean standards this is the scientific worldview. Its business is not to make compelling sense but to be empirically true — to simply be true about what is seen to be there, however little reason it has to be there. We observe it is there, that is all.

Kant's question about God in the fourth antinomy rises as a protest against this chaotic view of the world: the first conditions for things should be something other. But what is this other? What is better and more orderly, more rational, or somehow more neutral than the chaos of the world?

According to Kant (and numerous medieval authors before him), this is to say that something should *exist necessarily*, and such a necessary existent would be *God*. We may interpret this in the shape of a familiar type of series:

- a NECESSITATES b NECESSITATES c...,

    Its terminus is on the left:

- a NECESSITATES a...

a in aRa would now symbolize God. If a does not compel a first then none of b or c or d, etc., will come about. Thus a is the bedrock.

To be sure, Kant is again out to show with his antinomies that we do *not* know about this kind of thing. There is again a thesis and an antithesis. The thesis is that God exists first and conditions everything else, and the antithesis says there is no God and the whole show is only so much chaos, lotteries after lotteries.

Kant attacks the thesis in two well known ways, namely in opposing the 'ontological argument' and the 'cosmological argument'.

First the *ontological argument*.

This is due to Anselm of Canterbury (1033–1109). It aims to prove that God exists, thus: God is perfect, and therefore God is not only kind and omnipotent but also — existent! For a thing which does not exist is less perfect than a thing which does, Anselm says. Therefore God exists. (This was already the argument!)

Kant famously objects that existence is not a predicate:

> Being is evidently not a real predicate, that is, a conception of something which is added to the conception of some other thing. It is merely the positing of a thing, or of certain determi-

nations in it. Logically, it is merely the copula of a judgement. The proposition, God is omnipotent, contains two conceptions, which have a certain object or content; the word is, is no additional predicate—it merely indicates the relation of the predicate to the subject. Now, if I take the subject (God) with all its predicates (omnipotence being one), and say: God is, or, There is a God, I add no new predicate to the conception of God, I merely posit or affirm the existence of the subject with all its predicates—I posit the object in relation to my conception. The content of both is the same; and there is no addition made to the conception, which expresses merely the possibility of the object, by my cogitating the object—in the expression, it is—as absolutely given or existing.[1]

In other words:

> By whatever and by whatever number of predicates—even to the complete determination of it—I may cogitate a thing, I do not in the least augment the object of my conception by the addition of the statement: This thing exists. Otherwise, not exactly the same, but something more than what was cogitated in my conception, would exist, and I could not affirm that the exact object of my conception had real existence. If I cogitate a thing as containing all modes of reality except one, the mode of reality which is absent is not added to the conception of the thing by the affirmation that the thing exists...[2]

In the twentieth century G.E. Moore's version of this is often brought up. It is that lions are predators and mammals — such are their properties — but lions have no further property of *existing* alongside these other properties. For if some lion really is a predator then its existence comes along with this property. (If it is not really a predator then it does not exist.) Hence, existence is not a separate property.

In Frege's logically programmatic version existence is viewed as a second-order predicate, so that existence is indicated in logically formed statements but it is not one of the things described in them. The logical form is:

- (∃x) (x is a lion and x is tame)

---

[1] *Critique of Pure Reason* A598-599/B626-627.
[2] *Critique of Pure Reason* A600/B628.

This sentence means: *there is an x such that* x is a lion and x is tame. In this format, ∃ indicates existence, and this ∃ is not treated like lionhood and tameness — which are first-order predicates. (∃ is the 'existential quantifier'.)

So what?

Like Kant, both Moore and Frege strive to indicate that existence cannot be thought of in Anselm's manner.

Is this correct?

The reason to doubt it is that it *rules out all talk about* kinds or levels of being. Radhakrishnan states the general idea intuitively:

> Hindu thought admits that the immanence of God is a fact admitting of various degrees. While there is nothing which is not lit by God, God is more fully revealed in the organic than in the inorganic, in the conscious than in the unconscious, more in man than in the lower creatures, more in the good man than in the evil. But even the worst of the world cannot be dismissed as completely undivine. [...] There are divine potentialities in even the worst of sinners. No one is really beyond hope. The worst sinner has a future even as the greatest saint has a past.[1]

For the Hinduist, everything is divine, and everything has being — *some* being, that is, and *some* of the divine. Animals rank above rocks, humans rank above animals — and Brahman ranks above us. There is a graded evolution in thoughtfulness and responsibility, Radhakrishnan seems to mean.

Closer to Kant, the different levels of being could contain at least:

- the autonomous self as something higher than the more broken and less complete self that is heteronomous, or
- *Vernunft* versus *Verstand*,
- beauty or genius as something higher than ordinary objects like dishwashers or tires (I will come to beauty and genius in 3.9).

Many a classical philosopher and theologian would say that there is more being or more reality precisely in things that stand on their own as autonomous beings in this way, and like the Ideas, Gods are the very

---

[1] pp. 51-52.

paradigms of this kind of thinking. (Other things are not real *taken by themselves*, because they depend on other things. They are only relative and conditional.)

However, Kant's view of reality is not like this for — odd as this is — his view of reality is as poor as the empiricists'. For their part, the *empiricists* do not need any of these levels, whether of self-sufficiency or independence or whatever you may call it — because they *deal* only with the lowest level, that is with the most brutish facts. Thus they choose their yardstick, to which they give a monopology in the field. *Virtue or morality* for them is utility, *beauty* is but pleasure, the *self* is but a bundle of outer experiences, and *knowledge* is scientific prediction and control — because they insist that everything must be seen in a mechanical way. Using their standard they get all these results. For everything *must be* easy and coherent and there cannot be any of those extreme questions that the classical philosophers and theologians like to pose. (Recall that the empiricist does not prove this: he only *avoids* the hard issues, and chooses his low yardstick. He simplifies life.) But Kant cannot say this if he also has autonomy, *Vernunft*, genius, and such. Or does he not have them? Are they not there? (I will come to this again below.)

Cosmological arguments make for Kant's second main target in the world of religions and theologies.

These are a type of philosophical or theological argument which in the West goes back at least to Plato's *Laws* (cf. Ch. 2). Aristotle states his version of this, and so do his medieval Arab followers and prominent scholastics like Aquinas. The sixteenth-century rationalists Descartes, Spinoza, and Leibniz all use it. (Even Locke relies on one brand of it.)

In Kant's phrasing:

> If something exists, an absolutely necessary being must likewise exist. Now I, at least, exist. Consequently, there exists an absolutely necessary being. The minor contains an experience, the major reasons from a general experience to the existence of a necessary being. Thus this argument really begins at experience, and is not completely à priori, or onto-logical. The object of all possible experience being the world, it is called the cosmological proof.[1]

But Kant objects to the whole family. Why? He writes:

---

[1] *Critique of Pure Reason* A604/B632.

> In this cosmological argument are assembled so many sophistical propositions that speculative reason seems to have exerted in it all her dialectical skill to produce a transcendental illusion of the most extreme character.[1]

But why?

> What the properties of this being are cannot be learned from experience; and therefore reason abandons it altogether, and pursues its inquiries in the sphere of pure conception, for the purpose of discovering what the properties of an absolutely necessary being ought to be, that is, what among all possible things contain the conditions (requisita) of absolute necessity. Reason believes that it has discovered these requisites in the conception of an ens realissimum—and in it alone, and hence concludes: The ens realissimum is an absolutely necessary being. But it is evident that reason has here presupposed that the conception of an ens realissimum is perfectly adequate to the conception of a being of absolute necessity, that is, that we may infer the existence of the latter from that of the former.[2]

A cosmological argument begins from an empirical premise (like *I exist*, above) but next it idealizes that an absolutely necessary being ought to exist because of this (*if something exists then also a necessary being exists*), and this idealization is not at all part of the first experience. It is only a reasoned addition to the experience, and for Kant this means, once again, that it is a value and not a fact. God is what there *ought to be* if my existence made sense. But empirically and scientifically this about the *ought* can play no role. For my existence as it is need in fact make no sense! If we consider existence scientifically then this is how it will be: purely accidental, nothing more, as before.[3]

Is Kant correct now? It seems one can admit that reasoning sets values without agreeing that *all* existence questions (i.e. issues about what is real or not) must be settled by empirical science.

---

[1] *Critique of Pure Reason* A606/B634.

[2] *Critique of Pure Reason* A606-607/B634-635.

[3] In Kant's language: *All the examples adduced have been drawn, without exception, from judgements, and not from things. But the unconditioned necessity of a judgement does not form the absolute necessity of a thing* (*Critique of Pure Reason* A593/B621). A 'judgment' is a thought about what is or ought to be or could be, and a 'thing' is what there really is, but necessity about one is not necessity about the other. Mind and world stand apart.

Kant sounds much more compelling if he presents us with an intermi-nable inner conflict as in the antinomies:

> Unconditioned necessity, which, as the ultimate support and stay of all existing things, is an indispensable requirement of the mind, is an abyss on the verge of which human reason trembles in dismay. Even the idea of eternity, terrible and sublime as it is, as depicted by Haller, does not produce upon the mental vision such a feeling of awe and terror; for, although it measures the duration of things, it does not support them. We cannot bear, nor can we rid ourselves of the thought that a being, which we regard as the greatest of all possible exis-tences, should say to himself: I am from eternity to eternity; beside me there is nothing, except that which exists by my will; whence then am I? Here all sinks away from under us; and the greatest, as the smallest, perfection, hovers without stay or footing in presence of the speculative reason, which finds it as easy to part with the one as with the other.[1]

This describes a *crisis*. The questions will inevitably arise, but they cannot be answered. On the one hand we keep looking for final answers, but on the other hand we can always learn to ask why about each of them — so the game cannot end.[2]

But is there a way out of this crisis of the antinomies?

Especially in the earlier pages of the *Critique of Pure Reason* Kant sounds quite hopeless about this, saying that we humans cannot stop reasoning about ultimates in reality, that is even if we should!

> Human reason, in one sphere of its cognition, is called upon to consider questions, which it cannot decline, as they are presented by its own nature, but which it cannot answer, as they transcend every faculty of the mind. [...] It falls into this difficulty without any fault of its own. It begins with prin-ciples, which cannot be dispensed with in the field of expe-rience, and the truth and sufficiency of which are, at the same time, insured by experience. With these principles it rises, in obedience to the laws of its own nature, to ever higher and

---

[1] *Critique of Pure Reason* A613/641.

[2] This insight per se has nothing to do with empiricism or the view that all exis-tence issues must be settled empirically. For one does not need empiricism to generate antinomies: one needs dialectic. One needs regress arguments and ultimate terms, as in the Introduction.

more remote conditions. But it quickly discovers that, in this way, its labours must remain ever incomplete, because new questions never cease to present themselves; and thus it finds itself compelled to have recourse to principles which transcend the region of experience, while they are regarded by common sense without distrust. It thus falls into confusion and contradictions, from which it conjectures the presence of latent errors, which, however, it is unable to discover, because the principles it employs, transcending the limits of experience, cannot be tested by that criterion. The arena of these endless contests is called Metaphysic.[1]

The problem is more serious than some famous empirical illusions:

> This illusion it is impossible to avoid, just as we cannot avoid perceiving that the sea appears to be higher at a distance than it is near the shore, because we see the former by means of higher rays than the latter, or, which is a still stronger case, as even the astronomer cannot prevent himself from seeing the moon larger at its rising than some time afterwards, although he is not deceived by this illusion. [...] For we have here to do with a natural and unavoidable illusion...[2]

> It is not at present our business to treat of empirical illusory appearance (for example, optical illusion), which occurs in the empirical application of otherwise correct rules of the understanding, and in which the judgement is misled by the influence of imagination. Our purpose is to speak of transcendental illusory appearance, which influences principles—that are not even applied to experience, for in this case we should possess a sure test of their correctness—but which leads us, in disregard of all the warnings of criticism, completely beyond the empirical employment of the categories and deludes us with the chimera of an extension of the sphere...[3]

Optical illusions persist even if we are informed about them — but the illusions Kant means are not merely optical or otherwise empirical, for they go beyond experience and affect our very principles.

---

[1] *Critique of Pure Reason* Avii-viii.
[2] *Critique of Pure Reason* in A297/B354-355.
[3] *Critique of Pure Reason* A295/B351-352.

What is the outcome? It is as if we had an innate propensity to be religious and then the empirical facts of science refuted this, over and over, but without ever managing to uproot our innate inclination to believe in something higher.

This is how the story of the antinomies initially ends. But luckily, later portions of the *Critique of Pure Reason* do say that we can learn to view Ideas primarily as values, as we will now see.

From Ideas to Ideals

Here is Kant's overview of the questions of the antinomies:

> The brilliant claims of reason striving to extend its dominion beyond the limits of experience... [P]hilosophy discovers a value and a dignity, which, if it could but make good its assertions, would raise it far above all other departments of human knowledge—professing, as it does, to present a sure foundation for our highest hopes and the ultimate aims of all the exertions of reason. The questions: whether the world has a beginning and a limit to its extension in space; whether there exists anywhere, or perhaps, in my own thinking Self, an indivisible and indestructible unity—or whether nothing but what is divisible and transitory exists; whether I am a free agent, or, like other beings, am bound in the chains of nature and fate; whether, finally, there is a supreme cause of the world, or all our thought and speculation must end with nature and the order of external things—are questions for the solution of which the mathematician would willingly exchange his whole science; for in it there is no satisfaction for the highest aspirations and most ardent desires of humanity.[1]

If this could be made to work then the results would be glorious, by far more significant than what is discovered by the so much more modest methods of natural science. But as noted Kant does not believe that these questions are really about reality at all:

> In neither case—the regressus in infinitum, nor the regressus in indefinitum, is the series of conditions to be considered as actually infinite in the object itself. This might be true of things in themselves, but it cannot be asserted of phenomena, which, as conditions of each other, are only given in the

---

[1] *Critique of Pure Reason* A463-464/B490-491.

empirical regress itself. Hence, the question no longer is, "What is the quantity of this series of conditions in itself—is it finite or infinite?" for it is nothing in itself; but, "How is the empirical regress to be commenced, and how far ought we to proceed with it?"[1]

The question for *Vernunft* is a question about what ought ideally to be done, not what exists. This *ought* has little or nothing to do with reality:

> The question, "What ought to happen in the sphere of nature?" is just as absurd as the question, "What ought to be the properties of a circle?" All that we are entitled to ask is, "What takes place in nature?" or, in the latter case, "What are the properties of a circle?" [...] Reason will not follow the order of things presented by experience, but, with perfect spontaneity, rearranges them according to ideas, with which it compels empirical conditions to agree. It declares, in the name of these ideas, certain actions to be necessary which nevertheless have not taken place and which perhaps never will take place; and yet presupposes that it possesses the faculty of causality in relation to these actions.[2]

Empirical nature will be silent about the *ought*, like some kind of a desert or a quiet forest. It is only the reasoning human who will address his own reasoning needs. Nature will remain indifferent.

But this is already to say that *Vernunft* must teach *itself* — critique itself — so that it learns finally that its grandiose metaphysical or theological generalizations have been mere projections all along:

> It is, in fact, a call to reason, again to undertake the most laborious of all tasks—that of self-examination, and to establish a tribunal, which may secure it in its well-grounded claims, while it pronounces against all baseless assumptions and pretensions, not in an arbitrary manner, but according to its own eternal and unchangeable laws. This tribunal is nothing less than the *Critical Investigation of Pure Reason*.[3]

Vernunft has its own eternal, inner laws, which merely happen not to be the laws governing the physical universe.

---

[1] *Critique of Pure Reason* A514/B542.
[2] *Critique of Pure Reason* A547/B575.
[3] *Critique of Pure Reason* Axi-xii.

> We come now to *metaphysics*, a purely speculative science, which occupies a completely isolated position and is entirely independent of the teachings of experience. It deals with mere conceptions—not, like mathematics, with conceptions applied to intuition—and in it, reason is the pupil of itself alone. It is the oldest of the sciences, and would still survive, even if all the rest were swallowed up in the abyss of an all-destroying barbarism.[1]

This is to say that the dialectical reasoner has only himself to trust. His self-criticism has no outer reference point in nature. But also, Kant clearly supposes now that the reasoning individual *can* free himself of the illusions of the antinomies, because he *can* learn that the thesis side always represents an *ought* and not an *is* — contrary to the pessimistic pronouncements in the previous section!

What then is the precise status of this *ought*? It is not the same as autonomy, for with Kant autonomy is within every person's reach in everyday life. (Hence for him autonomy is not at a remote distance from us like an Idea.)

Kant's answer has more to do with his Enlightenment zeal for limitless questioning and responsibility or maturity, for at this juncture Kant introduces his famous term *regulative Idea* or *regulative ideal* for the optimum of higher reason which can never be matched exactly in concrete practice but which can forever be approximated more closely (this is often called *perfectibility* among Kant's French contemporaries). One such Idea or ideal may be associated with each antinomy, thus:

- *ANTINOMY 1:* You cannot ever confidently pronounce that you have identified the limits of space or time, but you can always expand further outwards *towards* such limits, getting to increasingly bigger units. (Thus the progress is comparative, not absolute. No Idea is matched, but there is more of something than before and the Idea is closer than before.)
- *ANTINOMY 2:* Never will you reach an element or atom which will have no parts at all, but you can always keep getting smaller in your units. In this sense Kant says that pure air or pure water are idealizations in his regulative sense: they are always abstractions from actual conditions, which are inevitably more complex. (Real life is never like ideal conditions but much messier.)

[1] *Critique of Pure Reason* Bxiv.

- *ANTINOMY 3:* Causal origins can be traced further and further in the past but — realistically — we can never bump into any final wall beyond which there is absolutely nothing. (Again the advance is graded. It is silly to believe that science will ever find final answers. It is not capable of that because it always conditions itself with further relative questions. It cannot deal in autonomous units.)
- *ANTINOMY 4:* A being to explain all other beings is for Kant an ideal which to us sounds theological, and which probably to most readers now seems quite exotic. None the less, the regulative thought is again the same, for Kant holds that this is an ideal that is always worth striving for even if it can never be reached. It would be perfection.[1]

Kant's spectrum of Ideas thus comes to resemble a grandiose map of everything, or metaphorically a windrose for seafarers with four radically different directions for travellers to head in — as it were, the East, West, North, and South. Such a windrose, however, is of course not to be confused with any *physical* windrose, for the directions now sought are Ideas and not places. They are not physical or geographical because they are types of question or cause.[2]

From Plato to Kant

Kant is well aware of his debts to Plato, and in the following passage he lays out very clearly how he values Plato precisely due to his Ideas — *as* ideals:

---

[1] Actually, Kant's most prominent version of a regulative Idea is censored here because it is built on a logical error which has major consequences for the higher culture of his time through German Idealism and Romanticism. This is an ideal of 'complete' or 'thoroughgoing' 'determination', as he calls it. He presents it at length (A571-583/B599-661) as his 'highest ideal' or 'the ideal of pure reason'. Where is the error? It is all about determining the *complete series* from (a-z) and not the *terminus* of the series (z). If Kant considered an Idea as the extreme of a series then he would not identify it with the whole of that series. A first cause is not the same as the chain of all causes.

German Idealists and Romantics after Kant very often make a similar error, namely in predicating *Vernunft* simply of the totality of things, as if the world taken as a whole were somehow identical to higher reasoning! (This is to err in a way that is analogical to the scientists of the next footnote!)

[2] This distinction may be difficult for scientists to observe, because they focus so keenly on physical reality and not on philosophical Ideas. In my own experience as a teacher, perhaps a half of the scientifically minded students typically prefer to avoid higher questions altogether, for their desire is rather to learn and discover concrete facts.

Plato employed the expression idea in a way that plainly showed he meant by it something which is never derived from the senses, but which far transcends even the conceptions of the understanding (with which Aristotle occupied himself), inasmuch as in experience nothing perfectly corresponding to them could be found. Ideas are, according to him, archetypes of things themselves, and not merely keys to possible experiences, like the categories. In his view they flow from the highest reason, by which they have been imparted to human reason, which, however, exists no longer in its original state, but is obliged with great labour to recall by reminiscence— which is called philosophy—the old but now sadly obscured ideas. I will not here enter upon any literary investigation of the sense which this sublime philosopher attached to this expression. I shall content myself with remarking that it is nothing unusual, in common conversation as well as in written works, by comparing the thoughts which an author has delivered upon a subject, to understand him better than he understood himself inasmuch as he may not have sufficiently determined his conception, and thus have sometimes spoken, nay even thought, in opposition to his own opinions.

Plato perceived very clearly that our faculty of cognition has the feeling of a much higher vocation than that of merely spelling out phenomena according to synthetical unity, for the purpose of being able to read them as experience, and that our reason naturally raises itself to cognitions far too elevated to admit of the possibility of an object given by experience corresponding to them—cognitions which are nevertheless real, and are not mere phantoms of the brain.

This philosopher found his ideas especially in all that is practical,[1] that is, which rests upon freedom, which in its turn ranks under cognitions that are the peculiar product of reason. He who would derive from experience the conceptions of virtue, who would make (as many have really done) that, which at best can but serve as an imperfectly illustrative example, a model for or the formation of a perfectly adequate

---

[1] *[Kant's original footnote.]* He certainly extended the application of his conception to speculative cognitions also, provided they were given pure and completely à priori, nay, even to mathematics, although this science cannot possess an object otherwhere than in Possible experience. I cannot follow him in this, and as little can I follow him in his mystical deduction of these ideas, or in his hypostatization of them; although, in truth, the elevated and exaggerated language which he employed in describing them is quite capable of an interpretation more subdued and more in accordance with fact and the nature of things.

idea on the subject, would in fact transform virtue into a nonentity changeable according to time and circumstance and utterly incapable of being employed as a rule. On the contrary, every one is conscious that, when any one is held up to him as a model of virtue, he compares this so-called model with the true original which he possesses in his own mind and values him according to this standard. But this standard is the idea of virtue, in relation to which all possible objects of experience are indeed serviceable as examples—proofs of the practicability in a certain degree of that which the conception of virtue demands—but certainly not as archetypes. That the actions of man will never be in perfect accordance with all the requirements of the pure ideas of reason, does not prove the thought to be chimerical. For only through this idea are all judgements as to moral merit or demerit possible; it consequently lies at the foundation of every approach to moral perfection, however far removed from it the obstacles in human nature— indeterminable as to degree—may keep us.

The Platonic Republic has become proverbial as an example— and a striking one—of imaginary perfection, such as can exist only in the brain of the idle thinker; and Brucker ridicules the philosopher for maintaining that a prince can never govern well, unless he is participant in the ideas. But we should do better to follow up this thought and, where this admirable thinker leaves us without assistance, employ new efforts to place it in clearer light, rather than carelessly fling it aside as useless, under the very miserable and pernicious pretext of impracticability. A constitution of the greatest possible human freedom according to laws, by which the liberty of every individual can consist with the liberty of every other (not of the greatest possible happiness, for this follows necessarily from the former), is, to say the least, a necessary idea, which must be placed at the foundation not only of the first plan of the constitution of a state, but of all its laws. And, in this, it not necessary at the outset to take account of the obstacles which lie in our way—obstacles which perhaps do not necessarily arise from the character of human nature, but rather from the previous neglect of true ideas in legislation. For there is nothing more pernicious and more unworthy of a philosopher, than the vulgar appeal to a so-called adverse experience, which indeed would not have existed, if those institutions had been established at the proper time and in accordance with ideas; while, instead of this, conceptions, crude for the very reason that they have been drawn from experience, have marred and frustrated all our better views and intentions. The more legislation and government are in harmony with this idea, the more rare do punishments become and thus it is quite reasonable to maintain, as Plato did, that in a perfect state no punishments at all would be necessary. Now although a perfect state may never exist, the idea is not on that account the less just, which holds up this maximum as the archetype or standard of a constitution, in order to bring legislative government always nearer and nearer to the greatest possible perfection. For at what precise degree human nature must stop in its progress, and how wide must be the chasm which must necessarily exist between the idea and its realization, are problems which no one can or ought to determine—and for this reason, that it is the destination of freedom to overstep all assigned limits between itself and the idea.

But not only in that wherein human reason is a real causal agent and where ideas are operative causes (of actions and their objects), that is to say, in the region of ethics, but also in regard to nature herself, Plato saw clear proofs of an origin from ideas. A plant, and animal, the regular order of nature—probably also the disposition of the whole universe—give manifest evidence that they are possible only by means of and according to ideas; that, indeed, no one creature, under the individual conditions of its existence, perfectly harmonizes with the idea of the most perfect of its kind—just as little as man with the idea of humanity, which nevertheless he bears in his soul as the archetypal standard of his actions; that, notwithstanding, these ideas are in the highest sense individ-ually, unchangeably, and completely determined, and are the original causes of things; and that the totality of connected objects in the universe is alone fully adequate to that idea. Setting aside the exaggerations of expression in the writings of this philosopher, the mental power exhibited in this ascent from the archetypal mode of regarding the physical world to the architectonic connection thereof according to ends, that is, ideas, is an effort which deserves imitation and claims respect. But as regards the principles of ethics, of legislation, and of religion, spheres in which ideas alone render expe-rience possible, although they never attain to full expression therein, he has vindicated for himself a position of peculiar merit, which is not appreciated only because it is judged by the very empirical rules, the validity of which as principles is destroyed by ideas. For as regards nature, experience presents us with rules and is the source of truth, but in relation to ethical laws experience is the parent of illusion, and it is in the highest degree reprehensible to limit or to deduce the laws which dictate what I ought to do, from what is done.

[...] A conception formed from notions, which transcends the possibility of experience, is an idea, or a conception of reason. To one who has accustomed himself to these distinctions, it must be quite intolerable to hear the representation of the colour red called an idea. It ought not even to be called a notion or conception of understanding.[1]

What is missing from this generalization is firstly the issue of the Copernican Turn for which Kant takes credit. For the irony is that if Kant agrees with Plato that Ideas are needed as perfect value-archetypes, it is *Plato* who sees this analogically to Copernicus, not Kant. After all, Plato's Ideas are real objects out there, not our mind-constructs in here. Kant's is in truth the Romantic Turn to the inner, to subjectivity — soon, with Schelling, to the subconscious, to art and myth. This is Copernicus reversed!

The second thing missing is that the Ideas in a sense revolve around *themselves:* after all, they are not only perfectionistic standards but also their perfect uses. This *double logic* is missing from Kant's Ideas, and in this way his world is much poorer than Plato's or Hegel's — who, as we will see, present not only theses and antitheses to form antinomies but also *syntheses* to solve them. In this sense, and compared to Hegel and Plato — both bolder idealists — Kant looks more like the great questioner (Socrates!) than a great answerer or visionary. But more exactly Kant's achievement is to systematically compare *Vernunft* downwards to *Verstand:* that is his unique ability. Meanwhile Plato soars higher, and Hegel ranges more widely. Each great idealist is in this way unmatched in its particular direction. (Thus we get a kind of Idealistic Pyramid, which I will return to in Ch. 4.)

Aesthetic Bridge to Later German Idealism and Romanticism

Kant's aesthetics has so far been downplayed in this book, but it certainly deserves to be in the limelight in Kant's aftermath for it is

---

[1] *Critique of Pure Reason* A313-320/B370-377.

premised on in so many places in German Idealism and earlier Romanticism.

One main cause of this period's general aestheticism is in Kant's suggestion that the two worlds of *is* and *ought* or *Verstand* and *Vernunft* may not need to be so far apart after all, for they are in certain ways brought together in the aesthetics of nature and or art.

What are the connections?

The bottom line is that in having aesthetic experiences we seem to find the patterns of *Vernunft* in empirical reality. This is understandable due to a number of separable factors.

Firstly, aesthetic experiences do not involve any strict types, so they always call forth reflective responses.[1] For instance, if you see an object which you recognize right away as a chair, then this is not aesthetic. For the aesthetic does not belong to any predetermined *kind*. Similarly, we may say that an object x is good for hammering and an object y is more or less good for that purpose and z is not good for that at all, but this that we have the function of hammering in place already before we look to x, y, and z is entirely opposed to aesthetics. We cannot have predefined aims or rules if we are to deal in aesthetic things, be they in art or nature. (In a nutshell: if you know what it is, it is not art.) In Kant's words:

> There can be no objective rule of taste which shall determine by means of concepts what is beautiful. For every judgement from this source is aesthetical; *i.e.* the feeling of the subject, and not a concept of the Object, is its determining ground. To seek for a principle of taste which shall furnish, by means of definite concepts, a universal criterion of the beautiful, is fruitless trouble; because what is sought is impossible and self-contradictory.[2]

---

[1] Kant writes that there are 'reflective' and 'determinative' 'judgments'. The determinative categorize things according to familiar types and the reflective ones do not. 'Judgments' abound in Kant's works, but as before I do not use his particular terminology because his philosophical insights seem to have value independently. (Cf. what I noted earlier about Al-Azm: it is not worthwhile to relativize Kant's first antinomy to the Newtonian influences of his day, for that would make it irrelevant to an Einsteinian age. Similarly, I would never teach youths to talk in 'judgments' in particular, as opposed to say views, theses, propositions, sentences, etc. This is not to say that the word 'judgment' means the same as these other words but that distinctions drawn on this level are not cardinal. They are very small stuff compared to the great issues of dialectical philosophy, and the first and grand issues must be the priority.)

[2] *Critique of Judgment* § 17.

Why would this be self-contradictory? Kant answers with his famous idea of 'free play':

> The cognitive powers [...] are here in free play, because no definite concept limits them to a particular rule of cognition. Hence, the state of mind in this representation must be a feeling of the free play of the representative powers in a given representation with reference to a cognition in general. Now a representation by which an object is given, that is to become a cognition in general, requires *Imagination*, for the gathering together the manifold of intuition, and *Understanding*, for the unity of the concept uniting the representations.[1]

Without free play your experience would be too dead to qualify as aesthetic in the first place. Without it you could not possibly experience that the top of your head has flown off (to borrow from Emily Dickinson). Why not? Well, you would be categorizing your experience by reference to familiar types. You would therefore not need to search for any rule to discover unity in what you experience. After all, it would be prepackaged for you like a Hollywood repeat! That is too safe for real art.

This is to say also that there cannot be rules for art. We cannot say that it should serve, say, particular decorative purposes, for instance by matching with currently fashionable shades of red. If piano concertos begin to follow a specific role model then they stop being art. Art is only there if no recognizable type is being followed. (One implication of this is that for instance harmonious color combinations or musical intervals cannot be intrinsic to art. All aesthetic events must live beyond any known rules.)

Producing art therefore requires *genius*:

> *Genius* is the talent (or natural gift) which gives the rule to Art. Since talent, as the innate productive faculty of the artist, belongs itself to Nature, we may express the matter thus: *Genius* is the innate mental disposition (*ingenium*) *through which* Nature gives the rule to Art.

> Whatever may be thought of this definition, whether it is merely arbitrary or whether it is adequate to the concept that we are accustomed to combine with the word *genius* (which is to be examined in the following paragraphs), we can prove already beforehand that according to the signification of

---

[1] *Critique of Judgment* § 9.

the word here adopted, beautiful arts must necessarily be considered as arts of *genius*.

For every art presupposes rules by means of which in the first instance a product, if it is to be called artistic, is represented as possible. But the concept of beautiful art does not permit the judgement upon the beauty of a product to be derived from any rule, which has a *concept* as its determining ground, and therefore has at its basis a concept of the way in which the product is possible. Therefore, beautiful art cannot itself devise the rule according to which it can bring about its product. But since at the same time a product can never be called Art without some precedent rule, Nature in the subject must (by the harmony of its faculties) give the rule to Art; *i.e.* beautiful Art is only possible as a product of Genius.

We thus see (1) that genius is a *talent* for producing that for which no definite rule can be given; it is not a mere aptitude for what can be learnt by a rule. Hence *originality* must be its first property. (2) But since it also can produce original nonsense, its products must be models, *i.e. exemplary*; and they consequently ought not to spring from imitation, but must serve as a standard or rule of judgement for others. (3) It cannot describe or indicate scientifically how it brings about its products, but it gives the rule just as nature does. Hence the author of a product for which he is indebted to his genius does not himself know how he has come by his Ideas; and he has not the power to devise the like at pleasure or in accordance with a plan, and to communicate it to others in precepts that will enable them to produce similar products.[1]

Like Bach in the Introduction, the genius does not state his rules, but he has them none the less because otherwise he would not produce compelling patterns but chaotic nonsense. He introduces them intuitively like a child, and he does not state them or teach them. He should be as astounded by his creation as anyone else! For it is a sudden discovery, a leap to an intuitive conclusion but without the graded steps of a ladder of proof.

However, to state this more exactly one should reflect that genius makes for but a *portion* of an aesthetic product:

---

[1] *Critique of Judgment* § 46.

Every one is agreed that genius is entirely opposed to the *spirit of imitation*. Now since learning is nothing but imitation, it follows that the greatest ability and teachableness (capacity) regarded *quâ* teachableness, cannot avail for genius. Even if a man thinks or invents for himself, and does not merely take in what others have taught, even if he discovers many things in art and science, this is not the right ground for calling such a (perhaps great) *head*, a genius (as opposed to him who because he can only learn and imitate is called a *shallow-pate*). For even these things could be learned, they lie in the natural path of him who investigates and reflects according to rules; and they do not differ specifically from what can be acquired by industry through imitation. Thus we can readily learn all that *Newton* has set forth in his immortal work on the Principles of Natural Philosophy, however great a head was required to discover it; but we cannot learn to write spirited poetry, however express may be the precepts of the art and however excellent its models. The reason is that *Newton* could make all his steps, from the first elements of geometry to his own great and profound discoveries, intuitively plain and definite as regards consequence, not only to himself but to every one else. But a *Homer* or a *Wieland* cannot show how his Ideas, so rich in fancy and yet so full of thought, come together in his head, simply because he does not know and therefore cannot teach others. In Science then the greatest discoverer only differs in degree from his laborious imitator and pupil [...].

Although mechanical and beautiful art are very different, the first being a mere art of industry and learning and the second of genius, yet there is no beautiful art in which there is not a mechanical element that can be comprehended by rules and followed accordingly, and in which therefore there must be something *scholastic* as an essential condition. For [in every art] some purpose must be conceived; otherwise we could not ascribe the product to art at all, and it would be a mere product of chance. But in order to accomplish a purpose, definite rules from which we cannot dispense ourselves are requisite. Now since the originality of the talent constitutes an essential (though not the only) element in the character of genius, shallow heads believe that they cannot better show themselves to be full-blown geniuses than by throwing off the constraint of all rules [...].[1]

---

[1] *Critique of Judgment* § 47.

Genius is not the same as chance, so we need it to *accompany* deliberate behavior, which must follow rules. However, this need of rules should not be overdone, and even the greatest scientists are all about following predetermined rules, Kant insists. It is only in the arts that we can find geniuses. (What then is Kant's view of himself? Is he a genius in his own eyes? I am sure he would deny this, for he certainly sees philosophy as a science, or a *Wissenschaft*: this German term encompasses the humanities.)

The *sublime* is a rather sensational aspect of Kant's aesthetics, standing for great magnitudes (the mathematical sublime: think of countless stars seen in the nighttime sky) or fearsome powers (the dynamic sublime: picture a thundering waterfall). These have to do with our sense for the infinite, which is in some connections inevitably involved in dialectics and *Vernunft*. The rush is experienced because the empirical data is experienced to be inadequate to the limitless Idea. No one can draw a picture of infinite complexity or power, for example, so the principle can be only suggested. Exactly this triggers the subjective sense of wonder. Accordingly, the sublime is in the seer, not in the seen thing, and the seer is a freely reasoning being — and this of course is authentic Kant once more. (For him the human self is always in the middle.)

Natural beauty is easily ranked above art on Kant's principles because of its spontaneity. Organic beings are for him in fact mechanistic, so they have no higher dignity in reality, but teleological principles can and must be used only heuristically (regulatively) in the life sciences. They are not in the things themselves. Kant's example is of a tree:

> In the first place, a tree generates another tree according to a known natural law. But the tree produced is of the same genus; and so it produces itself *generically*. On the one hand, as effect it is continually self-produced; on the other hand, as cause it continually produces itself, and so perpetuates itself generically.

> Secondly, a tree produces itself as an *individual*. This kind of effect no doubt we call growth; but it is quite different from any increase according to mechanical laws, and is to be reckoned as generation, though under another name. The matter that the tree incorporates it previously works up into a specifically peculiar quality, which natural mechanism external to it cannot supply; and thus it develops itself by aid of a material which, as compounded, is its own product. No doubt, as regards the constituents got from nature without, it must only be regarded as an educt; but yet in the separation

and recombination of this raw material we see such an originality in the separating and formative faculty of this kind of natural being, as is infinitely beyond the reach of art, if the attempt is made to reconstruct such vegetable products out of elements obtained by their dissection or material supplied by nature for their sustenance.

Thirdly, each part of a tree generates itself in such a way that the maintenance of any one part depends reciprocally on the maintenance of the rest. A bud of one tree engrafted on the twig of another produces in the alien stock a plant of its own kind, and so also a scion engrafted on a foreign stem. Hence we may regard each twig or leaf of the same tree as merely engrafted or inoculated into it, and so as an independent tree attached to another and parasitically nourished by it. At the same time, while the leaves are products of the tree they also in turn give support to it; for the repeated defoliation of a tree kills it, and its growth thus depends on the action of the leaves upon the stem. The self-help of nature in case of injury in the vegetable creation, when the want of a part that is necessary for the maintenance of its neighbours is supplied by the remaining parts; and the abortions or malformations in growth, in which certain parts, on account of casual defects or hindrances, form themselves in a new way to maintain what exists, and so produce an anomalous creature, I shall only mention in passing, though they are among the most wonderful properties of organised creatures.[1]

The tree looks so well organized, so purpose-built! But in reality this is all only about *reading things into* experiences of the tree:

This principle, which is at the same time a definition, is as follows: *An organised product of nature is one in which every part is reciprocally purpose, [end] and means.* In it nothing is vain, without purpose, or to be ascribed to a blind mechanism of nature.

This principle, as regards its occasion, is doubtless derived from experience, viz. from that methodised experience called observation; but on account of the universality and necessity which it ascribes to such purposiveness it cannot rest solely on empirical grounds, but must have at its basis an *a priori* prin-

---

[1] *Critique of Judgment* § 64.

ciple, although it be merely regulative and these purposes lie only in the idea of the judging [subject] and not in an effective cause. We may therefore describe the aforesaid principle as a *maxim* for judging of the internal purposiveness of organised beings.[1] (Italics in original.)

It is *as if* organic beings were means *and* ends or causes *and* effects — somewhat like autonomous beings, hence — but because this is only heuristically so, one should never take the analogy literally. Humans alone — not trees, not bees — are truly free and reasoning beings, Kant teaches. Nature like art comforts us because they *seem* to be like us. But they are not. (Again we project!)

However, Kant's contemporaries and followers are much too pleased by the prospect of unity to hold back in this way. The overall trend of the earlier German Romantics and Idealists is aptly summarized in a famous dispute between two early fans of Kant's aesthetic, Goethe and Schiller. Goethe seeks an *Urpflanze* — the original plant from which all other plants have evolved and simultaneously the model organism also for art (in Goethe nature and art are never far apart) — and believes that he actually finds it during his travels in Italy. However, his friend and younger collaborator Schiller stays clear of this, insisting with Kant that such a model of models is only a pure Idea, a thing of thought, not an empirical object or outer fact. Among the Romantics, it is usually Goethe's tendency that holds sway, and Kant's warnings are quickly buried.

---

[1] *Critique of Judgment* § 66.

Chapter 4. Hegel: A World Of Ideas

> The nothing longs for something.
> — Jakob Böhme

With the great philosophers it happens at times that the whole world changes in a decade or two. This is the revolutionary pace of change from Socrates to Plato to Aristotle in ancient Greece, and a comparable architectonic shift in horizons occurs in German Idealism from Kant via Fichte and Schelling to Hegel and Marx. Then the world rethought is a world remade.

Here is the shortest route to the dialectic of *Hegel*. With Kant, Plato, or Socrates, antinomies were patterns in thought, but in Hegel they become patterns in real things out there. Thus dialectic is not primarily a philosophical meditation, conversation, or lecture but rather a series of events outside speech and thought. History itself is philosophical. Hegel does not maintain that the historical events themselves always speak or represent themselves in this way, however. He says rather that there is a cunning of reason (German: *List der Vernunft*) in the real world, so that *Vernunft* only implicitly and unofficially orders the events. For example, when Caesar conquers much of Western Europe, he is not aware that he is spreading the seeds of Greco-Roman and Christian culture to those regions: his mind is on his personal merits, or on military affairs. Similarly for Napoleon. He need not *think* continually that he propagates the Enlightenment: it suffices that he does it. As Marx and Engels say, people are not to be judged by what they think of themselves but by their real and effective deeds. This is Hegelian thinking. It is the real affairs, and not anyone's particular words, that draw the main interest of Hegel. His wish is then to state *explicitly* just what the dialectical operations in life have always been, thereby achieving complete closure.[1] He does not make history, he only writes it. Before Hegel, high reasoning dominates the world, but not consciously, and with Hegel a full consciousness is reached but simultaneously the wheel grinds to a halt. Reasoning is always *ex post facto.*

Dialectically we may identify a single, grandiose *historical antinomy* in Hegel's books in order to locate its primary structure. For history, too, is a series, like the series of all the other antinomies: after all, one event or period does follow the next. But if this series ends somewhere then that is the aim or end of history. Is there such an end (4.1)? It is logically quite fitting for Hegel to say it is an Idea (4.2), for he defines Ideas in the familiar double sense. (They are therefore akin to Plato's.) However, Hegel rephrases his point also in terms of God (4.3), *Geist* (spirit), thought, and art (4.4). He does this because he views religions and arts as ways to reach the Ideas without philosophical technicalities.[2] Folksy dialectics are religious or artistic. If you go academic then you are left with nothing specifically artistic or religious anymore and all you have are dry and hard formats. Hegel at times phrases this as a contrast between children and adults. Children need the tall tales, adults do not. The higher truths are translated from myths into logic. Unlike so many current philosophers, he is convinced that the same Ideas are present already in the myths.[3]

---

[1] In passing, Hegel's use of the *word* '*dialectic*' (or *Dialektik*) and it cognates is not consistent, but this will not hamper my discussion due to what was noted already in the Introduction: reasoning dialectically is not the same as using the word 'dialectic'. (An unacceptably narrow use of the term is in Hegel's *Encyclopedia*.)

[2] Hegel's flexibility is an advantage *and* a disadvantage. His range is wider than anybody's, but he is not always precise. Without the former merit, many analytical or scholastic philosophers come to look like people playing on a Rubik's Cube or small chess problems compared to him. They are precise, right, but they are small, and Hegel's open-minded dynamism and fluidity are the antidote to this. But it also leads him to slip into positions at times which are not well founded or even well articulated. (There is a pro and a con, in Hegelian spirit!)

My personal response is to give Hegel his due without believing in him entirely or in everything. On my map, Kant is the idealist who compares *Vernunft downwards*, with *Verstand* and science. Plato soars *upward*, especially with his Agathon. Hegel expands *sideways*, comparing numerous cultures in history and their different levels. (One can picture this as an Idealistic Pyramid, as above. The height is Plato's, the width is Hegel's, and the hard bottom line is Kant's.)

[3] Children and primitives are not silly as they are in the light of modern science, for they are on to higher truths but in backward ways. For the scientist of course there are no higher truths at all: no Ideas, Gods, free wills, moral duties, aesthetic harmonies, etc. (Continued)

Things get more complicated and more uncomfortable with Hegel once we confront his generalizations about the *state* (4.5). He argues that there are no noble savages: uncivilized humans are merely brutes. We come to our own only in organized, law-bound societies. For that is when we state clearly how we want to live and also live that way in fact: we make and we follow our own nation's laws. These become our second nature, our local customs — our *Zeitgeist*. In this spirit, Hegel is full of praise for the "Germany" of his time, which — a slight irony — does not exist in his time (before Bismarck). However, the real trouble is not only with an inexistent "Germany". For while German Idealism and Romanticism are progressive and forward-looking cultural movements and diverse personalities like Beethoven and Goethe obviously innovate as geniuses, the laws of Prussia are backward and parochial by anyone's lights (except Hegel's). Hence Hegel's grand equation is ultimately wrong. *Vernunft* is not expressed in a national state. It is something far more dynamic and elevated. I will note that by and large states are actually closer to *Verstand*.[1]

Finally for this chapter I take a glimpse at Karl *Marx* (4.6-4.8), who understands the ironies of nation states very well. Like many others in his post-Hegelian age, he shifts from idealism to materialism, from romanticism to realism.[2] It is a new world of steel machines and congested cities. In this landscape states are mainly conservative forces, he writes. But unlike Hegel he does not say that the forward dynamo is

---

To be sure, despite this Hegel does call his studies scientific: they are *Wissenschaft*, in German. However, this German term (unlike 'science') covers not only the natural sciences but also the humanities and social sciences. I should also add that Hegel is all at sea about modern science, and that his views on physics, chemistry, and biology are in general not possible to take seriously. Hence I ignore them in this chapter. The dialectician who knows his science is Kant.

[1] An analogical case could be made about Hegel's view of *China*. For Hegel, China is a prosaic country in which the citizens act solely out of duty and have no inner, individual culture or *Geist*. (Hegel's India is the opposite of this: the land of dreams.) Only the emperor gives orders and everyone else obeys (thus Hegel's *Philosophy of History* Part I, Section 1). However, this simplistic sketch cannot encompass the dialectical philosophy of Daoism. Hegel does know about it and brings it up, but he cannot relate it to his model of the Chinese state. If the dao ruled in China then of course it would not be a hard dictatorship but something softer like an organic and reciprocal society — rather like a Hegelian social organism.

In saying this I am not claiming to know a great deal about Chinese history, but I have read enough of Daoist material (in translations, not in Chinese) to see that Hegel's story about China has very little to do with the dao. In other words: if that is the local politics then it does not accord with the local philosophy. (Hence the political *reduction* of philosophy does not work.)

[2] After a brief dispute among Left and Right Hegelians, Hegel is swiftly sidelined from the mainstream of philosophy due to the rise of materialistic scientism and NeoKantianism in Germany. Meanwhile in Italy, Britain, and the USA Hegel's reign continues until the early twentieth century. In Britain, analytic philosophy is born as a rebellion against Hegel's dominance (see Hylton).

idealistic. Rather innovation is powerfully driven by science and tech-nology. (Especially the steam engine revolutionizes production in Marx's time.) However, in saying this Marx does not slip to scientism, for his ultimate aim is to solve the same historical antinomy as Hegel. If tech-nology evolves sufficiently, then humans are freed for nobler pursuits, he writes. Machines can take over as the new slaves, doing all of the dirty and demeaning work. Hence, with Marx the means become material, but the ends remain quite idealistic, and this is how he is true to the dialec-tical tradition of Hegel, Kant, Plato, and Socrates.

Hegel's World

In Chapter 3, every antinomy in Kant was made out of a series like a MOVES b MOVES c... or a PROVES b PROVES c..., and in Plato's dialogues Socrates was seen to characteristically elicit each of these terms by means of a series of questions as in WHAT MOVES a?, WHAT MOVES b?, etc. The import was much the same, and I generalized that this is dialectical reasoning.

In coming to Hegel we need to picture dialectics like these as silent dialogues which the real world has with itself, so that history becomes a gradual progression towards an ultimate answer in time. This way we are able to structure Hegelian history in a manner that is analogical to the dialectics of Socrates and Plato as well as Kant — and simultane-ously we have an over arching order for interpreting Hegel's dialectical philosophy as a whole.

Hegel is not the first to picture history as a progression, of course, for that is normal to do already in ancient Christian and Jewish narra-tives. For them the human story begins with the Bible's *Genesis* and ends with its *Apocalypse*, and the Jewish or Christian historian is merely to read the signs in real life right. For the events alluded to in the Bible must have identifiable analogues in the process of the world. This way the Holy Book's omens can come true. Its words are confirmed. (On these premises ancient and medieval historians routinely pronounce about the imminent end of the world or misidentify someone or other as the Anti-Christ. For it is not easy to identify the parallels between the holy text and the real world. What does each Biblical symbol mean in real-world language? This involves plenty of guesswork.)

Closer to Hegel's own period, the eighteenth-century Enlightenment historians especially in France use the evolutionary narrative without religion, saying that the evolution in time is due not to God but to humans — or really to their increasingly enlightened ideas and habits. The key ideas are social or personal liberty and scientific experimentation. With Voltaire the medieval period is viewed as a dark age, and though traces of religion persist also in Voltaire's books, he is confident that the verifiable forces of progress are human.

With Hegel himself God comes back into the picture from another angle. He does not go back to looking for omens from the Holy Book like so many ancient Christians, for much like Plato in Chapter 2 he considers myths merely figurative. Like Plato's, Hegel's God is structural and philosophical, a representative of *Vernunft* — not a face but a formula. However, Hegel imagines that God or the Ideas can be realized on earth more thoroughly than Plato ever does. We saw that Plato has grave doubts about the rational potentials of the material or empirical world, but on the other hand he is sure that individual psyches or his social utopias — Atlantis, Kallipolis, and Magnesia — can abide by divine models or Ideas rather closely. With Hegel, empirical or material nature is usually set aside as irrelevant, and the progress of history is on the level human culture and social institutions. Hence it is at least roughly under-standable why Hegel believes in the possibility of an earthly paradise. It is realized in human history. In the end God will no longer be separate from the world. Thus the world is not only God's playground: it *is* God. He is but a different word for what will happen.[1]

The rising force of *reasoning* in human history is for Hegel not mainly a technocratic affair, and this contrasts again with the French Enlight-enment. The French *philosophes* typically mechanize whatever they touch, but already in his youth Hegel is keen on the Kantian agenda that true Christianity is manifested in living according to the Golden Rule (then the "kingdom of God will be among us", as Jesus says at Luke 17: 21). Miracles become unnecessary. It is not crucial to attend church on Sunday, for now 'religion' is out on the streets of every free city. But clearly reason in this sense is a dialectical and a reciprocal affair, not a function of computation, statistics, or probability. Hence, the *type* of reasoning that increasingly rules the world is in Hegel not like it is with the *philosophes.*

Next, *Vernunft* bears on *national customs and laws*, Hegel says, because as liberated beings we voluntarily and spontaneously fashion our own lives according to reasoned and moral principles. If we do this, the laws of our nation state will be our own laws. As a result of this, as good citizens we

---

[1] This is Hegel's Spinozism. Plato and Kant would never accept this, for they are committed dualists. Ideas cannot be realized concretely on earth, they write. For they can never have empirical equivalents, and the *ought* will never be the *is.*

should not so much as think of breaking them. To betray them would be to betray our own selves.

Hegel's *Germanic* emphasis is bolstered by the Napoleonic conquest of the German lands in Hegel's youth, for this triggers a patriotic reaction in Germany. The birth of the nation is still several decades away as noted, but it is popular to wish for German unity. In this phase, Germany becomes a thing of the mind, a cultural unit without institutional backing. It is the land of *Dichter und Denker* (poets and thinkers), an overachiever in all aspects of scholarship and high culture, from music and literature to theology, philosophy, and historiography — but an underachiever in politics, economics, and social affairs generally. It is a land of Ideas, an unrealistic island.

Hegel's views on *historiography* are in part quite ordinary for his time. Ranke and several others view history primarily as a function of statecraft — not say of cultural ideas or economic factors — and also Hegel adopts this view (cf. Iggers). This type of historiography is then viewed as the paradigmatic science or *Wissenschaft*. Ranke and the other 'historicists' at Berlin study and compare abundant sources meticulously and employ localist and organic models which contrast with the French Enlightenment universalism (exported by Napoleon). Hegel claims officially to oppose the historicist school, but like so often (and in accordance with his own dialectical philosophy!) he partly also sides with his opponents.[1]

Hegel's specifically *dialectical* addition to historiography lies partly in his emphasis on conflict. He says progress is never smooth or linear, though to be sure there are graded factors also. For instance, Luther's Reformation is anticipated by other figures numerous times (like Hus and Wycliffe), but Luther's systematic statement and the uncompromising zeal bring the development to a head. He cannot back away and there must be blood. Thus there is first an implicit period of maturation under the surface (this part many historians would probably not deny), and then there is the irrepressible breakthrough (this is the dialectical element of conflict and revolution). These are history's growing pains. (I will address Hegel's dialectical pattern fully below.)

An oddity of Hegel's historical view is that he imagines his own period to be historically *complete*. Here the human story ends, he says. We have 'Germany' — as noted, an inexistent state — and Protestant Christianity, the nuclear family, the established professions, the qualified adminis-

---

[1] This happens also with the *Romantics*, as is often noted: Hegel is officially against them but one sees their traces everywhere in his texts. The stress on local cultures (versus French universalism), on organic wholes (versus Enlightenment mechanisms), and on the spiritual side of things all testify to this. Major Romantics like Hölderlin and Schelling are his youthful friends.

trators and the stable social institutions. In the end history has only to quietly digest itself — primarily inside Hegel's own head. The storms are over, there is peaceful self-knowledge and self-acceptance, and everything grinds to a halt.[1]

From this position Hegel makes his confident declarations that world history (*Weltgeschichte*) is the world court (*Weltgericht*) and that the historically real is the rational — the *is* is the *ought*. The historical antinomy has been solved, the book of the world is closed.[2]

However, of course it only then needs to be opened up again, because things become much more complex very quickly! Marx more than anyone else reveals a rude new world which Hegel's fairy tale logic conceals only thinly. And then the wheel spins again.

Now let us consider a little more closely how Hegel *reasons*. What is his dialectic? In what way is it like Kant's or like Plato's? And why is he so influential and famous?

Hegel's Ideas

In his *Science of Logic* (§ 1631) Hegel states some elementary aspects of the Ideas that are familiar from *Kant*:

> The Idea is the *adequate Notion*, that which is objectively *true*, or the *true as such*. When anything whatever possesses truth, it possesses it through its Idea, or, *something possesses truth only in so far as it is Idea*. The expression 'idea' has often been employed in philosophy as in ordinary life for 'notion', indeed, even for a mere ordinary conception: 'I have no idea yet of this lawsuit, building, neighbourhood', means nothing more than the ordinary conception. Kant has reclaimed the expression Idea for the *notion of reason*. Now according to Kant, the notion of reason is supposed to be the notion of the *unconditioned*, but a notion *transcendent* in regard to phenomena, that is, no *empirical use* can be made of such notion that is *adequate to it*. The notions of reason are to serve for the comprehension of perceptions, the notions of the understanding for understanding them. (Italics in original.)

---

[1] This marks the *end of history*, which Hegelian doctrine is appropriated somewhat creatively by Fukuyama after the end of the Cold War.

[2] Hegel's *own role* in his narrative is always a curious affair. He is not one of the great agents of history like Napoleon and Caesar, and he merely interprets events after they occur — but how much of this is up to his own organization? History does not write itself, of course, and Hegel is an highly self-conscious (and elaborate) philosopher of history.

An Idea thus defined is not an ordinary idea. (Recall the contrast with Berkeley.) Ordinarily the word 'idea' is used for hunches or whichever light-minded associations, very loosely, but Kant makes an Idea an object of *Vernunft*. This means that it stands for an unconditional absolute, and per Kant this must be *super*-empirical. Hegel here also uses Kant's terms to distinguish *Vernunft* from *Verstand* and Platonic Ideas from Aristotelian categories: the former are for comprehending things and the latter are for merely understanding them.[1]

However, Hegel's Ideas accord better with Plato than with Kant in having a familiar *double logic*. This is from Hegel's *Encyclopedia* (§ 213):

> The Idea is truth in itself and for itself — the absolute unity of the notion and objectivity. Its 'ideal' content is nothing but the notion in its detailed terms: its 'real' content is only the exhibition which the notion gives itself in the form of external existence, while yet, by enclosing this shape in its ideality, it keeps it in its power, and so keeps itself in it. The definition, which declares the Absolute to be the Idea, is itself absolute. All former definitions come back to this. The Idea is the Truth: for Truth is the correspondence of objectivity with the notion — not of course the correspondence of external things with my conceptions, for these are only *correct* conceptions held by *me*, the individual person. In the idea we have nothing to do with the individual, nor with figurate conceptions, nor with external things. (Italics in original.)

This is already a pretty good example of 'Hegelese' — Hegel's personal way of stating things in his philosophy books, through thousands upon thousands of pages. It is usually dense — it is overkill. If one reads though a paragraph or a page in his book one quickly comes to realize that it is not possible to paraphrase, for Hegel typically tries to say so much at once. (He does not advance point by separate point in the manner of Plato's Socrates or Kant, because he is not as clear a thinker. His language is rich and he opens the whole box, and whatever is involved he will address without delay. In this sense his texts are full of life — or they are a kind of life: they are not educational tools like Plato's or Kant's but expressive manifestations of a form of life which celebrates itself.[2])

---

[1] Hegel presumably means that Ideas cover topics comprehensively as wholes as in Kant's idea of complete determination, see Ch. 3. As I explained there, this would be to confuse a totality with its extreme limit, or a series from a to z with its endpoint z.

[2] Hegel's predecessor in this is *Herder*, who influences Goethe and many others among the Romantics and Historicists in the later eighteenth century. Herder

What Hegel means in the above passage is that the Idea of truth is not simply a concept or theory (Hegel: notion) of truth but also *a* truth (Hegel: objective), or even *the* truth, the very truth *of* truths.

In similar spirit Hegel's *Philosophy of Right* begins with the statement that the Idea of Right is both the standard for all things that are right and something that *is* paradigmatically right[1] — and thus across the board.[2] In general, *wherever* we have an Idea, we have a scale and an optimal instance on that scale. Thus an Idea is again by its own lights a perfect circle: it is self-evident in saying what counts as evidence and providing just that kind of evidence, quite as in Plato.[3]

Thus Hegel takes up key leads from Kant *and* Plato. But also he learns also from numerous others. In accordance with this, he is typically aware that things can be stated in *various vocabularies.* He generalizes thus in his *Encyclopedia* ($ 214):

---

advocates expressivism *and* practices it — and unlike Hegel he can write.

[1] Hegel's *Philosophy of Right* begins with this statement (Introduction, $ 1): "The philosophic science of right has as its object the idea of right, i.e., the conception of right and the realisation of the conception."

This is clarified a little in his following remark:

> Philosophy has to do with ideas or realised thoughts, and hence not with what we have been accustomed to call mere conceptions. It has indeed to exhibit the one-sidedness and untruth of these mere conceptions, and to show that, while that which commonly bears the name "conception," is only an abstract product of the understanding, the true conception alone has reality and gives this reality to itself. Everything, other than the reality which is established by the conception, is transient surface existence, external attribute, opinion, appearance void of essence, untruth, delusion, and so forth. Through the actual shape [*Gestaltung*], which it takes upon itself in actuality, is the conception itself understood. This shape is the other essential element of the idea, and is to be distinguished from the form [Form], which exists only as conception [*Begriff*].

This is entirely systematic of Hegel, for as above *Verstand* (the understanding) deals in concepts, which are separate from their own uses ('one-sided', as 'mere conceptions') and *Vernunft* deals in realized Ideas, not in mere concepts.

[2] Here is the beginning of Hegel's aesthetics lectures:

> We called the beautiful the Idea of the beautiful. This means that the beautiful itself must be grasped as Idea, in particular as Idea in a determinate form, i.e. as Ideal. Now the Idea as such is nothing but the Concept, the real existence of the Concept, and the unity of the two. For the Concept as such is not yet the Idea, although 'Concept' and 'Idea' are often used without being distinguished. But it is only when it is present in its real existence and placed in unity therewith that the Concept is the Idea.

Again *concept: Idea:: Verstand: Vernunft.*

[3] This is not common knowledge among current Hegel scholars however. As remarked earlier, just as Plato scholars characteristically ignore or oppose the double logic of Plato's Ideas (see my *Plato's Logic*), Hegel scholars have a similar tendency (see, e.g., Beiser, Pinkard, Pippin, Brandom). However, in the Hegel literature there are exceptions, see for instance Arndt and de Vos.

> The Idea may be described in many ways. It may be called reason [*Vernunft*]; (and this is the proper philosophical signification of reason); subject-object; the unity of the ideal and the real, of the finite and the infinite [...]; the possibility which has its actuality in its own self; that of which the nature can be thought only as existent, etc. All these descriptions apply [...] .

Compare the sources:

- Reason is here *Vernunft*, from Kant, and the subject-object pair typifies Kant's ethics (the autonomous agent is his own patient) and aesthetics (aesthetic experiences project reason to external things).
- The ideal/real and infinite/finite dichotomies agree with Plato and Kant. In Kant the *ought* soars above the *is*, but in Plato the archetypal Ideas are the fundamental values *and* realities.
- Actuality/possibility is from Aristotle's theology (see Ch. 2).
- Necessity/existence is from Anselm's ontological argument (see Ch. 3).

Hegel is a full professor and an expert on these topics, so philosophy and theology are not mere occasional hobbies for him: he finds it easy to shift between numerous background theories, technical symbols, and natural languages. He knows his Latin and his Greek, and he has all the time and energy in the world to draw comparisons endlessly.

Having said that, Hegel is also an exceptionally *innovative* professor. He does not primarily know and report what has been or what is typically known or said in the journals, as more normal professors do. Rather, he has a revolution of his own to conduct. The Hegelian revolution in thought amounts to a *processual* turn (this too is from *Encyclopedia* § 214):

> The different modes of apprehending the Idea as unity of ideal and real, of finite and infinite, of identity and difference, etc, are more or less formal. They designate some stage of the *specific* notion. Only the notion itself, however, is free and the genuine universal: in the Idea, therefore, the specific character of the notion is only the notion itself — an objectivity, viz. into which it, being the universal, continues itself, and in which it has only its own character, the total character. The Idea is the infinite judgment, of which the terms are severally the independent totality; and in which, as each grows to the fullness of its own nature, it has thereby at the same time passed into the other. [Italics in original.]

In the first sentence an Idea is a unity of two functions, as I have called them. But in the second sentence Hegel does something new: he begins to view these as *temporal stages*, and this is not mirrored in Plato or anyone else before Hegel's time.

This takes us to Hegel's famous processual triplet: *thesis, antithesis, synthesis*. The double logic I described earlier leads to a strikingly coherent interpretation of this triplet: the thesis takes one function, the antithesis takes another function, and the synthesis takes these together. For example:

- THESIS: subject,
- ANTITHESIS: object,
- SYNTHESIS: subject & object.

If we compare this to Kant's antinomies, then the talk of theses and antitheses will of course sound familiar: these were for Kant the opposed sides in a dialectical dispute. However, with Hegel the synthesis is new. Thus from a Hegelian point of view Kant has no answers, only questions, for the double logic that is needed for complete answers is left missing.[1]

This is a major point in the history of dialectics. Kant said that dialectics are basically always only problems — without solutions. That is how he presented the antinomies. He never acknowledges the double logic of syntheses. (He never even brings it up.) Once Hegel comes along, he sees how the double logic of the synthesis is an exact match for the problems generated by theses and antitheses, and thus dialectic becomes something more competent and positive than it ever is in Kant.[2]

Hegel takes this rebellion quite far — indeed too far, as we will soon see.

His radicalism begins to show when we consider that for him an Idea *drives history*. (It is its dialectical pulse.) For history is the onward march of *Vernunft*.

For Hegel this means on one level that *entire periods or regions* may be one-sided altogether. Then further periods will come about which do just the reverse, and finally there will always be other places or times which

---

[1] As a much less relevant aside, Kant does use *the word 'synthetic'*, contrasting it with 'analytic', but this stands merely for non-logical relations. A synthetic a posteriori truth is only your ordinary empirical and contingent fact. A synthetic a priori truth is what is required for *Verstand* to operate, that is for empirical facts to attain intelligible structure. In general, the analytic and the synthetic are terms only in the first half of Kant's *Critique of Pure Reason* — the lower half, the half of *Verstand*, not of *Vernunft*.

[2] But as noted Hegel never sees that Plato has the double logic too.

succeed in living up to the whole Idea as a unity. For example, Hegel likes to say that in China there is an abundance of concrete thinking in daily affairs, whereas by contrast India is the very opposite of this, the land of dreams. Prussia or Germany supposedly is both: the land of precise organization but also of high culture and pure philosophy.

This is to favor *large* units, the macro over the micro. Entire civilizations are movers, and individuals usually live only as their little members. Thus most persons are made to seem passive and small, so for instance Chinese, Indian, and Prussian people do not each have their own little ideas, or if they do then those are not very significant in terms of the lives they lead in fact.

After World War II Hegel was often taken for an illiberal dogmatist by Anglo-American philosophers — a proto-fascist or totalitarian, an enemy, along with Plato and Marx –, but for decades this has no longer been in fashion. Despite this, Hegel's illiberal associations are in a sense clear: in his books most individual persons are small, and the grand isms always loom large in the background as the real forces. Instead of downplaying this, however, one may consider accepting it at least on some levels. For example, the dominance of large archetypes will be familiar to *movie* critics who can identify certain recurrent plot structures in different productions through the years. It is not outlandish to view *literature* in this way, for already the ancients outline the major types: what is a tragedy of comedy, how to write an epic, here is how you present the sublime, etc. (cf. Frye). Similarly, the catalogue of basic *political* constitutions is often said to remain changeless since ancient times (cf. Arent), and even the underlying *scientific* models of thought may be originally pre-Socratic (cf. Popper's "Back to the Presocratics" in his *Conjectures*).

What should sound shocking however is the idea that an Idea actually *does* any of this.

The first problem with this is that an Idea, being an atemporal archetype, should not at all move. How then can it do anything? In Plato, we saw, humans do things in the light of the Ideas. The utopias are not built *by* Ideas. Also, God shaped the cosmos in the light of the Ideas, in the myth of the *Timaeus*. The Ideas did nothing — they only stood there as final and formal causes. (They were never efficient causes.)

Why does Hegel not see this? It is his fashion to get carried away by bold analogies. Compare:

- GOD shapes the world in His own image in traditional myths (like the Bible's *Genesis* and Plato's *Timaeus*, but also elsewhere), just as
- THE HUMAN INDIVIDUAL finds himself (his 'voice') in the art he creates or else in a political or philosophical movement, and similarly
- AN IDEA differentiates itself from other things via theses, antitheses, and syntheses.

Thus the Idea — quite like God or the human personality — is made to seem like a self-realizing plan. It is first the hard and self-enclosed plan and then its total realization. (Hegel likes to compare seeds to fully grown plants.)

However, this cannot be quite right, not even internally to Hegel's viewpoint.[1] After all, an Idea is a standard *and* its instance, so it is a plan *and* the plan's implementation already! Hence the logic of the Ideas makes it natural to say that Ideas are perfect already in isolation — as Plato says. If God is like an Idea then He does not care about the world either. He is happy alone in heaven.

This concludes our brief survey of Hegel's general Idea idea.

Hegel's God

Hegel's philosophy of religion obeys the higher logic of the Ideas but in more colorful ways, for religion is *Vernunft* in ordinary life.

Hegel knows to appreciate everyday sentiments because he is aware that any official religion without authentically religious consciousness is like a hollow shell — a dead, robotic frame which no one likes or lives in (from *Lectures on the Philosophy of Religion*, Part A, III, 3).

> If the philosophical knowledge of religion is conceived of as something to be reached historically only, then we should have to regard the theologians who have brought it to this point as clerks in a mercantile house, who have only to keep an account of the wealth of strangers, who only act for others without obtaining any property for themselves. They do, indeed, receive salary, but their reward is only to serve, and to register that which is the property of others. Theology of this kind has no longer a place at all in the domain of thought; it

---

[1] Externally — i.e. without relying on Hegel's favorite premises — the point is as in the anti-Spinozist footnote above, due to both Plato and Kant.

has no longer to do with infinite thought in and for itself, but only with it as a finite fact, as opinion, ordinary thought, and so on. History occupies itself with truths which were truths namely, for others, not with such as would come to be the possession of those who are occupied with them. With the true content, with the knowledge of God, such theologians have no concern. They know as little of God as a blind man sees of a painting, even though he handles the frame.

Theorists of religion are like blind people dealing with paintings. Religious thought proper remains foreign to them, because for them the subjective side of things is missing (ibid.):

> the highest, the religious content shows itself in the spirit itself, that Spirit manifests itself in Spirit, and in fact this my spirit, that this faith has its source, its root is my deepest personal being, and that it is what is most peculiarly my own, and as such is inseparable from the consciousness of pure spirit. Inasmuch as this knowledge exists immediately in myself, all external authority, all foreign attestation is cast aside ; what is to be of value to me must have its verification in my own spirit, and in order that I may believe I must have the witness of my spirit.

The authentically religious personality has a private and personal certainty about his experience.

However, the Hegelian twist to this is that personal certainty must be supported by intrinsic knowledge about God — as God is quite alone –, so one's relations to God are not enough:

> In this sense it is stated, further, that we can only know our relation to God, not what God Himself is; and that it is only our relation to God which is embraced in what is generally called religion. Thus it happens that at the present time we only hear religion spoken of, and do not find that investigation is made regarding the nature of God, what He is in Himself, and how the Nature of God must be determined. God, as God, is not even made an object of thought; knowledge does not trench upon that object, and does not exhibit distinct attributes in Him, so as to make it possible that He Himself should be conceived of as constituting the relation of these attributes,

and as relation in Himself. God is not before us as an object of knowledge, but only our relation with God, our relation to Him; and while discussions of the nature of God have become fewer and fewer, it is now only required of a man that he should be religious, that he should abide by religion, and we are told that we are not to proceed further to get a know ledge of any divine content.

Hegel says it is in fashion in modern times to dwell on one's private feelings and to leave God out of the picture entirely, but this is not religion. (He probably means the sentimental Romanticism of Schleier-macher, his colleague and opponent in Berlin.)

But then who or what is God?

What is really contained in this position, and really consti-tutes its true kernel, is the philosophical Idea itself, only that this Idea is confined by immediate knowledge within limita-tions which are abolished by philosophy, and which are by it exhibited in their onesidedness and untruth. According to the philosophical conception, God is Spirit, is concrete; and if we inquire more closely what Spirit is, we find that the whole of religious doctrine consists in the development of the fundamental conception of Spirit. For the present, however, it may suffice to say that Spirit is essentially self-manifestation its nature is to be for Spirit. Spirit is for Spirit, and not, be it observed, only in an external, accidental manner. On the contrary, Spirit is only Spirit in so far as it is for Spirit; this constitutes the conception or notion of Spirit itself.

This should already sound familiar, for now Spirit (*Geist*) is being presented much like the Ideas above. Hegel states his lesson directly (*Lectures on the Philosophy of Religion*, Part I, Section A, 'Of God'):

For us who are already in possession of religion, what God is, is something we are familiar with a substantial truth which is present in our subjective consciousness. But scientifically considered, God is at first a general, abstract name, which as yet has not come to have any true value. For it is the Philosophy of Religion which is the unfolding, the apprehension of that which God is, and it is only by means of it that our philosophic knowledge of His nature is reached. God is this well known and familiar idea, an idea, however, which has not yet been scientifically developed, scientifically known.

Everyday consciousness of God is something different from a phil-osophical Idea, for it is only once folksy religion becomes thoroughly reflective that it turns into philosophy. The topic is the same however (ibid.):

> God is Spirit, the Absolute Spirit, the eternally undifferen-tiated Spirit, essentially at home with Himself; this ideality, this subjectivity of Spirit, which is, so to speak, transparency, pure ideality excluding all that is particular, is just the [...] pure relation to self, what is and remains absolutely at home with itself.

Like an Idea, God is a pure relation R to R — not a blank Thing or a simple quality like whiteness but a relation, and the relation is to the relation itself. The relation is pure and perfect because it satisfies its standard: its two functions correspond precisely with each other. Thus it has a 'home' in itself, in Hegel's figure. This is just as with the Ideas: it is perfect — up there, somewhere. (It is "shut up within itself", Hegel says.)

However, this is still to leave out one key aspect of the matter, one which Hegel seems rather to continually take for granted than to ever properly explain: for fundamentally Hegel's God is *not at all* a closed secret because he is more than anything the perfected dream of the thoughtful individual himself: "Reason is Thought conditioning itself with perfect freedom" (*Philosophy of History* § 17). This higher value is needed to confer value on life (*Philosophy of History*, Introduction):

> But from the fact that man is regarded as the Highest, it follows that he has no respect for himself; for only with the consciousness of a Higher Being does he reach a point of view which inspires him with real reverence. [...] Life has a value only when it has something valuable as its object [...].

The dialectical irony in this is that it is *we humans* who need God to rank above us. We need to hold Him up! (God does not need us, and he does not tell us any of these things.) This is probably best to picture as a kind of 'mirroring': if we are to see our lives as containing meaning and dignity then we need first to build a mirror which will make us look this way. But such a mirror is God — a God who values humans. If we had only humans with humans then this would not lead us to have any standards, and hence we would then run the risk of barbaric or animal relations. (Like in Plato's democracy things could shift in any possible direction.)

Hegel's Aesthetics

Perhaps surprisingly to modern readers, Hegel views art much as he views religion and philosophical Ideas, for he defines art as *spirituality which has been translated into empirical terms.*[1] In music one of course uses sound to do this, in paintings it is colors, and so on. Every time art is about communicating higher truths or higher realities (alternatively termed Gods or Ideas).

It is not far fetched to say that art is by definition empirical, but why is art spiritual? (How is serious art different from pretty ornaments?)

On one level this is due to its ancient origins, Hegel explains: "the artistic intuition as such, like the religious — or rather both together — [...] have begun in wonder." But this is not only a historical point. For religion and art are always born from a sense of distance:

> [...] wonder only occurs when man, torn free from his most immediate first connection with nature and from his most

---

[1] In his *Lectures on the Philosophy of Religion* (Part I, Section B, II, 2) Hegel says it thus:

> Art had its origin in the feeling of the absolute spiritual need that the Divine, the spiritual Idea, should exist as object for consciousness, and in the first place for perception in its immediate form. The law and content of art is Truth as it appears in mind or Spirit, and is therefore spiritual truth, but spiritual truth in such a form that it is at the same time sensuous truth, existing for perception in its simple form.

More exactly, art requires representational skills or techniques, but its message is spiritual:

> In what may be regarded as constituting the entire sphere of art, there may be other elements included than those which have just been alluded to. For truth has here a double meaning, and first of all that of accuracy, by which is meant, that the representation should be in conformity with the otherwise known object. [...] Here its law is not beauty. But in so far also as beauty is its law, art can be still taken as involving form, and have, moreover, a limited, well-defined content, as much as the literal truth itself. But this last in its true sense is correspondence of the object with its conception or notion, namely, the Idea. [...] The artist, then, has to present truth, so that the reality, in which the conception or notion has power, and in which it rules, is at the same time something sensuous. The Idea exists consequently in a sensuous form, and in an individualised shape, which cannot miss having the contingent character attaching to what is sensuous.

elementary, purely practical, relation to it, that of desire, stands back spiritually from nature and his own singularity and now seeks and sees in things a universal, implicit, and permanent element.

Like religion, art responds to the sense that we are not normal parts of his world, like animals among animals or things among things. If we felt at home there would be no religion or art.

But this asymmetry is sensed already by the earliest humans, Hegel supposes. For he finds that they strive to express themselves and to know themselves as spiritual, thinking beings — even if they have no language for this. They resort to empirical means — hence to art — because they have no language for stating their relations directly.[1]

Hegel often compares primitive humans to children. Like children they come to us with stories and questions, never with the law-like generalizations which must be stated by mature and reasoning adults. However, in a completely dialectical world we need both of these sides: questions and answers, children and adults, primitives and moderns. On Hegel's premises this means in effect that dialectical reasoning must be concerned also with the childhood of the human race and with art, for this is how we get the question-half of the equation.

The *growth process* is the next logical topic. What are the stages in which the human *Geist* evolves? How do questions turn into answers? On one level, one attains an overall impression of Hegel's examples from a series like this:

- primitives worship animal Gods in animistic religions (then God is identified with a particular animal or a plant, a river, a mountain, etc.),
- animal-human hybrids are symbolized in ancient Egypt (like the Sphinx: part animal, part human),
- anthropomorphism typifies ancient Greek art, where the Olympian or Homeric Gods are much like humans and the human form is studied in realistic sculptures, and still later
- Jesus is God born in the shape of man, and conversely there is something divine in humanity (according to Christian beliefs).

---

[1] This suggests that also in Hegel (like in Plato) the Ideas are innate. Cf. also *Encyclopedia* § 213: "When we hear the Idea spoken of, we need not imagine something far away beyond this mortal sphere. The Idea is rather what is completely present: and it is found, however confused and degenerated, in every consciousness."

However, of course Hegel cannot properly mean that an Idea has the exactly the shape of a human, with two eyes and a hat. Rather he thinks in more abstract patterns (the remaining quotations in this section are from his *Lectures on Fine Art*, Part I, Chapter 2):

> Regularity as such is in general sameness in something external and, more precisely, the same repetition of one and the same specific shape which affords the determining unity for the form of objects. [...] So, for example, among lines the straight line is the most regular, because it has only *one* direction, abstractly continually the same. Similarly, the cube is a completely regular figure. On all sides it has surfaces of the same size, equal lines and angles, which as right angles cannot be altered in size as obtuse or acute angles can.

> *Symmetry* hangs together with regularity; i.e. form cannot rest in that extreme abstraction of sameness of character. With sameness unlikeness is associated, and difference breaks in to interrupt empty identity. This is what brings symmetry in. Symmetry consists in this, that a form, abstractly the same, does not simply repeat itself, but is brought into connection with another form of the same kind which, considered by itself, is likewise determinate and self-same, but compared with the first one is unlike it. As a result of this connection, there must come into existence a new sameness and unity which is still further determinate and has a greater inner diversity. We have a sight of a symmetrical arrangement if, for instance, on one side of a house there are three windows of equal size and equidistant from one another, then there are added three or four higher than the first group with greater or lesser intervals between them, and then finally three higher once again, the same in size and distance as the first group. Therefore, mere uniformity and the repetition of one and the same determinate character does not constitute symmetry. Symmetry requires also difference in size, position, shape, colour, sounds, and other characteristics, but which then must be brought together again in a uniform way. Symmetry is provided only by the uniform connection of characteristics that are unlike one another. [...]

> In more detail, if we go briefly through the chief stages, minerals (crystals, for example) as inanimate productions have regularity and symmetry as their basic form. Their shape [...] is indeed immanent in them, and not determined by a

purely external influence; the form they acquire in accordance with their nature elaborates in secret activity their inner and outer structure. [...]

The plant, however, stands higher than the crystal. It has already developed to the beginning of an articulation and it consumes material in its continually active process of nourishment. But even the plant has not a really ensouled life, since, although it is organically articulated, its activity is always drawn out into externality. [...]

Finally, in the animal living organism there enters the essential difference of a double mode of the formation of the members. For in the animal body, especially at higher stages, the organism is, on the one hand, a self-related organism, more inner and self-enclosed, which, as it were, returns into itself like a sphere; on the other hand, it is an external organism, as an external process and a process against externality. (Italics in original.)

This describes a hierarchy from regularity to symmetry and then from minerals and crystals to plants and animals. The lowest type of structure, regularity, is merely repetitive, but symmetry is already more nuanced and analogical. Next, even minerals and crystals cause themselves to instance patterns, but with plants and animals the process of self-formation is more complex and systematic. Finally, it is at least vaguely intelligible that a positively free human individual, a *Geist*, a God, and ultimately an Idea can crown this series.

Another progression in Hegel runs from harmony to free subjectivity. First, harmony

consists, on the one hand, in the ensemble of essential elements, and, on the other hand, in the dissolution of their bare opposition, so that in this way their association and inner connection is manifested as their unity. In this sense we speak of harmony of shape, colours, notes, etc. [...] In them we have not just unlikenesses put together regularly into an external unity, as in symmetry, but direct opposites, like yellow and blue, and their neutralization and concrete identity. Now the beauty of their harmony consists in avoiding their sharp difference and opposition which as such is to be obliterated, so that in their differences their unison is manifested. For they belong together, since colour is not one-sided, but an essential

totality. The demand of such a totality can go so far, as Goethe
says, that even if the eye has before it only *one* colour as its
object, it nevertheless subjectively sees the others equally.
Among notes, the tonic, mediant, and dominant, e.g., are such
essential differences, which in their difference harmonize
unitedly into one whole. It is similarly the case with harmony
of [the human] figure, its position, rest, movement, etc. Here
no difference may come forward one-sidedly by itself, or
otherwise the harmony is disturbed.

But even harmony as such is not yet free ideal subjectivity and
soul. In the latter, unity is not just an association and an accord
but the positing of differences negatively, whereby alone their
ideal unity is established. To such ideality harmony cannot
attain. For example, every melody, although it has harmony as
its basis, has a higher and more free subjectivity in itself and
expresses that. Mere harmony does not in general manifest
either subjective animation as such or spirituality, although
it is the highest stage of abstract form and already approaches
free subjectivity.

Harmonies are projected systems, so that with Goethe's theory of
colors we 'see' more in things than they contain. For example, if we see
blue, we need to see orange too: we insist on finding the balance between
the opposites. (In experiments long after Goethe if persons constantly
wore red sunglasses for two weeks they did not see everything as red
anymore but if they then took off the red sunglasses everything looked
green.) In music, chords, melodies, and rhythms are of course systems of
intervals — distances between individual notes or beats. They too are
harmonies. However, free subjectivity leaps beyond such empirical givens
and individuates and differentiates itself actively from within, so it does
not merely project outward to colors and sounds, pretending passively
to find the systems that please it. For it is not merely perceptual. It is
Geist, it is agency. It is inward and abstract — again somewhat like an
Idea — thus Hegel. But this is already to state why art, being empirical,
will always have to be deficient. True, it can evolve, yes, but only to a
point. At its highpoint, art self-destructs and becomes something else.

One of Hegel's many famous teachings is that of the *end of art*. Art ends
with the realization that empirical means do not suffice for *Geist*, God,
or the Ideas. We need 'concepts': verbal structures, arguments, formulas.
People will still continue to produce works of art but the sense of alarm
they trigger is gone if we already have the mature, adult laws to explain

and justify things generally. Then we do need art any longer — and it becomes mere entertainment or ornamentation.

The final twist to Hegel's philosophy comes from his political philosophy — his view of the *state*.

Hegel's State

The first step now is to see why Hegel does not believe in the French Enlightenment myth of the noble savage:

> The first error that we encounter is the direct contradiction of our principle that the State is the realization of freedom: the view, namely, that man is free by nature but that in society and in the state, to which he necessarily belongs, he must limit this natural freedom. That man is free "by nature" is quite correct in the sense that he is free according to the very concept of man, that is, in his *destination* only, as he is, in himself; the "nature" of a thing is indeed tantamount to its concept. But the view in question also introduces into the concept of man his immediate and natural way of *existence*. In this sense a state of nature is assumed in which man is imagined in the possession of his natural rights and the unlimited exercise and enjoyment of his freedom. This assumption is not presented as a historical fact; it would indeed be difficult, were the attempt seriously made, to detect any such condition anywhere, either in the present or the past. Primitive conditions can indeed be found, but they are marked by brute passions and acts of violence. Crude as they are, they are at the same time connected with social institutions which, to use the common expression, restrain freedom. The assumption (of the noble savage) is one of those nebulous images which theory produces, an idea which necessarily flows from that theory and to which it ascribes real existence without sufficient historical justification.

> Such a state of nature is in theory exactly as we find it in practice. Freedom as the *ideal* of the original state of nature does not *exist* as original and natural. It must first be acquired and won; and that is possible only through an infinite process of the discipline of knowledge and will power. The state of nature, therefore, is rather the state of injustice, violence, untamed natural impulses, of inhuman deeds and emotions. (Italics in original.)

The natural setting of humans is not free but brutish. Properly freedom begins only in an organized and civilized entity:

> The idea of freedom necessarily implies law and morality. These are in and for themselves universal essences, objects, and aims, to be discovered only by the activity of thought, emancipating itself from, and developing itself in opposition to, the merely sensuous [...].

We are free not as sensual animals but as moral and thinking beings. Our freedom is spiritual — it is in our *Geist*. An object has a mass, and it obeys the laws of gravity, Hegel writes, but a *Geist* has freedom and it obeys higher laws, the laws of *Vernunft*. As above, we instance this in religion or art to the extent that we have not yet learned to do it properly in philosophy. But animals do not philosophize. They instance no higher thinking. And where are their Gods and artworks? Where are their priorities or first principles? They show no interest in such things, and rather they are enslaved by their low impulses for food etc. But that is not freedom — rather it is slavery to the body. Though it is of course nice to be nice to animals, it is only a misunderstanding to say that as animals we are free. This is a difference in kind.

But now, what of the state? How does the state participate in the liberation of human beings?

One of Hegel's statements is that religion and art and philosophy amount to only the *subjective* or inner, spiritual side of free life, whereas the *objective* or outer conditions are supplied by state institutions.

> We have established as the two points of our discussion, first, the idea of Freedom as absolute final aim, and, secondly, the means of its realization, the subjective side of knowledge and volition with their vitality, mobility, and activity. We then discussed the State as the moral whole and the reality of freedom, and thus as the objective unity of the two preceding factors. Although for analysis we separated the two elements, it must be well remembered that they are closely connected and that this connection is within each of them when we examine them singly. On the one hand we recognized the Idea in its determination, as self-knowing and self-willing freedom which has only itself as its aim. As such, it is at the same time the simple idea of reason and likewise that which we have called subject, the consciousness of self, the Spirit existing in

the world. On the other hand, in considering this subjectivity, we find that subjective knowing and willing are Thinking. But in thoughtful knowing and willing I will the universal object, the substance of actualized rationality (of what is in and for itself rational). We thus observe a union which is in itself, between the objective element, the concept, and the subjective element. The objective existence of this unity is the State. The State, thus, is the foundation and center of the other concrete aspects of national life, of art, law, morality, religion, science. All spiritual activity, then, has the aim of becoming conscious of this union, that is, of its freedom.

Hegel may mean (with his talk of 'foundations') that if the right objective social institutions are not in place then philosophy and art cannot operate. But would this be true? Is there philosophy only if there are universities first? Do we have art only if there are museums and galleries? To have religion do you need to have church? No, no, no. This is all too easy to argue given that the archetypal names in ancient Greece predate Plato's Academy, that Jesus and the Buddha too must come earlier than all the schools that claim to follow them, that so many great names even oppose all institutions they can find, declining even to write things down (thus Socrates, Jesus, Buddha). And of course countless artistic movements begin and bloom without any institutional support at all. (Incidentally, this is a very Berlin thing to say — two centuries after Hegel it has turned upside down in this way!)

What adds to the puzzle is that Hegel is not unfamiliar with the heroic independence of many philosophical personalities. This is from the Introduction to Hegel's *Lectures on the History of Philosophy*:

> What the history of Philosophy shows us is a succession of noble minds, a gallery of heroes of thought, who, by the power of Reason, have penetrated into the being of things, of nature and of spirit, into the Being of God, and have won for us by their labours the highest treasure, the treasure of reasoned knowledge. [...]

> There is an old tradition that it is the faculty of thought which separates men from beasts; and to this tradition we shall adhere. In accordance with this, what man has, as being nobler than a beast, he has through thinking. Everything which is human, however it may appear, is so only because the thought contained in it works and has worked. But thought,

although it is thus the essential, substantial, and effectual, has many other elements. We must, however, consider it best when Thought does not pursue anything else, but is occupied only with itself — with what is noblest — when it has sought and found itself. The history which we have before us is the history of Thought finding itself, and it is the case with Thought that it only finds itself in producing itself; indeed, that it only exists and is actual in finding itself. These productions are the philosophic systems; and the series of discoveries on which Thought sets out in order to discover itself, forms a work which has lasted twenty-five hundred years.

We may put this as a counterfactual: *if* the philosophies (and the religions and the arts) did *not* evolve independently, that is, if they were *not* self-movers capable of new insights and innovations unaided, and if they did *not* fight their way against hostile material and social environments, then where would be their heroism or nobility? If a philosopher (or an artist or a believer or a saint) is only someone who gets paid by the state then there are no real or authentic philosophers (or artists etc.) in any fully respectable or autonomous sense at all.

Hegel seems to know this. None the less, he is also positioned at the pinnacle of academic power at Berlin's state-owned university (where he is rector from 1829) and this imposes its duties. A little earlier he says this about his German nationality in his inaugural address at Heidelberg university in 1816:

> Philosophy, excepting in name, has sunk even from memory, and [...] it is in the German nation that it has been retained as a peculiar possession. We have received the higher call of Nature to be the conservers of this holy flame [...]. We have already got so far, and have attained to a seriousness so much greater and a consciousness so much deeper, that for us ideas and that which our reason justifies, can alone have weight; to speak more plainly, the Prussian State is a State constituted on principles of intelligence.

It is true that the German Idealists make advances in philosophy which are in some ways comparable to the ancient Greeks, but Hegel is wrong to suggest that this has to do with the Prussian (or 'German') state or nation. They are dynamic and progressive, it is stagnant and traditional. It is closed, but they are open to the future. Hence they are not the same: here there is no organic whole no matter what dialectical tricks Hegel might try.

Hence we face an either/or: dialectical philosophizing may be combined with religion and with aesthetics or art, and also quite obviously with ethics, morality, and the psyche (or *Geist*), but the state is something else. Hegel's dialectic of a totalized both/and is an error in the end.[1]

We may reach a similar conclusion by comparing Hegel's historical narrative about modern times since the Renaissance. The story Hegel

---

[1] A different line of argument would be to premise not so much on Hegel's view of the state but rather on the things he says about *organic social patterns*.

The famous *master-slave dialectic* is popular among some schools especially in twentieth century France and Germany but also among current scholars in the USA. (In France Kojeve popularizes the master-slave dialectic in 1934. The current American Hegelians — like Pippin, Pinkard, and Brandom — seem to see the master-slave dialectic as Hegel's very center. As noted they do not discuss Ideas, Gods, or dialectics, and their 'Hegel' is by and large democratic and pragmatic, much like Dewey's and Rorty's before them.) It is presented in Hegel's early work, the *Phenomenology of Spirit*:

Self-consciousness exists in itself and for itself, in that, and by the fact that it exists for another self-consciousness; that is to say, it is only by being acknowledged or "recognized". (From § 178.)
Self-consciousness has before it another self-consciousness; it has come outside itself. This has a double significance. First it has lost its own self, since it finds itself as an **other** being; secondly, it has thereby sublated that other, for it does not regard the other as essentially real, but sees its own self in the other. (This is § 179.)
But this action on the part of the one has itself the double significance of being at once its own action and the action of that other as well. For the other is likewise independent, shut up within itself, and there is nothing in it which is not there through itself. The first does not have the object before it only in the passive form characteristic primarily of the object of desire, but as an object existing independently for itself, over which therefore it has no power to do anything for its own behalf, if that object does not per se do what the first does to it. The process then is absolutely the double process of both self-consciousnesses. Each sees the other do the same as itself; each itself does what it demands on the part of the other, and for that reason does what it does, only so far as the other does the same. Action from one side only would be useless, because what is to happen can only be brought about by means of both. (From § 182.)
Each is the mediating term to the other, through which each mediates and unites itself with itself; and each is to itself and to the other an immediate self-existing reality, which, at the same time, exists thus for itself only through this mediation. They recognize themselves as mutually recognizing one another. (From § 184.)
The reader grasps what Hegel wishes to say: there is never self-consciousness in isolation, but only in interaction with someone else. But in such interactions one needs to see oneself in the other, and this leads to reciprocal recognition. Even the slave-owner or 'master' (*Herr*) must find his own reflection in his slave (*Knecht*), and the slave must actively participate in the relationship (§§ 178-193).

The *status* of Hegel's assertions in these passages is a little puzzling, however. Social reciprocation may be ethical in some versions of the Golden Rule, but it is hardly clear that there is no self-consciousness without it. (Perhaps there is, perhaps not.) Hence, fascinating though Hegel's expressions are, I will leave them aside here.

wishes to tell (in his *Philosophy of History*, Chapter III, 'The Éclaircissement and Revolution') is one in which the human spirit learns gradually to identify with its earthly conditions in modern history. In abstract terms his lesson would be this:

> But in Thought, Self moves within the limits of its own sphere; that with which it is occupied — its objects are as absolutely present to it [as they were distinct and separate in the intellectual grade above mentioned]; for in thinking I must elevate the object to Universality. This is utter and absolute Freedom, for the pure Ego, like pure Light, is with itself alone [is not involved with any alien principle]; thus that which is diverse from itself, sensuous or spiritual, no longer presents an object of dread, for in contemplating such diversity it is inwardly free and can freely confront it. [...] — Consequently, the *ne plus ultra* of Inwardness, of Subjectiveness, is Thought. Man is not free, when he is not thinking [...].

Much as in Kant, we are thinking beings who assign laws to empirical phenomena. In thus reasoning about events we are free beings, for this is how we come to our own.

In natural science the meaning of this would be as follows (ibid.):

> It seemed to men as if God had but just created the moon and stars, plants and animals, as if the laws of the universe were now established for the first time; for only then did they feel a real interest in the universe, when they recognized their own Reason in the Reason which pervades it. The human eye became *clear*, perception quick, thought active and interpretative. The discovery of the laws of Nature enabled men to contend against the monstrous superstition of the time, as also against all notions of mighty alien powers which magic alone could conquer. [...] Thus all miracles were disallowed: for Nature is a system of known and recognized Laws; Man is at home in it, and that only passes for truth in which he finds himself at home; he is free through the acquaintance he has gained with Nature.

It is as if humans woke up with the discoveries and innovations of Renaissance science! No more childish dreams and miracles, and no more baseless authorities, but reasoned intelligence everywhere — finally! The moon, the stars, seasons, the tides, etc. would all make sense. This would be Hegel's earthly paradise for the reasoning mind.

His political narrative is analogical to the above scientific narrative, so there is a double emancipation (ibid.):

> Nor was thought less vigorously directed to the Spiritual side of things: Right and [Social] Morality came to be looked upon as having their foundation in the actual present Will of man, whereas formerly it was referred only to the command of God enjoined *ab extra*, written in the Old and New Testament, or appearing in the form of particular Right [as opposed to that based on general principles] in old parchments, as *privilegia*, or in international compacts. [...]

> These general conceptions, deduced from actual and present consciousness — the Laws of Nature and the substance of what is right and good, have received the name of *Reason*. The recognition of the validity of these laws was designated by the term *Éclaircissement* (*Aufklärung*). From France it passed over into Germany, and created a new world of ideas. The absolute criterion — taking the place of all authority based on religious belief and positive laws of Right (especially political Right) — is the verdict passed by Spirit itself on the character of that which is to be believed or obeyed.

Even ordinary people come to realize that all they have to obey is their own selves — their own larger selves, that is, for the key is to realize that freedom always requires the realization of concrete rights and duties (ibid.):

> This formally absolute principle brings us to *the last stage in History, our world, our own time.*

> Secular life is the positive and definite embodiment of the Spiritual Kingdom — the Kingdom of the *Will* manifesting itself in outward existence. Mere impulses are also forms in which the inner life realizes itself; but these are transient and disconnected; they are the ever-changing applications of volition. But that which is just and moral belongs to the essential, independent, intrinsically universal Will; and if we would know what Right really is, we must abstract from inclination, impulse and desire as the particular; *i.e.*, we must know what the Will is in itself. [...] What the Will is in itself can be

known only when these specific and contradictory forms of volition have been eliminated. Then Will appears as Will, in its abstract essence. The Will is Free only when it does not will anything alien, extrinsic, foreign to itself (for as long as it does so, it is dependent), but wills itself alone — wills the Will. This is absolute Will — the volition to be free. Will making itself its own object is the basis of all Right and Obligation — consequently of all statutory determinations of Right, categorical imperatives, and enjoined obligations. The Freedom of the Will *per se,* is the principle and substantial basis of all Right — is itself absolute, inherently eternal Right, and the Supreme Right in comparison with other specific Rights; nay, it is even that by which Man becomes Man, and is therefore the fundamental principle of Spirit. But the next question is: How does Will assume a definite form? For in willing itself, it is nothing but an identical reference to itself; but, in point of fact, it wills something specific: there *are,* we know, distinct and special Duties and Rights. (Italics in original.)

However, Hegel's knotty phrases do not cover up the elementary disparacy which I have alluded to above. For just as modern natural science since the Renaissance has been increasingly mechanical, modern politics is in fact closer to *Verstand* than it is to *Vernunft.* Modern natural science has done well to sidestep dialectical reasoning and Gods, because in this way it has flourished in its own direction. Prediction and control are actually managed in many areas, and this conquest will of course continue to the future. But similarly, the modern state with its institutions is not primarily about serving any higher purposes, and this too is just as well. For in its particular arena it too has been a success story since the French Revolution! Yet the liberal state is unquestionably about protecting negative liberties — about confining greedy animals, as it were - and not about positive liberties or Ideas etc. A French parallel illustrates the point well: in Paris' Pantheon a large mosaic depicts Jesus with the angel of France standing at its center. One marvels: France? Who would bow to that? Of course nationalists quite like advertizers will produce these kinds of exaggerations about 'national' meanings, and they are clearly needed if anyone is to sacrifice his life for his country on the battle front — but Hegel is a rare philosopher to take them seriously. The cost of this is high, for Hegel inspires nationalists throughout Europe in the nineteenth century, thereby certainly contributing to the polarizations that lead to the World Wars.

Marxist Materialism

Hegel dies in 1831, leaving Berlin, Germany, and much of Europe ablaze with his ideas. The question of questions then is how to appropriate him. His Leftist or Young Hegelian followers interpret dialectics as a critical tool, not as stamp of approval for whatever may happen to be the status quo, which is the Old or Right Hegelian view of their opponents. The major Left Hegelians often cited include the Bible critic David Strauss, the atheistic materialist Ludwig Feuerbach, the moral radical Bruno Bauer, and the individualist-anarchist Max Stirner, but the greatest name by all accounts has of course been Karl Marx.

Marx studies philosophy under Hegel in Berlin along with hundreds of others, but his bombastic radicalism is fairly conventional until he begins to appropriate more of the new doctrines from further in the West, notably French utopianism and British economics. Within a few years he has the maturity to state original and systematic positions such as these from his *German Ideology* (1846, co-authored with his friend Friedrich Engels, like most of his works):

> In direct contrast to German philosophy which descends from heaven to earth, here we ascend from earth to heaven. That is to say, we do not set out from what men say, imagine, conceive, nor from men as narrated, thought of, imagined, conceived, in order to arrive at men in the flesh. We set out from real, active men, and on the basis of their real life-process we demonstrate the development of the ideological reflexes and echoes of this life-process. The phantoms formed in the human brain are also, necessarily, sublimates of their material life-process, which is empirically verifiable and bound to material premises. Morality, religion, metaphysics, all the rest of ideology and their corresponding forms of consciousness, thus no longer retain the semblance of independence. They have no history, no development; but men, developing their material production and their material intercourse, alter, along with this their real existence, their thinking and the products of their thinking. Life is not determined by consciousness, but consciousness by life. In the first method of approach the starting-point is consciousness taken as the living individual; in the second method, which conforms to real life, it is the real living individuals themselves, and consciousness is considered solely as their consciousness.

History is divided into two levels:

- an economic *basis* (*Basis*), which determines
- a *cultural superstructure* (*Überbau*).

Idealists like Hegel merely pretend that the cultural level of Ideas and principles rules in the material domain, but the true situation is the reverse. Thus Hegel is turned upside down, or really right side up, as Marx puts it in a famous afterword to *Capital*.

Marx never claims that the materialistic method of inquiry is morally neutral. On the contrary, it has very clear moral bearings. But reality itself is like this, so all this about facts being distinct from values is not for Marx (in the manner of Kant!). Rather, the world of facts is and remains purely factual — but it generates its own values from within (ibid.):

> The premises from which we begin are not arbitrary ones, not dogmas, but real premises from which abstraction can only be made in the imagination. They are the real individuals, their activity and the material conditions under which they live, both those which they find already existing and those produced by their activity. These premises can thus be verified in a purely empirical way.

> The first premise of all human history is, of course, the exis-tence of living human individuals. Thus the first fact to be established is the physical organisation of these individuals and their consequent relation to the rest of nature. Of course, we cannot here go either into the actual physical nature of man, or into the natural conditions in which man finds himself — geological, hydrographical, climatic and so on. The writing of history must always set out from these natural bases and their modification in the course of history through the action of men.

> Men can be distinguished from animals by consciousness, by religion or anything else you like. They themselves begin to distinguish themselves from animals as soon as they begin to produce their means of subsistence, a step which is condi-tioned by their physical organisation. By producing their means of subsistence men are indirectly producing their actual material life.

Real, living individuals do not distinguish themselves from animals or from natural conditions in consciousness or Ideas — for they do not typically philosophize. Rather, the tool-making animal operates in concrete practice. We are not thinkers but workers, Marx means. We labor under certain conditions, each of us. Some things are given, and out of these we make what we can.

But this is to say that though we are material we are also creative beings. We are inventive animals: we do not only seek food or survival, for we also invent tools. Indeed we go so far as to invent art and religions and philosophies! The irony in human history is always, Marx says, that we tend to believe in our creations. We create God, so God does not create us, and nonetheless we bow down before Him. Similarly, *we actively hold up* the economy which presses us down. It is not neutral. It is not just there like the sun or the seas. It is all only a human creation: we live in a man-made world, though it is material. We as makers are also only material! This is not an entirely easy equation!

But let us move on. The next step is to see that the — material and creative! — practices vary by historical period because the tools forged and used in labor are different in each: "The hand-mill *gives* you society with the feudal lord; the steam-mill society with the industrial capitalist" (Marx in *The Poverty of Philosophy*). In the feudal period it is fitting to think in terms of landed aristocracies and chivalric virtues, but in capitalism both the aristocratic class and its values fall out of fashion — ultimately because the productive technology is different. (Ariosto and Cervantes are correct to mock medieval chivalry in the new world! Hegel realizes this clearly but he has no notion of the driving material forces which Marx exposes.) Now the motor of history of the human world is in the hands of the capitalist class, which takes power from the blue-bloods and the Church officially in the French Revolution. Technological innovation goes hyper in the competitive market conditions, and this should ultimately lead to the liberation of the human species as a whole, Marx writes (this is again from *The German Ideology*):

> We shall, of course, not take the trouble to enlighten our wise philosophers by explaining to them that the "liberation" of man is not advanced a single step by reducing philosophy, theology, substance and all the trash to "self-consciousness" and by liberating man from the domination of these phrases, which have never held him in thrall. Nor will we explain to them that it is only possible to achieve real liberation in the real world and by employing real means, that slavery

cannot be abolished without the steam-engine and the mule and spinning-jenny, serfdom cannot be abolished without improved agriculture, and that, in general, people cannot be liberated as long as they are unable to obtain food and drink, housing and clothing in adequate quality and quantity. "Liberation" is an historical and not a mental act, and it is brought about by historical conditions, the development of industry, commerce, agriculture, the conditions of intercourse [...].

Real liberation is material, not spiritual. Hence idealists like Hegel exist in a fictional world:

In Germany, a country where only a trivial historical development is taking place, these mental developments, these glorified and ineffective trivialities, naturally serve as a substitute for the lack of historical development, and they take root and have to be combated.

The grandiose rhetoric only thinly conceals the inferior reality.

Marxist Praxis

Marx's views on the basis side are extensive and systematic, but not so his views on the side of the superstructure (*Überbau*). The large lower half takes up more than 99 per cent of his writing but the tiny top half gets less than one per cent. I will now make only a few generalizations about the top half.

Marx's works are rife with Biblical-sounding pronouncements, many of them too famous to bear repetition. To get their general tone, *Eye for eye* seems to be echoed for example here: "The expropriators are expropriated" (from *Capital*). Similarly: "The weapons with which the bourgeoisie felled feudalism to the ground are now turned against the bourgeoisie itself" (*Communist Manifesto*). There is something circular about the historical events thus described, and such circles have Marx's stamp of approval. Things should close in upon themselves. (This kind of thing is entirely absent from the classical British economists from whom Marx learns so much. They do social science scientifically, so they observe what happens and try to formulate larger laws. They do not try to state how things would occur justly or symmetrically, but Marx always comes back to this.)

If we turn this same value around then it becomes a critical tool: "Landlords' right has its origin in robbery. The landlords, like all other men, love to reap where they never sowed, and demand a rent even for the natural produce of the earth" (*Paris Manuscripts*). Marx documents in detail how English aristocrats do not come by their property by fair methods: they do not reap what they sow (another Biblical figure of course). Rather, they *steal* the common lands, and then they demand rent — i.e. for what is not rightfully theirs in the first place. Thus the land-owning aristocrats are thieves!

Notice that in using *patterns* like these Marx does not need any idealistic rhetoric abut God, *Geists*, or Ideas: he can take a feudal practice and use it against itself for example.[1] For no keyword is dialectical, nor any literary style. It is pure syntax — as reasoned patterns always need to be.

Is this the heart of Marx's *dialectic*? I am personally not entirely sure how to assess this, so it is safer to say that it is one level of it. In other places Marx also uses higher level relations and reciprocal relations, such as: "The materialist doctrine concerning the changing of circumstances and upbringing forgets that circumstances are changed by men and that it is essential to educate the educator himself" (*Theses on Feuerbach*). Thus educators are to be educated, but also: we are made by our circumstances and we make our circumstances, so the effects go both ways. A further trick especially in his *Paris Manuscripts* is to shift subject and object positions in expressions, like here: "The weapon of criticism cannot, of course, replace criticism by weapons, material force must be overthrown by material force; but theory also becomes a material force as soon as it has gripped the masses" (*Paris Manuscripts*). Here force and criticism shift roles, but they are not equals and criticism must first materialize by becoming popular socially. Marx's different pronouncements are often dense and knotty, and there is no passage or document in which all these different threads are pulled together in his corpus.[2]

However, it is gratifying to report that we also find larger panoramas, like the following — which includes premises of the historical antinomy discussed in this chapter (this is from "Critique of Hegel's Philosophy in General" in the *Paris Manuscripts*):

---

[1] However, in this rare passage (from the *Paris Manuscripts*) Marx adopts Kant's language: *The criticism of religion ends with the teaching that* man is the highest essence for man — *hence, with the* categoric imperative to overthrow all relations *in which man is a debased, enslaved, abandoned [...].* (Italics in original.) Based on this Marx is exceptionally easy to interpret, but there is also the illusory impression that Marx is only a kind of liberal — only after the elimination of material obstacles and for not any dialectical symmetries.

[2] There are famous passages in which Marx says seemingly representative things about dialectics, e.g., that his dialectic is Hegel's turned upside down (or right side up, in *Capital*), However, this is not to systematize the structures.

The outstanding achievement of Hegel's *Phänomenologie* and of its final outcome, the dialectic of negativity as the moving and generating principle, is thus first that Hegel conceives the self-creation of man as a process, conceives objectification as loss of the object, as alienation and as transcendence of this alienation; that he thus grasps the essence of *labour* and comprehends objective man — true, because real man — as the outcome of man's own labour. The *real, active* orientation of man to himself as a species-being, or his manifestation as a real species-being (i.e., as a human being), is only possible if he really brings out all his *species-powers* — something which in turn is only possible through the cooperative action of all of mankind, only as the result of history — and treats these powers as objects: and this, to begin with, is again only possible in the form of estrangement. (Italics in original.)

In this passage, self-creation (*Selbsterzeugung*) may at first seem like aRa if a = self and R = CREATES, but in fact Marx means that it is labor in the abstract which evolves thus, and not merely any individual laborer. Hence it is the creative relation itself that gets created (as in RR). That said, the creative relation is here presented as the motor of history, not as its outcome, so things are not quite as one would expect based on Plato or Aristotle. (It is a means to means, not an end of ends.)

Marx's organic ideal for the outcome of human history is perhaps most fully expressed here (from "Money" in the *Paris Manuscripts*):

He who can buy bravery is brave, though he be a coward. As money is not exchanged for any one specific quality, for any one specific thing, or for any particular human essential power, but for the entire objective world of man and nature, from the standpoint of its possessor it therefore serves to exchange every quality for every other, even contradictory, quality and object: it is the fraternisation of impossibilities. It makes contradictions embrace. Assume *man* to be *man* and his relationship to the world to be a human one: then you can exchange love only for love, trust for trust, etc. If you want to enjoy art, you must be an artistically cultivated person; if you want to exercise influence over other people, you must be a person with a stimulating and encouraging effect on other people. Every one of your relations to man and to nature must be a *specific expression*, corresponding to the object of your will, of your *real individual* life. If you love without evoking love in

return — that is, if your loving as loving does not produce
reciprocal love; if through a *living expression* of yourself as a
loving person you do not make yourself a *beloved one*, then your
love is impotent — a misfortune. (Italics in original)

If this is the center of Marx's dialectical philosophy, then the final
realization of human potentials will come in organic relationships,
symmetric (as in love or art) or asymmetric (as in leadership). However,
as this passage makes clear, the tyranny of money must first become a
thing of the past.

Marx's Aftermath

Things do not turn out as Marx predicts. Highly developed Western
societies never undergo revolutionary periods in the way that Marx says
(only more backward places do), and though leisure time per worker
is greatly increased and the physical working conditions for Western
workers are so markedly improved (not least by Marx-inspired reformers,
especially the Kautskyan–Bernsteinian social democratic parties which
create the welfare state, cf. Sassoon) this does not in general lead to a new
dawn of higher culture which Marx's materialistic premises would seem
to entail. Instead, American popular culture experiences an amazing
boost through new technologies in unforeseen areas like the radio and
movie cinemas, and later the television and the internet. (Frankfurt
School authors call this a 'culture industry'.) In this way materialism
takes a kind of cultural turn: it is no longer about steel factories and war
machines or bread and school and medicine but something much softer
or more optional, like consumer friendly advertizers and service robots.
This goes beyond Marx.

APPENDIX A. QUOTATIONS FROM THOREAU'S WALDEN

Quotation 1:

John Farmer sat at his door one September evening, after a hard day's work, his mind still running on his labor more or less. Having bathed, he sat down to re-create his intellectual man. It was a rather cool evening, and some of his neighbors were apprehending a frost. He had not attended to the train of his thoughts long when he heard some one playing on a flute, and that sound harmonized with his mood. Still he thought of his work; but the burden of his thought was, that though this kept running in his head, and he found himself planning and contriving it against his will, yet it concerned him very little. It was no more than the scurf of his skin, which was constantly shuffled off. But the notes of the flute came home to his ears out of a different sphere from that he worked in, and suggested work for certain faculties which slumbered in him. They gently did away with the street, and the village, and the state in which he lived. A voice said to him,—Why do you stay here and live this mean moiling life, when a glorious existence is possible for you? Those same stars twinkle over other fields than these.—But how to come out of this condition and actually migrate thither? All that he could think of was to practise some new austerity, to let his mind descend into his body and redeem it, and treat himself with ever increasing respect.

Quotation 2:

Our inventions are wont to be pretty toys, which distract our attention from serious things. They are but improved means to an unimproved end, an end which it was already but too easy to arrive at; as railroads lead to Boston or New York. We are in great haste to construct a magnetic telegraph from Maine to Texas; but Maine and Texas, it may be, have nothing important to communicate. Either is in such a predicament as the man who was earnest to be introduced to a distinguished deaf woman, but when he was presented, and one end of her ear trumpet was put into his hand, had nothing to say. As if the main object were to talk fast and not to talk sensibly. We are eager to tunnel under the Atlantic and bring the old world some weeks nearer to the new; but perchance the first news that will leak through into the broad, flapping American ear will be that the Princess Adelaide has the whooping cough.

Appendix B. Quotations From Kierkegaard's Either/Or

Quotation 1:

> A fire broke out backstage in a theater. The clown came out to
> warn the public; they thought it was a joke and applauded. He
> repeated it; the acclaim was even greater. I think that's just how
> the world will come to an end: to general applause from wits who
> believe it's a joke.

Quotation 2:

> ... while everyone wants to rule, no one wants the responsibility. It is
> still fresh in our memory that a French statesman, on being offered
> a portfolio for a second time, declared that he would accept on
> the condition that the secretary of state be made responsible. The
> King of France, we know, has no responsibility, while his minister
> has; the minister does not want to be responsible but wants to
> be minister provided the secretary of state becomes responsible.
> Naturally, the end result is that the watchmen or street wardens
> become responsible. What a subject for Aristophanes, this upside-
> down tale of responsibility!

Quotation 3:

One is tired of living in the country, one moves to the city; one is tired of one's native land, one travels abroad; one is *europamüde* [tired of Europe], one goes to America, and so on; finally one indulges in an endless travel from star to star. Or the movement is different but still in extension. One is tired of dining off porcelain, one dines off silver; one tires of that, one dines off gold; one burns half of Rome to get an idea of the conflagration at Troy.

Quotation 4:

Ask any question you will, just don't ask me for reasons. A young girl is excused for not being able to give reasons, they say she lives in her feelings. It is different with me. Generally, I have so many and usually mutually contradictory reasons that, for that reason, it is impossible to give reasons.

Appendix C. Quotations From Heine's History Essay[1]

Quotation 1:

> On the one hand, we do not wish to be inspired uselessly and stake the best we possess on a futile past. On the other hand, we also demand that the living present be valued as it deserves, and not merely serve as a means to some distant end. As a matter of fact, we consider ourselves more important than merely means to an end. We believe that means and ends are only conventional concepts, which brooding man has read into nature and history, and of which the Creator knows nothing. For every creation is self-purposed, and every event is self-conditioned, and everything — the whole world itself — is here, in its own right.

Quotation 2:

> Life is neither means nor end. Life is a right. Life desires to validate its right against the claims of petrifying death, against the past. This justification of life is Revolution. The elegaic indifference of historians and poets must not paralyze our energies when we are engaged in this enterprise. Nor must the romantic visions of those

---

[1] This was written in the early 1830s and published in 1869 as "Verschiedenartige Geschichtsauffassung".

who promise us happiness in the future seduce us into sacrificing the interests of the present, the immediate struggle for the rights of man, the right of life itself.

BIBLIOGRAPHY

Aristotle. *The Works of Aristotle*, 2 Vols., transl. W.D. Ross. London: Britannica, 1952.

Arndt, Andreas. *Dialektik und Reflexion*. Zur Rekonstruktion des Vernunftbegriffs. Hamburg: Meiner, 1994.

Ayer, A. J. *Language, Truth, and Logic*. New York: Dover, 1952.

Ayer, A. J., ed. *Logical Positivism*. New York: Free Press, 1959.

Barnes, Jonathan. "Imperial Plato". *Apeiron: A Journal for Ancient Philosophy and Science*, Vol. 26, No. 2 (June 1993), pp. 129-151.

Barnes, Jonathan. *The Pre-Socratic Philosophers*. London: Routledge, 1983.

Beiser, Frederick C. *German Idealism:* The Struggle against Subjectivism. Cambridge, Mass.: Harvard University Press, 2002.

Benson, Hugh, ed. *A Companion to Plato*. Oxford: Wiley-Blackwell, 2008.

Berlin, Isaiah. *Four Essays on Liberty*. Oxford: Oxford University Press, 1969.

Berlin, Isaiah. "Two Concepts of Liberty", in *Four Essays on Liberty*, pp. 118-172.

Beversluis, John. *Cross-Examining Socrates:* A Defense of the Interlocutors in Plato's Early Dialogues. Cambridge: Cambridge University Press, 2000.

Bhaskar, Roy. *Dialectic:* The Pulse of Freedom. London: Routledge, 2008.

Bobonich, Christopher. *Plato's Utopia Recast:* His Later Ethics and Politics. Oxford: Oxford University Press, 2002.

Bostock, David. *Plato's Phaedo*. Oxford: Oxford University Press, 1986.

Brandom, Robert. *A Spirit of Trust:* A Reading of Hegel's *Phenomenology.* Cambridge, Mass.: Harvard University Press, 2019.

Buck-Morss, Susan. *The Origin of Negative Dialectics:* Theodor W. Adorno, Walter Benjamin, and the Frankfurt Institute. New York: Free Press, 1977.

Camus, Albert. *The Myth of Sisyphus and Other Essays.* London: Vintage, 1991.

Carnap, Rudolf. "The Old and the New Logic," reprinted in A. J. Ayer (ed.), pp. 133–146.

Edgerton, Franklin. *The Beginnings of Indian Philosophy.* London: George Allen and Unwin, 1965.

Feibleman, James K. *Religious Platonism:* The Influence of Religion on Plato and the Influence of Plato on Religion. London: Routledge, 2013.

Fine, Gail, ed. *Plato,* 2 Vols. Oxford: Oxford University Press, 2000.

Frege, Gottlob. "On Sense and Reference," transl. M. Black in Translations from the Philosophical Writings of Gottlob Frege, P. Geach and M. Black, eds. and transl., pp. 25-50.

Friedländer, Paul. *Platon,* 3 vols. Berlin: Gruyter, 1960.

Fromm, Erich. *Marx's Concept of Man.* New York: Frederick Ungar, 1961.

Frye, Northrop. *Anatomy of Criticism:* Four Essays. Princeton: Princeton University Press, 2000.

Gaiser, Konrad, ed. *Das Platonbild:* Zehn Beiträge zum Platonverständnis. Hildesheim: Georg Olms, 1969.

Geach, Peter, and Black, Max, eds. and transl. *Translations from the Philosophical Writings of Gottlob Frege,* 3rd Ed. Oxford: Blackwell, third edition, 1980.

Glasenapp, Helmut von. *Die Philosophie der Inder.* Stuttgart: Kröner, 1974.

Greene, Brian. *The Elegant Universe:* Superstrings, Hidden Dimensions, and the Quest for the Ultimate Theory. New York: Norton & Company, 1999.

Gregory, Andrew. *Plato's Philosophy of Science.* London: Bloomsbury, 2001.

Gulyga, Arseni. *Die klassische deutsche Philosophie:* Ein Abriss. Leipzig: Reclam, 1990.

Guthrie, W. C. K. *A History of Greek Philosophy,* Vol. 4. Cambridge: Cambridge University Press, 1975.

Guyer, Paul, ed. *The Cambridge Companion to Kant's Critique of Pure Reason.* Cambridge: Cambridge University Press, 2010.

Habermas, Jürgen. *The Theory of Communicative Action,* 2 Vols. Boston: Beacon, 1985.

Hanhijärvi, Tommi Juhani. *Dialectical Thinking:* Zeno, Socrates, Kant, Marx. New York: Algora, 2015.

Hanhijärvi, Tommi Juhani. *Plato's Logic.* Lanham: Hamilton, 2019.

Hanhijärvi, Tommi Juhani. *Socrates' Criteria.* Lanham: University Press of America, 2012.

Hansen, Chad. *A Daoist Theory of Chinese Thought:* A Philosophical Interpretation. Oxford: Oxford University Press, 2000.

Hegel, Georg Wilhelm Friedrich. *Hegel's Science of Logic,* transl. A. V. Miller. New Work: Prometheus, 1991.

Hegel, Georg Wilhelm Friedrich. *Hegel's Lectures on the History of Philosophy,* transl. E.S. Haldane. London: Routledge & Kegan Paul, 1955.

Hegel, Georg Wilhelm Friedrich. *Lectures on Fine Art,* transl. T.M. Knox. Oxford: Oxford University Press, 1975.

Hegel, Georg Wilhelm Friedrich. *Lectures on the Philosophy of Religion,* transl. E.B. Speirs and J. Burdon. London: Routledge & Kegan Paul, 1895.

Hegel, Georg Wilhelm Friedrich. *Philosophy of History,* transl. Robert S. Hartman. Indianapolis: The Bobbs-Merrill Company, Inc., 1953.

Hegel, Georg Wilhelm Friedrich. Phenomenology of Mind, translated by J. B. Baillie. London: Harper & Row, 1967.

Hegel, Georg Wilhelm Friedrich. *Philosophy of Right,* transl. W.W. Dyde. London: Bell, 1896.

Heimsoeth, Heinz. *Transzendentale Dialektik.* Ein Kommentar zu Kants Kritik der reinen Vernunft, 4 Vols. Berlin: de Gruyter, 1966–1971.

Heine, Heinrich. *The Poetry and Prose of Heinrich Heine,* selected and edited by Frederick Ewen. New York: The Citadel Press, 1948.

Horkheimer, Max and Theodor W. Adorno. *Dialectic of Enlightement.* New York: Herder & Herder, 1972.

Horstmann, Rolf-Peter. *Ontologie und Relationen:* Hegel, Bradley, Russell und die Kontroverse über interne und externe Beziehungen. Hain: Königstein, 1984.

Hylton, Peter. *Russell, Idealism, and the Emergence of Analytical Philosophy.* Oxford: Clarendon, 1990.

Irwin, Terence. *Aristotle's First Principles.* Oxford: Clarendon, 1990.

Jacquette, Dale, ed. *A Companion to Philosophical Logic.* Oxford: Blackwell, 2002.

Jaeger, Werner. *Paideia,* 3 Vols., transl. Gilbert Highet. Oxford: Oxford University Press, 1944.

Kant, Immanuel. *Critique of Judgment*, transl. J. H. Bernard. London: Macmillan, 1892.

Kant, Immanuel. *Critique of Pure Reason*, transl. John Miller Dow Meiklejohn. New York: Prometheus, 1991.

Kant, Immanuel. *Fundamental Principles of the Metaphysic of Morals*, transl. Thomas Kingsmill Abbott. London: Longmans, Green & Co, 1895.

Kierkegaard, Søren. *Either/Or*: A Fragment of Life. London: Penguin, 1992.

Kim, Alan. *Plato in Germany*: Kant— Natorp—Heidegger. Sankt Augustin: Academia, 2010.

Kline, Morris. *Mathematics for the Nonmathematician*. New York: Dover, 1967.

Kneale, William and Kneale, Martha. *The Development of Logic*. Oxford: Oxford University Press, 1962.

Kolakowski, Leszek. *Main Currents of Marxism*, 3 Vols., transl. P.S. Falla. Oxford: Clarendon Press, 1978.

Krämer, Hans Joachim, and Catan, John R., eds. *Plato and the Foundations of Metaphysics*: A Work on the Theory of the Principles and Unwritten Doctrines of Plato with a Collection of the Fundamental Documents. Albany: State University of New York Press, 1990.

Legge, J., ed. *Sacred Books of the East*, Vol. 39. Oxford: Oxford University Press, 1891.

Losee, John. *A Historical Introduction to the Philosophy of Science*. Oxford: Oxford University Press, 1972.

Lutoslawski, Wincenty. *The Origin and Growth of Plato's Logic*. London: Longmans, Green, and Co., 1905.

Magnus, Bernd. *Nietzsche's Existential Imperative*. Indianapolis: University of Indiana Press, 1978.

Manuel, Frank E. and Manuel, Fritzie P. *Utopian Thought in the Western World*. Cambridge, Mass.: Belknap Press, 1982.

Marcuse, Herbert. *One-Dimensional Man*. Boston: Beacon, 1964.

Marcuse, Herbert. *Reason and Revolution*: Hegel and the Rise of Social Theory. Boston: Beacon, 1968.

Marx, Karl and Engels, Friedrich. *Collected Works*. London: Lawrence and Wishart, 2005.

Moore, G. E. *Principia Ethica*, Revised Edition. Cambridge: Cambridge University Press, 1993.

Murdoch, Iris. *The Sovereignty of Good*. London: Routledge & Kegan Paul, 1970.

Natorp, Paul. *Platons Ideenlehre: Eine Einführung in den Idealismus*. Hamburg: Meiner, 1922.

Nietzsche, Friedrich. *The Birth of Tragedy: Out of the Spirit of Music*, transl. Shaun Whiteside. London: Penguin, 1994.

Owen, G. E. L. *Logic, Science, and Dialectic:* Collected Papers in Greek Philosophy, ed. Martha Nussbaum. Ithaca: Cornell University Press, 1986.

Paramananda, Swami, ed. *The Upanishads*. Frankfurt: Aeterna, 2010.

Pinkard, Terry. *Hegel's Phenomenology:* The Socialty of Reason. Cambridge: Cambridge University Press, 1996.

Pippin, Robert B. *Hegel's Idealism:* The Satisfactions of Self-Consciousness. Cambridge: Cambridge University Press, 1989.

Plato. *The Complete Works of Plato*, transl. Benjamin Jowett. New York: Scribner's, 1871.

Popper, Karl. *Conjectures and Refutations:* The Growth of Scientific Knowledge. London: Routledge, 1963.

Popper, Karl. *The Logic of Scientific Discovery*. London: Routledge, 1959.

Popper, Karl. *The Open Society and its Enemies*, 2 Vols., 5th Ed. Princeton: Princeton University Press, 1971.

Prior, William. *Virtue and Knowledge:* An Introduction to Ancient Greek Ethics. London: Routledge, 1991.

Quine, Willard van Orman. *Word & Object*. Cambridge, Mass.: MIT Pres,s 1960.

Radhakrishnan, Sarvepalli. *The Hindu View of Life*. London: George Allen & Unwin Ltd., 1926.

Reeve, C.D.C. *Philosopher-Kings:* The Argument of Plato's Republic. Indianapolis: Hackett, 2006.

Rey, Georges. *Contemporary Philosophy of Mind:* A Contentiously Classical Approach. Oxford: Blackwell, 1997.

Russell, Bertrand. "Mathematics and the Metaphysicians," in *Mysticism and Logic*, pp. 74-96. Russell, Bertrand. *Mysticism and Logic and Other Essays*. London: Allen & Unwin, 1918.

Russell, Bertrand. *The Principles of Mathematics*. Cambridge: Cambridge University Press, 1903.

Ryle, Gilbert. *The Concept of Mind*. Chicago: University of Chicago Press, 1949.

Sassoon, Donald. *One Hundred Years of Socialism:* The West European Left in the Twentieth Century. New York: Tauris, 1996.

Scheibe, Erhard. "Über Relativbegriffe in der Philosophie Platons," *Phronesis*, Vol. 12, No. 1 (1967), 28–49.

Schopenhauer, Arthur. *The World as Will and Idea*, vol. 1, transl. R. B. Haldane and J. Kemp. London: Kegan Paul, Trench, Trübner & Co., 1909.

Sedley, David. *Creationism and Its Critics in Antiquity*. Berkeley: University of California Press, 2007.

Shanahan, Timothy. *The Evolution of Darwinism:* Selection, Adaption, and Progress in Evolutionary Biology. Cambridge: Cambridge University Press, 2004.

Sieroka, Norman. *Philosophie der Physik:* Eine Einführung. Beck: Munich, 2014.

Snell, Bruno. *The Discovery of the Mind:* The Greek Origins of European Thought, transl. T.G. Rosenmeyer. London: Blackwell, 1953.

Solmsen, Friedrich. *Plato's Theology*. Ithaca: Cornell University Press, 1942.

Tarski, Alfred. "On the Calculus of Relations," *The Journal of Symbolic Logic*, Vol. 6, No. 3 (Sep., 1941), 73–89.

Taylor, A.E. *Plato:* The Man and His Work. London: Methuen, 1926.

Taylor, Charles. *Hegel*. Cambridge: Cambridge University Press, 1975.

Thoreau, Henry David. *Walden, Or, Life in the Woods*. New York: Signet, 1963.

Tucker, Robert C. *The Marxist Revolutionary Idea*. New York: Norton, 1969.

Vlastos, Gregory. *Socrates:* Ironist and Moral Philosopher. Ithaca: Cornell University Press, 1991.

Vos, Ludovicus de. *Hegels Wissenschaft der Logik, die absolute Idee:* Einleitung und Kommentar. Bonn: Bouvier, 1983.

Watts, Alan. *The Way of Zen*. New York: Random House, 1957.

Wiedmann, Franz. *Hegel*. Reinbeck bei Hamburg: Rowolt, 1965.

Wilamowitz-Moellendorff, Ulrich von. *Platon:* Leben und Werk. Berlin: Weidmannsche Buchhandlung, 1920.

Wittgenstein, Ludwig. *Philosophical Investigations*, transl. G.E.M. Anscombe, 2nd Ed. London: Basil Blackwell, 1968.

Wood, Allen W. "The Antinomies of Pure Reason", in Paul Guyer (ed.), pp. 245-265.

Woodruff, Paul. *Plato:* Hippias Major. Indianapolis: Hackett, 1982.

Zaehner, R.C. *Hinduism*. Oxford: Oxford University Press, 1962.

Zeller, Eduard. *Outlines of the History of Greek Philosophy*, transl. Wilhelm Nestle. Mineola, N.Y.: Dover, 1980.

INDEX

Printed in the United States
by Baker & Taylor Publisher Services